Basic Automotive WELDING

Jeffrey Zurschmeide

S-A DESIGN

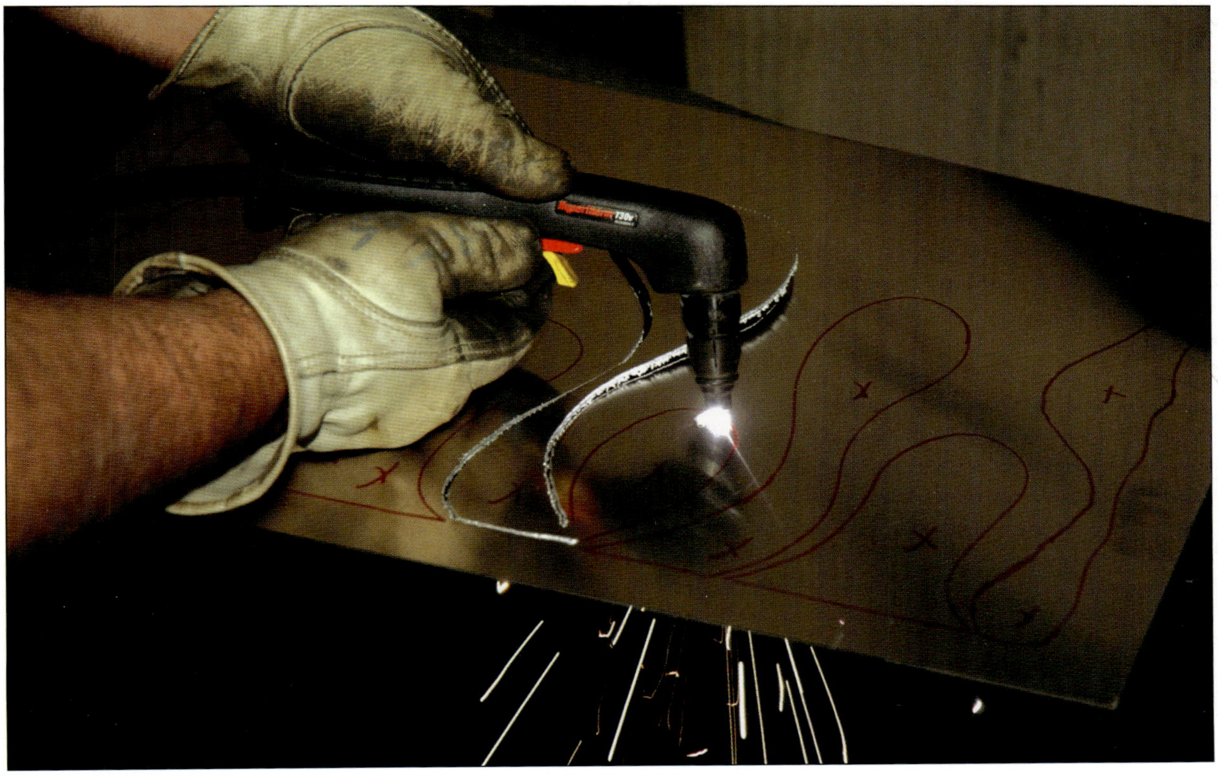

CarTech®

CarTech®

CarTech,® Inc.
39966 Grand Avenue
North Branch, MN 55056
Phone: 651-277-1200 or 800-551-4754
Fax: 651-277-1203
www.cartechbooks.com

Edit by Josh Brown
Layout by Monica Bahr

ISBN 978-1-932494-86-0
Item No. SA159

Library of Congress Cataloging-in-Publication Data

Zurschmeide, Jeff.
Automotive welding : a practical guide / by Jeffrey Zurschmeide.
p. cm.
ISBN 978-1-932494-86-0
1. Automobiles--Welding--Handbooks, manuals, etc. 2. Automobiles--Bodies--Maintenance and repair--Handbooks, manuals, etc. 3. Metal-work--Handbooks, manuals, etc. I. Title.
TL278.Z87 2009
629.28'7--dc22

2008039230

Printed in China
10 9 8 7 6 5 4

Title Page:
Using a plasma cutter allows you to make precise cuts in both aluminum and steel. The price of plasma tools has now dropped enough to make these tools a practical addition to the hobbyist's arsenal.

Back Cover Photos

Top Left:
Instructions are provided to create structures out of basic forms to allow the novice automotive enthusiast to effectively customize any kind of car.

Top Right:
Lessons are included on how to cut and grind to prepare for welding and to dress up your work after it's welded.

Middle Left:
Simple tools such as bead rollers help you add a professional touch to your work. Tips and procedures are documented to help you get the most from these tools.

Middle Right:
Practical real-world examples are described to illustrate how to turn the basic skills into actual automotive projects.

Bottom Left:
Exercises are detailed to allow you to practice and gain confidence in your skills before you weld on your important projects.

Bottom Right:
Reinforcement of stock pieces is as important as fabrication, and this process is covered in detail, with instructions for inspection and crack repair.

CONTENTS

ACKNOWLEDGMENTS

Very few books could be written without the help and support of a whole cast of individuals. In this case, those individuals start with Dave Uebele of Port Orchard, Washington, and Judd Weld of Grindesigns in Bend, Oregon. These patient people reviewed and commented on every page of this work.

Rob Zeller of Godspeed Customs in Portland, Oregon, graciously let us crawl all over and under his 1937 Chevrolet gasser drag racing project. Russ LaFontaine of the Highwallers Racing Team (www.highwallersracing.com) demonstrated his sheetmetal skills while restoring the team's circle track race car. John Masterman of Team Lowered Expectations in Milwaukie, Oregon, also gave us access to his drag racing cars. Dave Franks of Durham, Oregon, let us use the lower control arm from his Sprite race car. Bill Becker of Becker's Auto Restoration (www.beckersauto.com) in Beaverton, Oregon, offers fantastic hands-on classes in bodywork and paint preparation. Bill taught me the hot-shrinking dent technique described in Chapter 6.

I would also like to thank Kirk McNeill of Freedom Forge in Santa Cruz, California, who first taught me to handle a hammer and a coal forge.

INTRODUCTION

Metalworking is the fundamental process by which automobiles are made. Whether they're made entirely of rolled and stamped steel and cast iron or hand-crafted from beaten, cast, and machined aluminum, every car is an amalgamation of metalworking techniques.

Yet metalworking is among the most difficult skills to master for the automotive hobbyist. Metalwork requires specialized tools and the skill to use them correctly. Many people try to compensate for poor metalworking skills—usually by drastically overbuilding—but the truth is that with just a little practice and some patience almost anyone can do

Most automotive metalwork projects start out looking like this. It will take a lot of work to get this into shape.

After who knows how many hours and thousands of dollars in frame, tube, and bodywork, this project is completed. It's a singular work of art and craftsmanship.

good metalwork. Expensive metalworking tools such as welders are available to rent by the day or week, and professionals are usually happy to meet you halfway if there is a part of the project you can complete on your own.

Your first efforts may not be beautiful, but with practice you can take pride in your own metalwork.

A Note About this Book

This book describes the tools used to perform most automotive metalworking tasks and how to use them to do the job right. Then, we have laid out a number of simple projects, ranging from basic welding technique and cutting out parts to creating your own bulkheads, switch boxes, dashboards, and roll bars.

There is not space in this book for an exhaustive examination of all metalworking techniques. There are big, thick books that detail welding techniques for all kinds of situations, whole shelves of books devoted to automotive bodywork and sheetmetal fabrication, and hundreds of articles, standards, and specifications published by metalworking trade organizations such as the American Welding Society (AWS), American National Standards Institute (ANSI), and American Society for Testing Materials (ASTM). There are also tremendous resources available online, published by the welding manufacturers and on forums frequented by professional metalworkers.

This book is designed as a starting point for the amateur automotive metalworker. You should feel free to mark it up with notes about what works for you and what does not. In short, don't think of this book as the last word in metalworking—rather, it's a resource for learning.

Topics Covered in this Book

This book covers the most common tasks faced by automotive hobbyists. From repairing and augmenting a car's frame to basic aluminum sheetmetal fabrication, the projects in this book cover the needs of most amateur racers, hot rodders, and tuners.

Chapter 1 starts the book off with a brief tutorial on common automotive metal alloys and metalworking techniques.

Chapter 2 offers a complete rundown on the tools and supplies referred to throughout the book. It's true that many of the tools described are priced out of the budget of the amateur enthusiast, but many of these tools can be rented. Rentals may be by the hour, by the day, by the week, or longer. You should always compare the price of rental and supplies against the cost of having a professional shop perform the work for you—it's often cheaper to hire the pro.

Metalwork is a tool-intensive hobby or profession. Be prepared to spend a lot of money to get a complete set of tools. Fortunately, you can build up your tool kit over time.

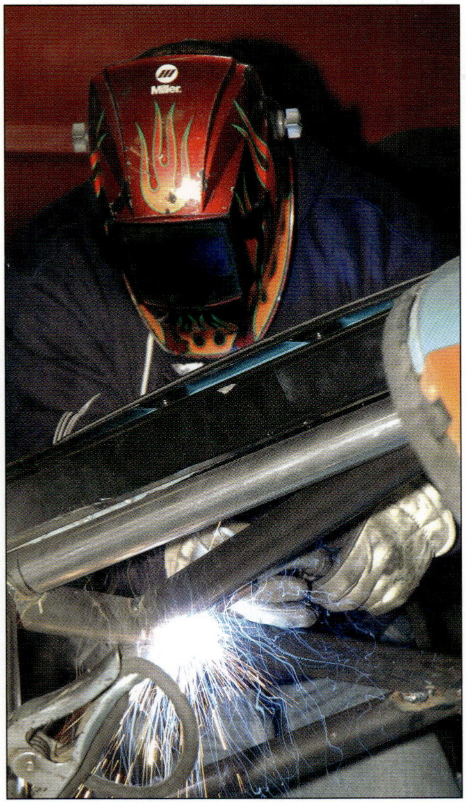

Like any skill, welding takes practice to do well. Give yourself time and some basic projects to work on before you take a welder to your pride and joy.

Grinding is an essential part of metalwork. Be sure to get good grinding tools to make short work of whatever metal you need to remove.

Good sheetmetal work is both easy and rewarding. Sheetmetal fabrication skills allow you to create a professional look in your home garage with just a few inexpensive tools.

Rolla Vollstedt built this Track-T Roadster recently. Vollstedt used to build Indy cars back when a man could build a race car in his garage and race it in the Indianapolis 500. To build this roadster, he used frame reinforcement, tube steel, bodywork, and sheet metal fabrication skills—and there's no fiberglass anywhere on it.

The nose of this completed Track-T roadster was made on an English wheel and the body-work restored from an original Model T.

At left is an example of the kind of rust that can be repaired with a simple project to cut and weld a patch panel into place.

This "basket of snakes" style of exhaust header takes skill, planning, and patience to create, but it can be done with practice.

Where it is possible, the book lists less-expensive alternatives and techniques. Many of those less-expensive tools and techniques also yield less satisfactory results, and where this is the case, we suggest that you seek out a professional shop to perform those tasks.

Chapter 3 offers a brief tutorial on welding and working with ferrous metals. This information has been covered many times before in textbooks and how-to manuals, and this book is not intended to be a complete treatise on every welding technique—just an introduction. Included are several exercises designed to let you practice good welding technique before you dive in and start welding for keeps on your car.

Because there's more to metalwork than welding, Chapter 4 covers grinding and cutting to remove unwanted material and Chapter 5 covers the important work of manipulating sheetmetal to make your own bulkheads, boxes, and dashboards. Several more practice projects are included here to offer you some practice in cutting and grinding using various tools.

Chapter 6 offers a set of projects specifically related to automotive frame and body repair. There are many books on automotive bodywork, so this book covers just a few specific projects related to welding and fabrication, such as frame reinforcement and welding in a replacement panel.

Chapter 7 deals with the special techniques used to build structures out of round steel and aluminum tubes. Round tubes can be bent as a single piece, unlike square or rectangular stock, and the round shape makes the parts strong for their weight. Projects in this chapter include making your own roll bar and subframe brace.

Chapter 8 covers the issues around working with cast iron and other cast alloys. Modern cars use a great number of aluminum parts, usually cast, and classic cars use many cast iron and cast steel parts. These parts require special techniques to weld and manipulate, and the chapter covers several common repair and fabrication projects using cast materials.

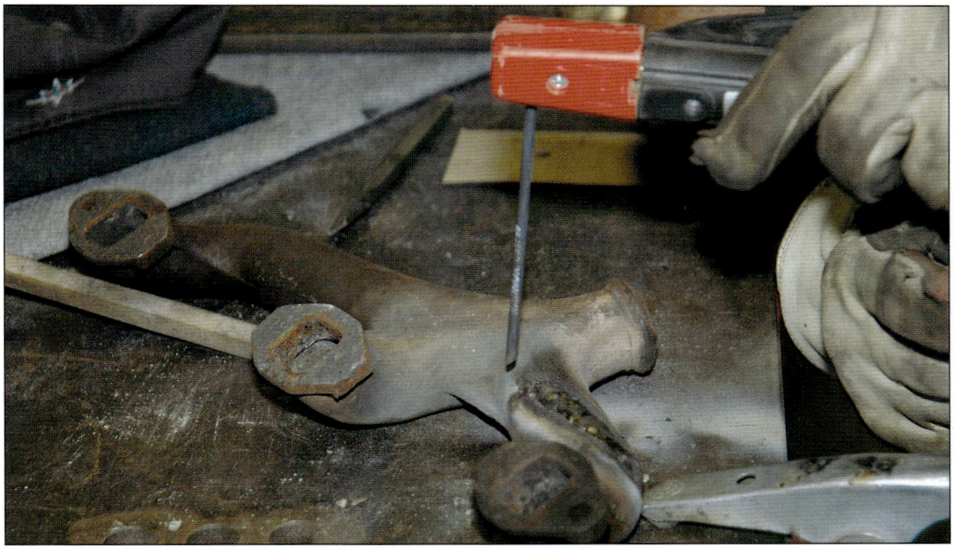

Cast metals pose their own challenges for the professional or amateur welder, but work with care and a little practice and you can repair cast parts with a basic stick welder.

The structural strength and light weight of tube-frame structures makes it popular with race car builders.

CHAPTER 1

Metalworking Overview

Simply put, metalworking is anything you do with metal. Bend it, hammer it, weld it, or drill a hole in it—it's all metalwork. Welding, on the other hand, is more specific. Because metal melts when it is sufficiently heated, two or more pieces of metal can be fused together into one piece. This property of metals has dominated human history and enabled our modern technological world.

For most of history, iron and its derivatives have been relatively rare and expensive. Many means have been used to mine and refine iron ore, but one of the most common was to simply drag a magnet through a muddy riverbed. Small bits of iron would stick to the magnet and could be easily separated from the surrounding earth. Then a blacksmith would heat the mass of iron fragments and begin to work it, eventually forming it into a single piece of metal.

As you might imagine, this method of mining for iron was time- and labor-intensive. A fine implement such as a sword took hundreds of hours to create. The biblical proverb about beating swords into plowshares reflects this truth: when iron is precious, you must recycle even your sword when you don't need it any more.

Iron was rare and valuable enough to recycle through most of history, and steel has been even more valuable yet. Pure iron (correctly called wrought iron—the term has only lately come to mean railings and gates) is a comparatively soft and malleable substance compared to steel. Blacksmiths on several continents developed welding techniques to merge iron and steel for maximum benefit well before the common era. In order to make an axe or a sword, the smith would take a small quantity of precious steel and make the cutting edge of the tool, and then make the body of the tool out of plain iron. Then the hard steel edge would be joined to the body through a process known as forge welding. This process (in various forms) was separately developed in Scandinavia, the Middle East, India, China, and Japan. Products like Damascus steel and the legendary Japanese samurai swords are results of forge welding.

The process of forge welding is relatively straightforward. The pieces to be welded are heated in a forge using charcoal or coal. When they are white-hot and on the verge of melting, the smith dusts the parts with a flux material (charcoal ash or borax, typically) and hammers the parts together. The surfaces melt a little bit and weld the separate pieces into one. Before the advent of oxygen-acetylene and electric arc welding in the early 20th century, this is how all welding was accomplished.

These processes used by smiths back to the beginning of recorded history still inform the practice of metalworking today. With all of the exotic alloys available to the modern metalshop, the fundamental properties of ferrous metals have not changed. The hammer and anvil still have a place in the shop next to the TIG welder.

Blacksmiths created the first steel alloys simply by working the raw iron they had. When a smith works iron in a charcoal or coal fire, carbon from the burning fuel is introduced into the iron, making it harder. The amount of carbon put into (or taken out of) a piece of iron depends on the fuel being used and on the temperature to which the material is heated. By manipulating these simple variables, ancient and medieval smiths made tools and developed techniques that are still in use today.

That's enough of a history lesson—we're lucky to have access to modern equipment and materials, and that's what this book is about.

The Physical Structure of Steel

Think of a piece of iron or steel as a block of cheese with a melting point at about 2,500 degrees F. Heat that block of cheese and it will get soft and ultimately melt.

When the cheese is soft, you can shape it into any form you want. When the cheese melts, you can merge it with other pieces of melted cheese and then let it cool. The result is a single, larger piece of cheese. That's the basis of welding.

Iron and its alloys have a crystalline structure. You can't see this structure except under a microscope, but it's there. You can get a hint of it by looking at the end of a broken steel tool. When you heat up a piece of steel, that crystalline grain begins to melt and you can form the material easily. At a certain point, the crystals melt and become a thick liquid. When they solidify again, new crystals form.

Welding is just the process of melting the steel to a white-hot liquid form and allowing it to cool in a single piece.

Some characteristics of steel result from the composition of the alloy. Add different amounts of carbon, and the hardness of the steel changes. Add in a little nickel, chromium, or other elements and you can make the steel rust-resistant and much harder yet.

But other characteristics of the steel happen because of the way it's worked. You've probably heard of quenching and annealing and relieving (or normalizing) a piece of steel. Those terms all apply to the speed with which you cause the crystal structure of the metal to form.

A white-hot piece of steel that is quenched (dunked) into cold water or oil cools quickly and forms many small crystals. This promotes hardness for sharp edges, but the resulting steel is brittle, like glass. On the other hand, if you take a piece of white-hot steel and put it into an oven so it can slowly cool (or anneal) over a period of hours, the resulting steel is made of longer, larger crystals. This promotes toughness—the ability to withstand shocks and bending without breaking. Toughness is a tradeoff against hardness.

Finally, normalizing or relieving may need to take place when you have welded two pieces together without heating all the metal to a soft state. As the welds are heated and then cool, stresses are placed on the surrounding metal that can pull it out of shape. So, you can place an entire piece into an oven and heat it until all the metal relaxes enough to normalize to its new configuration. Then the piece is cooled and the grain forms to hold the new shape.

These are the central facts that govern everything we do with steel. We can bend it, pound it, melt it, and cool it to make things we want. The concepts are simple, but getting the execution right takes practice. It's not magic and almost anyone can learn to do it.

There are a variety of materials and techniques used in automotive metalworking. The materials are collectively called *alloys*. An alloy is simply a mixture of metallic and other elements. The nature and interaction of the various elements in the mixture gives the alloy its specific attributes and characteristics. For example, the presence of a small amount of carbon in iron makes the material harder than pure iron, and we call the alloy steel. The presence of chromium in addition to carbon in iron makes the material more resistant to rust and corrosion, and we call the alloy stainless steel. There are hundreds of alloys in use, but relatively few are common in automotive work.

The techniques used to work the alloys commonly found in automotive applications are variations on the themes of pouring molten metals into shapes, beating or pressing hot or cold metal into shape, cutting and grinding to size, and melting pieces of metal together to join multiple pieces together. Respectively, these four fundamental techniques are called casting, forging, machining, and welding.

This chapter offers some details on the alloys and the processes used to fabricate these metals for automotive use.

Commonly Used Automotive Alloys

The following metals are frequently used in automotive construction and in automotive projects. These metals are commonly available in a variety of forms such as round tube, box tube, square and flat stock, and in sheets of different thickness.

The American Iron and Steel Institute (AISI) and the Society of Automotive Engineers (SAE) have developed a standard for classifying steel alloys. The AISI-SAE system uses a numeric series to quickly identify commercially produced alloys. The full listing of alloys is very long, but what you need to know for automotive projects is that carbon steel means that the alloy contains up to about 2 percent carbon. Stainless steels contain about 10 percent chromium. Only a few alloys are inexpensive and readily available for automotive projects.

Mild Steel

The most common steel used for automotive projects is called mild steel. Mild steel generally has about .1 percent to .2 percent carbon. Carbon steels are given four-digit numeric designations beginning with 1. For example, basic cold-rolled mild steels are commonly available in 1018 or 1020, which have .18 percent and .20 percent carbon content, respectively. There are small amounts of other elements such as silicon and manganese as well.

The American Society for Testing and Materials (ASTM) has a mild steel standard for hot-rolled steel called A36, which is .26 percent carbon and small amounts of other elements. Hot-rolled steel generally has more surface scale present than cold-rolled, and should be brushed clean before welding.

Mild steel is the workhorse metal of automotive projects. Because it bends and welds easily, you can use it for projects such as this suspension tower reinforcement. Simply weld the steel firmly in place on one side, wrap it around the tower, and complete the welds.

Almost all automotive projects are made using some grade of mild steel. This is the universal material for good results. It's easy to work with, readily available anywhere, and economically priced.

Tool Steel

Tool steel is a general term for the higher-grade steel alloys known for hardness and toughness. The name is applied because tool applications require a higher grade of steel than basic structural work. Anyone who has ever watched a cheap wrench gouge or bend on a grade 8 bolt head understands the value of good tool steel. Tool steel has between 1 percent and 1.5 percent carbon, plus traces of other elements, primarily manganese. Chrome vanadium (AISI 6100 series) falls into this category.

Spring Steel

There is a special application in the automotive world for spring steel. Springs are made of steel with about 1.5 percent to 2 percent silicon, about 1 percent manganese,

Many auto parts such as these brake shoes are made from stamped and machined mild steel. It's cheap, welds easily, and is available everywhere.

Tool steel is known for exceptional hardness, but can be correspondingly brittle. With the exception of the rawhide mallet, all these items are made from tool steel

about .5 percent carbon and up to .5 percent chromium. The AISI-SAE code for most automotive spring steels is 9255. Anti-sway bars are frequently made of spring steel.

But to make steel into a spring requires more than just the proper alloy. Springs are precisely heat-treated to obtain the desired shape retention properties. If you heat a spring to red-hot to make it malleable, you will change those properties—usually a heat cycle makes the metal less springy. You may have heard that you can heat up a spring and quench it in water or oil, or even by blowing compressed air on it, but the fact is that the amateur simply cannot get the precise timing and conditions necessary to make a good, consistent, reliable spring. However, if you decide to make your own custom tools such as chisels or drifts, old coil and leaf springs make good starting material.

Several types of automotive metal are shown in this photograph. The red spring has been powder coated, but underneath is a high quality spring steel. You can see the upper and lower control arms, stamped from mild steel, and the cast steel brake rotor.

Stainless Steel

Stainless steel has a 3-digit identifier from 200 to 665 for its alloys. To be considered stainless, a steel must generally have at least 10 percent chromium content, and less than .15 percent carbon content. Additionally, stainless steels include other elements such as nickel, phosphorus, sulphur, silicon, and manganese. T-304 stainless steel is the most common formulation used for automotive purposes such as exhaust pipes. Unlike some stainless alloys, T-304 is easily weldable, machinable, and offers good rust resistance. However, T-304 is not recommended for saltwater use. T-316 is a popular saltwater marine-grade alloy.

Chrome-Molybdenum

Another material commonly used for automotive projects is 4130 chromium-molybdenum alloy. This alloy contains between .50 percent and .95 percent chromium and .12 percent to .30 percent of molybdenum, as well as traces of other elements. Chrome-moly is often selected for roll structures because sanctioning bodies allow thinner chrome-moly tubes than the same cage design built from mild steel, and the chrome-moly cage is therefore lighter.

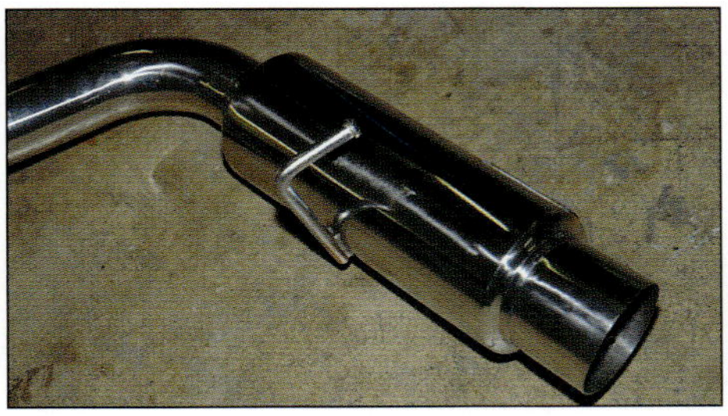

T-304 stainless steel is used to make exhaust systems like this unit from CorkSport in Vancouver, Washington. Stainless is preferred for exhausts because of its excellent rust resistance and great shiny appearance. Most stock exhausts are made of aluminized steel, which is mild steel coated with a mixture of aluminum and silicon.

Cast Iron

Cast iron has been popular for decades in the manufacture of engine blocks, manifolds, older transmission bodies, suspension components, and many other auto parts. Repairing broken cast parts is one of the most common automotive welding tasks. Cast iron contains 2 to 4 percent carbon and 1 to 3 percent silicon. Because most hobbyists do not have access to the equipment necessary to make iron castings, automotive cast-iron work is generally limited to repair welding.

Chrome-molybdenum steel looks just like other steels, but is harder because of its additional alloyed elements. Because of its composition, chrome-moly requires TIG welding to maintain its strength.

Cast iron is everywhere in automotive applications. Most engine blocks are made of cast iron or steel, as are intake and exhaust manifolds, suspension and steering components, and many internal engine parts as well.

Wrought Iron

The term wrought iron is generally taken to refer to decorative railings and fences, but it has a specific meaning when referring to iron alloys. Wrought iron is almost pure iron, with some traces of impurities such as carbon, silicon, and other elements. Wrought iron used to be readily available, and very old brass era antique cars with wooden frames may have some wrought iron fittings. Wrought iron can be welded easily, but be aware that it becomes soft at much lower temperatures than steel.

Aluminum

Aluminum is a metal element extracted from bauxite ore. It's two thirds lighter by volume than steel, but also less strong than steel. But if you use sheet aluminum that is 50 percent thicker than steel, it will be about 50 percent of the weight of steel and give you the same strength. For example, .090 steel and .125 aluminum have about the same strength, but a .125 aluminum sheet weighs less than half as much as a .090 steel sheet of the same area.

In situations where maximum strength is not needed, aluminum makes a great choice for custom automotive work. You can machine, weld, and braze aluminum, but it's tricky to bend if it's thicker than 10 gauge sheetmetal, and aluminum is virtually impossible to forge by hand.

Aluminum is prized for its light weight and relative strength, which is why it's used to make critical assemblies such as this wheelchair. Aluminum is best welded with the TIG process.

Aluminum alloys are defined according to a series of numbers that specify the additional elements in the alloy. Alloys named with a number between 1000 and 1999 are almost pure aluminum, with just a little bit of a few other elements. Alloys in the 2000-series contain more copper, and have gone by the trade name Duralumin. The 3000-series aluminums are mixed with more manganese and 6000-series metals are mixed with magnesium and other elements for strength.

The 4000-series aluminum alloys are often used in the manufacture of pistons because these alloys contain more silicon. The silicon content helps the metal flow easily into castings. Pistons advertised as hypereutectic have been made with a high-silicon aluminum alloy and a special casting process.

Some of the common alloys used in automotive work are shown in the table below.

Common Aluminum Alloys and Their Uses

Alloy	Description	Uses
1100	Almost pure aluminum, nice finish	Trim pieces
3003	Alloyed with manganese and magnesium	All-purpose sheetmetal
6061-T6	Alloyed with silicon, magnesium, copper, and chromium	Frames/Structures

Automotive Metalworking Techniques

Every metalworking technique is a variation on one of the following processes. If the metal is hot enough to flow into a mold, it's casting. If the metal is being beaten or pressed into shape, it's forging, which can be done with hot or cold metal. If part of the metal is being heated to the melting point to join otherwise solid pieces together, it's welding. And if you're cutting or grinding metal into shape, it's machining.

Casting

Casting is not typically a process that an amateur or even a professional welding and metalworking shop can perform. The tremendous energies and specialized skills and equipment required to run an industrial foundry mean that making your own cast-iron or steel parts is impractical. However, small-scale sand-casting of aluminum and other metals can be performed, and combined with machining can produce high-quality custom parts for unstressed applications such as trim pieces, shift knobs, and support braces.

Hot Forging

Hot forging takes in a number of related techniques. The common factor is that the metal is heated to red-hot or greater temperatures, which renders it malleable. The metal is then beaten or pressed into shape and hardens as it cools.

Traditional or hammer forging is done by hand, sometimes using a power hammer in a well-equipped shop, but the defining characteristic is that someone holds the metal and shapes it. This technique is often used in combination with welding to fit flat or bar steel into place. For example, this technique is used when fitting a mounting plate for a roll cage onto an uneven surface. The fabricator welds one edge into position, then heats the whole plate and beats it into shape against the backing structure before welding the remaining edges into place.

Drop forging involves taking a blank piece of heated metal and placing it in a pre-formed set of dies, and then striking the dies together to shape the piece. Excess metal is then trimmed off and the piece is finished with machining. This technique produces a stronger part than casting, so it is often used to create suspension components and other stressed parts.

Hot stamping or pressing is closely related to drop forging, except that it typically uses sheetmetal instead of billet steel, and the stamping/pressing process is more precise and gentle to the material than drop-forging. But the metal is still heated to make it soft and then stamped into shape. As the metal cools, it hardens into its new shape. This method is used to make everything from uni-body chassis to hoods, door skins, and any other stamped sheetmetal part on an automobile. Both sheet steel and aluminum may be hot-stamped.

Cold Bending, Stamping, Pressing and Forging

If you apply enough pressure, you can bend, stamp, or beat steel at room temperature. Performing the shaping while cold has a different effect on the internal structure of the metal than hot-forging, so this technique is not generally used on critical stressed parts such as engine or suspension components. But it is commonly used on many automotive fabrication projects, and many of the projects covered in this book use some form of cold-forming.

Cold-forming steel affects the crystalline structure of the metal—it literally breaks crystals and fibers at the bend. This is why you can tear steel if you bend it back and forth several times. This is called metal fatigue—and if you look at the ragged ends of a torn piece of metal, you can see where the tiny crystalline fibers have stretched and broken. Obviously, you want to avoid fatiguing the metal in any critical stressed part on your project car, but you have some leeway before a bent piece of metal becomes too fatigued to serve your purposes.

Cold-forming techniques include bending tube steel, brake-bending and bead-rolling sheetmetal, hammer-forming steel plate, and bending steel bars. In general, aluminum is not as bendy as iron-based alloys and fatigues sooner. Other materials have different characteristics. Copper is very malleable, but its alloy brass is not.

Welding

Welding refers to any technique whereby two or more pieces of metal are joined together by melting the edges into each other. Welding is also used to repair cracks in a single piece of metal.

There are several varieties of welding, characterized generally by the equipment used to perform the weld. But whether you use oxy-acetylene gas, an electric stick welder, or some form of wire-feed, MIG, or TIG welder, you're using the machine to create localized heat sufficient to melt the metal being welded, and usually introducing some new metal into the molten area as filler.

The exception to all this is forge welding, which is an advanced blacksmith's skill. In forge welding, the entire body of metal to be joined is heated to near-molten temperatures and joined by pressing the pieces together with hammer blows.

Machining

Machining metal is fundamentally different from other metalworking techniques. Casting, welding, and hot forging all involve heating metal until it is molten or at least ductile and then shaping or joining the metal while it is hot. Cold working metal involves beating or bending it into shape by force. In machining, metal is simply cut away from an existing piece until the desired shape is obtained.

For our purposes, we use the term "machining" to cover all work that involves cutting, grinding, or otherwise removing metal from a piece.

But in the strictest terms, machining is performed on a mill or a lathe. A mill is similar to a large drill press with a very adaptable platform for the part. Milling bits fit into a chuck on the mill and perform a variety of different cuts. A lathe spins the piece of metal being worked, and is used to create perfectly round pieces with cutting bits.

The other common factor with a mill is that the work platform can be adjusted to within 1/1000 inch and moved in the same precise increments during the cutting process. This allows the machinist to cut a part to very precise standards.

Remember that machining can only remove existing material, it cannot be used to add metal to any piece.

CHAPTER 2

Tools of the Trade

Welding and metalworking in general are tool-intensive skills. The most experienced and talented welder in the world can't do much without at least a basic set of tools. Plus, the tools used in metalworking tend to be expensive. If you plan to do your own metalwork, you need to budget quite a bit of money (and space in your shop or garage) for tools.

On the other hand, you don't need to spend a fortune to get started and achieve good results on basic projects. While a top-quality TIG welder costs several thousand dollars, you can purchase a basic 110-volt wire-feed welder new for less than $200. Used oxygen-acetylene welding sets are available for well under $500, and a basic stick arc welder can be purchased from the classified ads for less than $100.

Along with the big purchases like a welder, there are also investments to be made in hammers, chisels, shears, and clamps. These low-cost tools can be bought one at a time, and often turn up at garage sales and swap meets at extremely affordable prices. At the other end of the spectrum are specialized tools like English wheels, sheetmetal brakes, and blacksmithing anvils. Generally these tools cost more and occupy a lot of precious shop space.

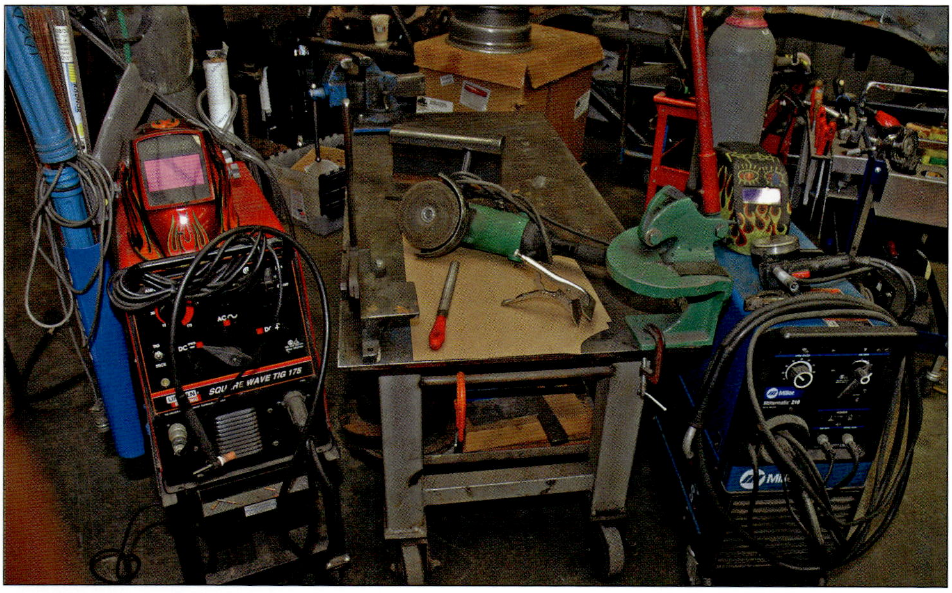

Metalworking of any kind is a tool-intensive proposition. Luckily, you can get started with just a few basic tools and build your collection over time.

As a general rule, you should buy the best tools you can afford, and generally try to get tools that are more capable than you think you'll need. It's frustrating and often unsafe to try to weld with a tool that is inadequate to the task at hand. When it comes to clamps and shears and other tools, good equipment saves you both in time and money in ruined or poor quality results. There's no shame in starting with a basic set of tools, but even if you have to build your tool set slowly, it's best to build it right.

This chapter describes some of the tools found in a metalworking shop. Some of the tools described here may be new to you, and others are found in virtually every home, but are mentioned here because of specific uses in automotive metalworking.

You can use this chapter to generate a shopping or wish list for your shop, but remember that most hobbyists build up their tool collection over many years, and you can find bargains on used tools at garage sales and swap meets.

A Word About Renting

If you're looking at a special project or simply need to weld only infrequently, you can rent MIG, TIG, oxy-acetylene, and stick welders from many tool rental centers and welding shops. This is often an affordable alternative to buying your own equipment, but be prepared to leave a large deposit. There are also equipped metal shops and studios that rent out working space. These businesses provide varying levels of equipment and assistance, but can also be useful if you don't have a working space.

Safety Gear

Working with any kind of tools can be dangerous, and welding is more dangerous than most undertakings. Mostly this is because welding involves extreme heat, but you're also at some risk for cuts, crushing injuries, and radiation burns from your welding arc.

Getting hurt is no fun at all and an injury can put your project on indefinite hold, so it's important to purchase good safety gear and then use it as designed at all times.

Fire Extinguishers and First Aid Kits

First on your list should be a pair of fire extinguishers. One should be a dry chemical or carbon dioxide B-C rated extinguisher, preferably the 5 pound size. These are good for grease, plastic, and other materials. The other should be an A-rated water-based fire extinguisher for wood, paper, and just for cooling hot metal. You can recharge a water-based extinguisher with your air compressor and a hose. Just be sure that you grab the right extinguisher when a fire happens. Pouring water on a kerosene, gasoline, or other chemical fire can turn a small fire into a huge fireball.

Keep a good first aid kit in your shop, and keep it stocked. Burns and cuts are common when working with metal.

Know Your Bubba Ring

Roger Welsch describes the concept of the Bubba Ring in his excellent series of books on farm tractor restoration. Simply put, your Bubba Ring is a circle of friends who borrow each other's tools. If you've got a group of like-minded friends, consider the benefits of purchasing only those tools that your friends don't own. If each member of a group buys a different tool, then everyone has access to a full set of tools without the expense of duplication. This works best with large, expensive tools such as MIG or TIG welders, rather than hammers and files, but it holds true for any tool that you don't use all the time, such as bodyworking dollies or a bead roller. Always take good care of your Bubba Ring and you'll never lack for tools or an extra hand when you need one.

Aloe Vera

Metalworking has always been a safety-conscious profession. Many years ago, I was a docent in the blacksmith shop at Wilder Ranch State Park outside Santa Cruz, California. The shop was outfitted with all the latest technology of 1902, but if you walked out the front door, right across the yard was a huge aloe vera plant. I like to think that the blacksmith planted that aloe back in the day to deal with his minor burns. I know I used it more than once.

If you plan to do a lot of work with hot metal, an aloe plant on the windowsill is a good addition to your first aid kit. Just cut off a chunk and rub its juice straight onto your burn. It kills the pain, soothes the wound, and aids in healing.

Gloves

A good set of gloves is a basic part of your safety kit. Buy several pairs because gloves get lost more than anything else in your shop. Any kind of animal skin gloves are good, but cowhide seems to be the toughest against heat. Pigskin works well, but the surface tends to be more porous and the gloves do not last as long as cowhide.

Special TIG welding gloves are made from thinner material to provide more tactile sensitivity. This helps when TIG welding because the rods are finer and TIG is often used for welding very fine sheetmetal or other delicate tasks.

Avoid any kind of synthetic material for welding gloves—many of these materials may melt or catch fire. Some welders keep a supply of thick cotton gloves, which may catch fire if used carelessly, but are much less expensive to replace. Wool gloves are even better, as they will smolder but not catch fire.

Some welding gloves come to the wrist, but traditional welder's gloves are insulated and have a skirt to protect the welder's forearms. These are most useful when you have to work in a very hot area or you have another need to protect your forearms, but you trade off dexterity for insulation.

Owning a variety of high-quality gloves allows you to choose the best option for any given job.

Welding Hoods, Masks and Goggles

First on the list of required safety equipment is high-quality eye protection rated for the type of welding you're doing. A pair of sunglasses simply will not do, and you can damage your eyesight permanently if you don't use appropriate protection. All quality welding lenses protect your eyes from ultraviolet and infrared radiation as emitted by the welding process, and that's something your sunglasses just aren't designed to do.

Welding Lenses for Different Operations

Lens Rating	Activity
2–4	Propane soldering and brazing, some spot welding,
5–9	Oxy-acetylene welding, higher numbers for cutting
10–11	Stick welding up to 75 amps, MIG welding
12–13	Stick welding over 75 amps, TIG welding
14	Stick welding over 400 amps

Fortunately, appropriate protection does not have to be expensive. A basic welding helmet with replaceable lenses costs about $30, and just a few dollars more for a complete selection of lenses. Also, most welding units come with at least a basic hood or handheld mask, which is usually enough to get you started.

You can select from a wide variety of helmets, goggles, and masks. Prices have come down sharply on auto-darkening hoods, and they're worth the investment compared to goggles or conventional hoods.

The lenses used for welding are numbered in ascending order by the amount of light they block. Thus, a #8 lens suitable for allows more light to pass through than a #12 lens. In general, as the amperage of your welder increases, so should your lens number. For example, depending on the amperage being used, a TIG welder requires a #10 to #12 lens, and a MIG welder from #10 to #13. Stick welders require lenses from #9 to #14. Lighter lenses can be used for gas welding and brazing. The standard lens that comes in most welding helmets is usually a #10. Follow the recommendations in your welding machine's operator's manual.

No matter what brand of helmet you choose, make sure that your helmet is lightweight and fits well. You'll be wearing it a lot, and if it's uncomfortable or unwieldy, you'll be tempted to weld without it, and that's a bad choice.

Hand-Held Masks and Goggles

Many low-cost welders come with a handheld mask rather than a welding hood. These masks can be handy for working in close quarters, but you should be aware that the radiation from Stick, MIG, and TIG welding is dangerous for your skin as well as your eyes, so you should cover all your skin to avoid a welding "sunburn." This means that you really do need a full hood to cover your face and neck. A handheld mask or a set of goggles does not provide the necessary protection for arc welding of any kind. If you are using oxy-acetylene gas, a set of goggles or a handheld mask is sufficient.

Auto-Darkening Hoods

With most hoods, you have to position your welding tip, then flip down the lens before you start to weld, but an auto-darkening hood allows you to see what you're doing before you strike an arc, and then the lens turns dark within 1/1000 of a second as you begin to weld. The better auto-darkening helmets cost more than $200, but most serious welders choose these hoods for convenience. Bargain tool stores sometimes carry less expensive auto-darkening hoods, but these trade off features for low cost. They do work, however, and can be a good choice for the hobbyist welder.

Better auto-darkening hoods allow you to set the total sensitivity and the re-lightening delay. The lens sensitivity setting is so that nearby welders do not set off your hood. With a fully adjustable helmet, you can also set the lens rating for the work you're doing. Setting the re-lightening delay allows your helmet to re-lighten shortly after you stop the arc, protecting your eyes from residual glow but allowing convenient work.

Coats and Aprons

As mentioned before, the radiation from arc welding is dangerous for your skin as well as your eyes. Also, welding frequently involves splattering molten metal, so you really want to protect your entire body from burns. A good coat or apron (or both) is an important part of your welding safety kit. Most welding aprons are made of leather, and work very well. Cotton clothing is preferred because while it will burn, it's easily extinguished and unlike synthetics, will not melt onto your skin. Wool is even better than cotton because it will not catch fire, and military surplus stores have 100 percent wool pants and coats at low prices. If you're not sure of the material, cut a small bit off and try to light it with a match—if it melts and burns, it's synthetic and not wool!

A good welding apron helps keep your clothes and your skin clean and free from burn holes. You can buy one or make your own from bulk leather.

Hats and Hair Control

Your hair is flammable. Because you're likely to have your head near your welding project, it's important to cover your hair and your scalp when welding. Cotton is the preferred material for a dedicated welding hat. Most welding shops offer inexpensive beanie-like hats that do not interfere with a welding helmet and protect your scalp from splatter and sparks. As always, avoid synthetic materials, because they burn and melt.

Hearing Protection

Probably the most overlooked safety item is hearing protection. Metal shops are noisy places, and a $1 investment in a pair of nice ear plugs will help save your hearing. If you plan to spend a lot of time in the shop, keep a stash of earplugs or external hearing protectors. Gun shops have a great selection of hearing protection designed to be comfortable for extended use. As a side benefit, reducing the noise level in your head also reduces fatigue. You can do better work for more hours if you wear hearing protection.

Shoes

You need good leather shoes to work safely around metal. Beyond the fire hazards of synthetic materials and rubber soles, a metal shop always has splinters and shards on the floor. Get a shoe with protective steel toes if you plan to work with heavy parts such as brake discs, flywheels, engines, and so on. A good set of work boots can be found used at thrift stores for just a few dollars.

Cold Tools

All the basic hand tools used in automotive metalworking come under the heading cold tools. These include the hammers, files, dollies, chisels, and other unpowered tools that date back to the beginning of civilization. A few notes are listed below about these tools as they relate to automotive work.

Hammers

You should have a good selection of hammers in your shop. You need a variety of sizes, from small 8-ounce hammers for tapping pieces into place to 4- or even 8-pound sledge hammers for serious persuasion.

A variety of hammer face designs are also useful. The most common designs are ball peen and cross peen hammers. A cross peen hammer has a flat face and a V-shaped face with the point of the V perpendicular to the hammer handle. Less common is a straight peen hammer, where the V-face is parallel to the handle.

You also need at least one dead blow or soft face hammer for moving material that you do not wish to mark with hard hammer blows. Such hammers may have bronze, lead, or plastic faces.

If you plan on doing your own welding, you need a chipping hammer for use with stick welders and flux-core wire feed welders. A chipping hammer has a chisel end and a pointed end. Sometimes they include a wire brush as well. You use a chipping hammer to chip away the crust of flux slag left behind by a stick or flux-core wire welder.

As you collect a shop full of tools, you may also want a slide hammer—this is a shaft with a threaded end and an end with a mushroomed cap. There is a heavy handle that slides along the shaft, and various tools can be attached to the threaded end. These are useful for pulling on dents and other difficult pieces that cannot be pushed with hammer blows.

Sheetmetal Hammers and Dollies

If you plan to work with sheetmetal, you need a set of dollies and bodywork hammers. You can purchase a basic kit of body tools at discount tool stores or online, but there is no end to the variety of dollies that you can find.

Dollies and spoons are portable, handheld anvils for shaping sheetmetal. To fit a wide range of curvatures, you need a selection of dollies. These come in handy whether you're fabricating your own sheetmetal parts or repairing existing panels. They're also useful any time you need a solid backing to a part you're fitting into place.

Sheetmetal hammers are different from general purpose hammers; they are lighter and frequently have a pick on one side of the head and a coin-sized flat surface on the other. These hammers are designed to do fine work without leaving marks on the surface. Consult a bodywork and paint manual for detailed instructions on using these tools on automotive bodywork.

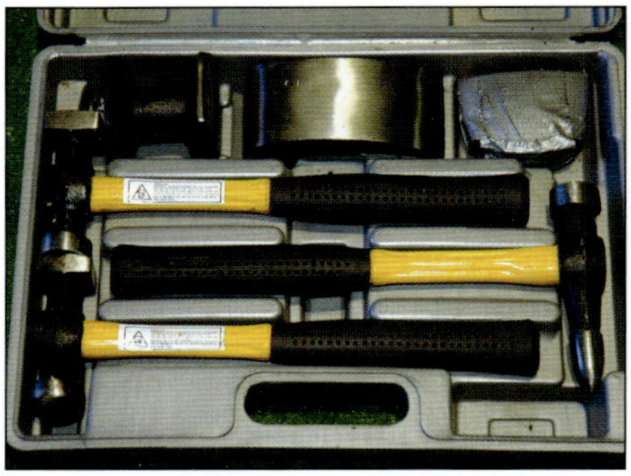

A basic bodywork kit is enough to get you started. You can add to your dolly and spoon collection at garage sales and swap meets.

Files

You will want to accumulate a good assortment of quality files in your shop. Keep a separate box of files for use with aluminum and other non-ferrous metals. Those files don't wear as much, so they last longer. You don't want to mix your files because small particles of iron, aluminum, or other metals remain in the file and can be transferred to other pieces you're working. If you try to weld a steel piece with bits of

A good selection of hammers is always useful. Get some very small ones and at least a couple 3- and 4-pound sledgehammers.

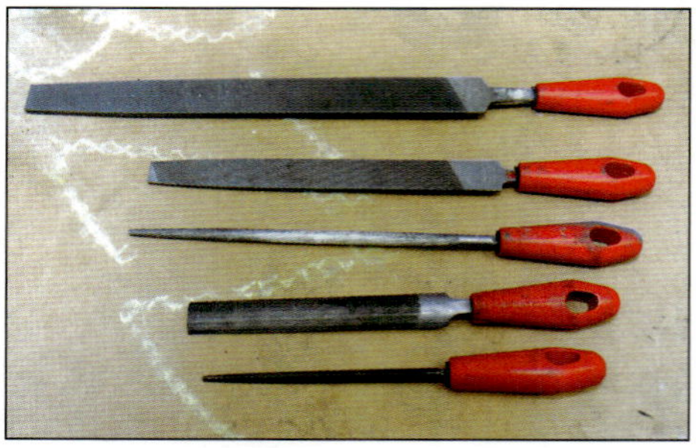

Buy a good selection of quality files with handles. Broken hammer handles can often be cut down and used as file handles. Keep a separate set of files for use with aluminum.

aluminum wedged in it, or aluminum with bits of iron, your weld quality will suffer.

Even with all the gadgets and grinders and power tools, the basic file is still an indispensable tool for shaping metal.

Vises

A well-supplied shop also has at least one vise. There are two kinds of vises commonly used in metal shops. By far the most common is a machinist's vise, also called a bench vise. These are typically bolted to a workbench or table, and they are designed to hold a part while you work. Most include a flat surface for chiseling or hammering, but do not mistake a bench vise for an anvil. If you use a hammer to beat a piece held in the vise jaws, some of the blow is transferred to the vise screw, and it can bend.

You can get a machinist's vise in any size from a jewelry vise to vise with an 8-inch opening and heavy jaws. Different vises also offer a variety of adjustments to hold materials at any angle. In general you get what you pay for, but estate and garage sales are good places to find an older high-quality vise.

A machinist's vise is handy to hold pieces while you work. Larger vises and smithing vises can also serve as small anvils.

A blacksmith's leg vise is great if you can find one. You can hammer on this tool like an anvil without damaging the screw mechanism.

The other type of vise is more archaic, but also more useful. It's called a leg or blacksmith's vise, and it's easily identified because it has a support leg that stands on the ground, while the body of the vise is still mounted to a bench or table. The key difference is that a leg vise is designed to be used as an anvil surface as well as to hold your work. This is also sometimes called a blacksmith's vise. If you find one of these, it's likely to be at a farm sale or antique store, and they are likely to be expensive. But those who use them value them highly.

Clamps

Clamps are constantly used in metalworking. Holding your work together while you weld, grind, and fit the parts is critical to a high-quality outcome. Luckily, if you have a selection of woodworking clamps, these can generally be used for metalwork as well.

Basic woodworking clamps with a wide opening are good to have, along with a selection of C-clamps and spring clips. Handheld Vise-Grip clamping pliers are very convenient, and come with a variety of jaw designs. Most commonly sold Vise-Grips have plier jaws, but you can also purchase models with flat plate

You can never have too many clamps. Clamps are useful when you're measuring, cutting, pounding, riveting, welding, and painting. Garage sales are great places to pick up clamps on the cheap.

jaws for holding sheetmetal and with large open jaws for clamping parts to be welded.

Diagonal Cutters

These go by a dozen different names—clippers, dikes, wire cutters, and so on. They are indispensable for wire-feed and MIG welding because you frequently have to trim the wire coming out of the gun. Get a pair with a little spring that holds the jaws open for easier use when you're wearing heavy gloves. A good set of lineman's pliers are also handy.

Most welders keep several sets of diagonal cutters around the shop. It's nice to have a pair close at hand when welding.

Welder's Magnets

One of the benefits of working with ferrous metals is that you can take advantage of magnets. Most welding shops have a selection of magnetic tools that are designed to hold parts in perfect 15-, 30-, 45-, 60-, and 90-degree orientations while you weld. Magnetic clamps and even magnetic studs allow you to ground your arc welder to an otherwise smooth piece.

Finally, invest in a magnetic dish to hold small parts as you work on your car. The dish will stick to your work and all the nuts and bolts you don't want to lose will stay in the dish until you're ready for them again.

A set of welder's magnets like these help hold your work in place while you weld, and help you achieve consistent angles in your finished work. Get a few of these—you'll use them.

Angle Finders and Protractors

A carpenter's angle finder is a basic tool with an adjustable (and clampable) pivot. Simply place it against any arbitrary angle and clamp it down. Then you can take the finder and use it as an angle template to repeat the exact angle or its complementary angle. A protractor may be fixed or adjustable, but is graduated with degrees and allows you to measure any angle.

A carpenter's angle finder is perfect for matching existing angles, and a protractor such as this laser unit is good for determining the degrees of an angle.

Sheetmetal Shears

It's almost impossible to work with sheetmetal without a variety of shears. You can use the most basic scissor-design tin snips, or you can purchase a set of aircraft sheetmetal

Whether you choose hand shears or the more expensive electric shear tool, you will need several sets of these to work with sheet metal. Remember that the color of the handle dictates the direction of the cut. Red is left-cutting, green is right-cutting, and yellow is for straight cuts.

shears with special designs optimized for cutting left or right, or straight. Complete sets are available at any tool store.

Many metal shops or industrial suppliers cut sheet steel to your specifications at a small added cost over the price of the material, but they do expect to sell you the basic material if they are asked to cut it.

Seamers and Folders

Heating and air-conditioning sheetmetal workers use some tools that are handy for automotive metalworking. A seamer or seamer tongs looks like pliers with flat wide jaws. They are available in 1 to 6 inch jaw widths. The jaw depth usually less than two inches, but they are useful for making small straight bends along edges. Folders slip over the edge of the metal to a depth of 3/8 or 1 inch and then are used to fold over the edge. This is particularly useful for making hems in small pieces.

Anvils

One tool that is harder to find in the modern era, but which remains one of the most useful tools you can own is an anvil. Anvils come in a variety of sizes and designs, and even a small anvil is useful for home-shop metalworking projects.

Modern metalworking shops still find a traditional anvil useful for everyday work because the basic mechanics of shaping metal have not changed. This particular anvil was made by the Acme company.

Many different shapes and designs have been used over the centuries, but the most common anvil used by blacksmiths is called the London or American pattern, with a round, pointed horn at one end and a hard, flat rectangular working surface. Often, these anvils have other features such as a smaller, flat chiseling surface

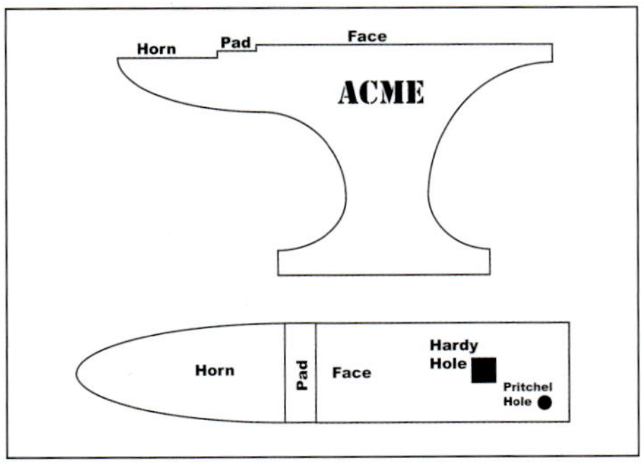

This drawing shows the standard American or London pattern anvil, with the parts labeled. The horn is used for forming bends, while the pad is used as a safe place to chisel without damaging the hard face. The hardy and pritchel holes are labeled.

called a pad and a pair of square and round holes in the anvil's face.

The square hole is called a hardy hole and it is used to hold hardies—small tools with square tangs that sit in the hole. Common hardies include chisels, shaping tools, and conical vertical horns. The smaller round pritchel hole is used for punching holes and can also be used to secure a working piece to the anvil with a piece of bent rebar.

A traditional blacksmithing anvil is made of forged iron or steel, with a hard steel working face, but many modern anvils sold in discount stores omit the hard face. A modern farrier's (horseshoe) anvil may have a bulge on one side for shoe forming. The face of a farrier's anvil need not be as hard as a smith's anvil, because it is designed to modify premade horseshoes, not for heavy work with steel.

If you go to buy an anvil, you can generally purchase a new European anvil for about the same or less money than an antique. Avoid cast iron anvils and those sold at discount tool stores for more than the lightest work.

Setting up your anvil is also important. Your anvil should be mounted securely to a sturdy base. A section of log makes a good anvil stand. Cut the base so that the top of the anvil is dead level and about at knuckle height when you stand next to it and let your arms hang at your sides.

If a true anvil is beyond your means, Chapter 4 includes a project to make one out of a piece of railroad track, or you can make do with just about any large, heavy piece of steel with a flat face. Search your local steel scrapyard for a big chunk that you can cut to meet your needs.

Lead Shot Bags

Another tool for forming sheetmetal (and weighting down light parts) is a lead shot bag. These bags are usually leather, although a heavy canvas bank coin bag also works well. Because it is filled with lead shot, you can form the bag and it tends to hold its shape. You can form your sheetmetal using the shot bag as a backing that yields against your hammer blows. This tool is especially handy for dishing sheetmetal.

A big leather ravioli filled with lead shot works great for dishing metal with minimum blemishing. After using the shot bag, move on to the planishing tools.

Planishing Tools

A planishing stake is a smooth round surface used to smooth indentations and irregularities from a piece of formed sheetmetal. Think of a tennis ball on a stick and you've got the idea. A planishing hammer is a special hammer with a rounded face that is kept free of blemishes and used to smooth metal over the planishing stake.

You can make your own planishing stakes to fit the hardy hole in your anvil or fit into your bench vise or other sturdy support. Because planishing is a gentle process, it's OK to use a conventional machinist's bench vise.

Alternately, you can buy an electric or air-powered planishing tool.

These sometimes go by the name smoothers. They are simply a framework that holds an air-powered hammer and a rounded die beneath. You simply insert the sheetmetal to be planished between the air hammer and the die and actuate the machine. The hammer gently and repeatedly strikes the metal on the die and by moving the metal back and forth, you can smooth out small imperfections.

Deburring Tools

A deburring scraper is an important and inexpensive tool if you are working with sheet metal. When you use shears or a nibbler on sheetmetal, you leave behind a sharp and somewhat jagged edge—perfectly made to slash open your hand. You don't want to cut yourself while working or leave that edge on your finished product, and running the deburring tool along the sharp edge helps to avoid that. The tool works like a potato peeler, simple and easy.

A deburring tool like this costs just a few dollars and can save you from painful injury.

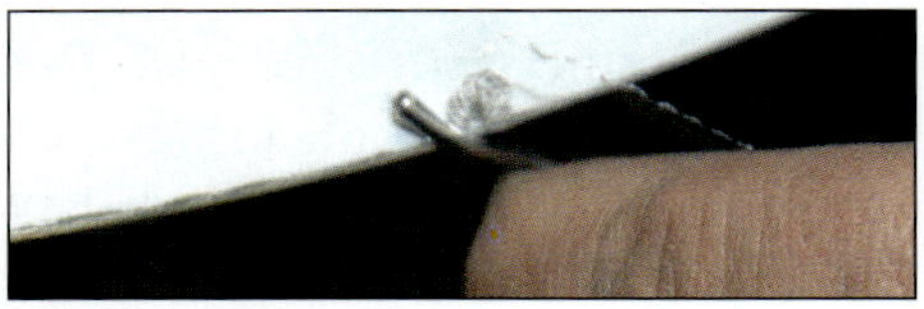

Just run the deburring tool along the cut edge of sheet aluminum to remove the razor sharp edge.

Wire Brushes

You will want to accumulate a good supply of wire brushes, including some that are dedicated to cleaning grunge off of cars and parts, and others that you keep clean to use when you're welding. Get a supply of steel-bristled brushes in large and small sizes, but also get some with brass and nylon bristles for more delicate work.

Be sure to keep some of your wire brushes clean for welding work, and devote some to removing crud from cars and parts.

Bench and Free-Standing Tools

You can do a lot with hand tools, but when you start doing more and larger projects, you will find that your results are better and easier with larger bench-mount or free-standing tools. Of course, these tools are correspondingly more expensive than hand tools. While the prices may be intimidating, you can often find these tools for less on the used market, and you can build up your shop over time.

Welding Tables

A welding table may be any size, and the structure may be made of any material, but it has a flat rectangular surface made of 1/4-inch or thicker steel on top. The steel surface allows you to use magnets or even tack welds to hold your pieces in place for welding. The steel surface also allows you to weld without fear of setting your workbench on fire.

If your tabletop is perfectly rectangular, you can align your parts and be confident that they're square to each other. When you're through welding, you can break or grind your parts free of the table and grind the table smooth again for the next

Even a basic welding table knocked together from angle iron works better than a table made of wood. Note the spaces between the slats that allow for cutting and clamping. (Photo courtsey of Dave Uebele)

project. A project to create a welding table is detailed in Chapter 3.

Bench-Mount Sheetmetal Shears

For thicker sheetmetals, you may need a bench-mounted shear (also known as a "throatless" shear and by the popular brand name Beverly shear). The term "throatless" means simply that you do not feed the metal through the body of the shear as you do with a free-standing shear. These use leverage and heavy-duty edges to cut thicker gauges of sheet steel or aluminum than hand-held shears can manage. A bench shear also allows you to cut a curve into your metal. You can buy a high-quality bench-mount shear for about $650 or an imported throatless shear suitable for light work for about $100 through discount tool stores.

For cutting heavier sheet steel and aluminum, a bench shear such as this Beverly model is handy.

Free-Standing Sheetmetal Shears

If you have a great deal of free space and you think you will do a lot of large-scale sheetmetal work, you may want to invest in a free-standing sheetmetal shear, often called a jump shear because of its foot-operated action. You can buy a new 8-foot shear that cuts up to 16 gauge sheet steel for about $3,000. Used shears occasionally turn up at shop sales for less. These large tools make clean straight cuts in sheet aluminum or steel and allow you to buy your sheetmetal in larger sizes, which can save you some money.

A large free-standing shear allows you to cut straight lines in sheet metal up to 6 or 8 feet long.

Sheetmetal Notchers

Professional shops also have a 90-degree corner notcher, which uses replaceable dies to shear perfect interior corner cuts out of sheetmetal. Again, if you plan to do a great deal of professional-quality sheetmetal work, this tool makes a good investment. You can find a basic notcher for about $700.

This notcher is used to cut perfect 90-degree angles (or other shapes by replacing the dies) out of sheet metal. This is useful when you're creating boxes and other shapes that require removing sections of metal.

Louver Punches

Perhaps the ultimate tool for outstanding automotive sheetmetal work is a louver punch. This tool allows you to take any piece of sheetmetal, such as your car's hood, and punch professional-quality louvers into it. Race car and hot rod fabricators always find a good use for a louver punch. You can find this kind of tool starting at about $1,500.

Sheetmetal Brakes

A brake is a tool used to make straight, crisp, accurate bends in sheetmetal. You can purchase small bench-mounted brakes (up to 36 inches) for less than $200 at discount tool stores. These are perfectly adequate for the occasional job—making a switchbox or heat shield, for example. Larger brakes cost many thousands of dollars and you're better off taking work of that size to a professional metal shop for bending.

When shopping for a brake, be sure to recognize the difference between a press brake and a leaf brake. A press brake uses hydraulics or other force to pinch a bend into the metal. A leaf brake clamps the metal and then you lift a hinged leaf to make the bend. A special type of leaf brake is the box and pan brake. This brake has removable and adjustable fingers that allow you to make bends of precise width and let previous bends move into the machine without interference.

Some bargain brakes also incorporate a bead roller and/or a shear in their construction. You can use pieces of angle iron held in a vise as a makeshift brake, but your results

A large free-standing brake like this one can cost thousands of dollars. If you're not bending thick or large pieces, a discount bench-mount unit will work.

Replaceable dies on this bead roller allow you to make various depths of roll, ridges, and raised or lowered areas.

are likely to be uneven if the piece is much larger than the vise.

Bead Rollers

A bead roller is an important tool if you want to achieve a finished, professional-looking result with sheetmetal. Using interchangeable rollers, this tool can roll the sharp edges of cut sheetmetal under and fold the material, leaving a smooth edge. You can also use a bead roller with different spools to create raised or depressed sections for cross-sectional rigidity. Bead rollers are available in a variety of styles, and a bench-mounted roller can be purchased at a discount tool store for under $100. High-quality motorized units cost more than $500, but a manual roller is sufficient for most hobbyists.

A basic bead roller like this one doesn't cost much and adds a professional touch to your sheetmetal work.

An electric bead roller like this costs more, but is smoother in its operation because it's controlled by a foot pedal.

Slip Rollers

A slip roller is used to make smooth even-radius curves in sheetmetal. These tools start at about $650 for a small unit. However, to make compound curves, you need a set of planishing tools or an English wheel.

English Wheel

An English wheel is a large tool used to form long smooth curves in sheetmetal. Using a wheel requires patience, however. Historic and vintage race cars with sheet aluminum bodies and fenders were often handmade by English wheel experts. You can buy an English wheel kit for about $500. The kit includes the wheels, but you need to weld it together. Sometimes discount tool stores carry English wheels, but these are often flimsy when assembled. You can, however, reinforce these as a practical welding project.

This English wheel is a craftsman's tool, and when you get good at it, you can make beautiful compound curves in sheet aluminum. Russ created this wheel from downloadable plans and purchased the wheel dies separately.

Replaceable wheels allow you to change the arc of the curve you're working into your sheet metal.

Power Tools

English wheels and anvils are all very well and good, and they are irreplaceable for fine work, but one of the benefits of the modern world is the availability of power tools. Most automotive hobbyists and all professionals are short on time, and power tools cut down the time required to do any given job.

Body Grinders

The body grinder (also known as an angle grinder) is probably the most basic power tool to have in an automotive metal shop. This is simply a tool with a replaceable rotating disc and an extra handle you can grab for support. You can install a disc that grinds on its face, one that grinds on its edge, a disc of overlapping pieces of sandpaper, or any of several kinds of wire wheel or cup-shaped wire brushes. With this variety of abrasives, you can easily grind away metal, rust, or grunge, clean off paint, or rough up a surface. These tools are also handy for cleaning up the slag and crust left over from stick welding, but be sure to wear your eye protection! These tools come in a variety of sizes. Larger units are good for getting a lot of work done fast, while smaller tools allow you to get into tight spaces.

Body grinders are one of the basic tools of modern automotive metal-working. They come with a removable side handle for stability, but this is often removed to work in tight places.

Wire Wheels

Wire wheels and brush cups that attach to your body grinder, power drill, and bench grinder are critical for removing rust, paint, and grunge before you weld. You can also use a wire wheel to clean up the slag left

Wire brush wheels for power tools make welding prep go much faster. Get a selection of these to attach to your body grinder for convenient work.

over from stick welding. A wire cup or wheel on a body grinder makes short work of anything standing between you and clean metal. Unfortunately, it can also make short work of paint, chrome, and skin that you didn't intend to remove, so use these tools with care and wear your safety glasses.

Belt Sanders and Grinders

A good bench-mounted belt sander or grinder is always useful around automotive projects. Belt grinders are more precise than a stone bench grinder or a body grinder. If you plan to weld thin materials, you can use the belt grinder for making bevels for your weld beads and to clean up and smooth your welds.

Your belt grinder doesn't have to be this fancy, but make sure it uses a commonly-available belt size and has enough power to get the job done.

Nibblers

A nibbler is designed to cut sheetmetal by taking little bites out of the sheet. Nibblers make a ragged cut and also leave thousands of little sheetmetal nibbles all over your shop. You can get nibblers that work on compressed air or on electricity. When using a nibbler, always be sure to remember that the width of the bite is lost from your work and take that into account when you measure and cut.

If you have access to compressed air, an air nibbler doesn't cost much, and is much easier than using aircraft shears or snips.

Power Shears

Probably the nicest tool available for cutting sheetmetal is a set of power shears. These are similar to aircraft shears, but powered by air or electricity instead of your forearm muscles. Most power shears cut a small section from the sheetmetal, so keep them to the outside of your desired cut line, and leave space between cut lines on the same sheet of metal.

You can also buy a shearing attachment that fits onto your handheld electric drill. The attachment converts the drill's rotational movement into a scissors action shear. These attachments cost about the same as a pneumatic shear. Electric shears are more expensive, but if you have air power, it's always better to have a tool designed explicitly for the job.

Power shears are the best tool going for cutting sheetmetal, but they cost more than a nibbler, and a lot more than a set of hand shears.

Power shears work quickly and easily, and yield great results. You want to have a deburring tool handy, though, as power shears leave a razor-sharp edge on your material.

Bandsaws and Chop Saws

Two power saws are used most often with metal. A standard bandsaw is handy for cutting aluminum and other non-steel metals. You can get by with a saber saw or a reciprocating (Sawzall) saw, but the band saw allows you to do finer work.

A bandsaw allows you to turn material and make detailed cuts. You can get the job done with a handheld saber saw, but it's harder and takes longer.

A chopsaw is generally cheaper than a steel-cutting bandsaw, and works just as well. You can also get by with a table saw or circular saw, but a chopsaw works better for mitered cuts.

Handheld band saws are also available, and these allow you to cut substantial cross sections of metal that for whatever reason you cannot maneuver into a shop tool.

Within your shop, a straight metal-cutting bandsaw is handy for cutting box and tube steel. But you can get results just as good with a chop saw. There are abrasive blades for use cutting steel and you can also spend a little more and get a carbide or diamond-tipped metal blade and a saw body that spins slower (about 1,300 rpm). The metal blade lasts longer than the consumable abrasive blades and produces less dust, but the price difference is significant.

You can also get by with an abrasive blade on a table saw or even with a handheld circular saw, but these are dangerous due to their high rotation speed. If the blade comes apart, you (or bystanders) could be injured. There are now special handheld circular saws on the market that spin at the lower speed and are designed to use the same kind of metal-cutting blades found on cold-cutting chop saws.

Drill Presses

Every metal shop needs a good large drill press. Get the biggest and most powerful drill press you can afford and find a vise or clamp attachment to hold parts. Countless metalworkers have been injured when a drill press grabbed the part and swung it around to hit their hands! Get a good set of high-speed hardened drill bits with plenty of spares for the small and often-used sizes (1/4, 5/16, 7/16, 1/2, 9/16, and so on). You can also invest in a set of step-bits, which have a small pilot section to start a hole accurately before the main bit cuts the hole to size.

You will find your life is much easier if you get a large free-standing drill press. Bench-mounted units are also useful.

Tubing Notchers

If you plan to make roll bars and cages, tube-frame chassis, or any kind

This is a basic tube-notching press. It's got a clamp that allows you to mount the tube at any angle, and then a drill press that uses a standard drill. The tool also uses a standard metal-cutting hole saw. Remember that you need a selection of hole saws to notch tubing of different diameters.

This is the result when you use a tubing notcher. You can simulate this result with a bench grinder, body grinder, files, and other tools, but it takes a long, long time and the results are not nearly as accurate.

of figures using round tube steel, you need a tubing notcher. This is a ream or a drill with an attachment to hold a piece of round tube at a fixed angle. This allows you to create the perfect-fit fishmouth ends for great-looking tube projects. A good tubing notcher with a hole-saw end can cost as little as $200. Reamer-style units cost substantially more.

Tubing Bender

The corresponding tool to a tubing notcher is a tubing bender. If you plan on making a lot of roll bars or

This tubing bender uses a moving die and hydraulic power. It costs a lot of money and makes very accurate bends that do not crush the tube. You can spend less and get a hand-operated bender, but it's still hundreds of dollars. The kind that use a bottle jack and a fixed mandrel will crimp your tube.

tube-frame chassis, this is a good investment. Manual tubing benders start at about $300, while a professional-quality power unit costs up to several thousand dollars.

Welders

A welder is one of the largest investments the automotive hobbyist may make in shop equipment. Over time, some enthusiasts collect a selection of welders including a basic wire feed welder, TIG welder, and an oxy-acetylene rig. You can find these tools through classified ads, at swap meets, or through welding shops. Obviously, buying used through a reputable welding shop is the safest route.

You may already own a welding setup of some kind. But if you start to weld regularly, chances are good you'll be in the market for a second welder shortly, because different welding rigs are good for different purposes. If you plan to weld a wide range of materials, you'll have your wallet out soon. The table below lists the most common types of welding setups and their best uses.

Of all these types of welding, the MIG and flux-core processes are the easiest to learn. In basic terms, these are point and shoot welders. Flux-core welders are cheaper to buy, but MIG delivers substantially better results. The best option for the amateur automotive metalworker is to buy a low-cost electric welder with both MIG and flux-core capabilities. That way, you can get started practicing with flux-core welding and then add a gas bottle and solid-core wire as your budget allows. But if at all possible, spring for the MIG setup from the beginning and make your life easier. Used welders are a good way to start.

Stick welding takes a little more skill, but it's very inexpensive, especially if you buy your stick setup through an online market like Craigslist.org Oxy-acetylene setups are expensive and tricky to use. At the top of the heap, there's TIG welding. These welders are precise, fun to use, and they offer beginners very good results on simple tasks. As you gain experience, you can weld difficult materials such as chrome-moly and titanium or magnesium alloys with TIG.

Oxy-acetylene is still a popular method for cutting large chunks of steel. Plasma cutting is fast overtaking it as the price of basic plasma cutters comes down.

Welding Rigs and Their Uses

Welder	Uses
Oxy-Acetylene	Mild steel, stainless, aluminum, cast
Stick (SMAW)	Mild steel, stainless, aluminum, cast iron, nickel alloy
Flux-Core (FCAW)	Mild steel, stainless
MIG (GMAW)	Mild steel, stainless, aluminum, nickel alloy, brass
TIG (GTAW)	Mild steel, stainless, aluminum, nickel alloy, brass, chrome-moly, exotic alloys

Oxy-Acetylene & Oxy-Propane

Automakers do not typically use gas welding to make cars. It's just too expensive and fiddly a process to be part of an assembly line. But hot rodders, race car builders and home mechanics can make good use of gas welding and cutting in projects. A well-formed gas weld with the proper rod is strong enough for most automotive purposes. Professionals shy away from gas welds on structural or safety pieces such as roll bars because gas welding can oxidize metal, removing carbon and leaving the welded area brittle. However, it's just the ticket for many repairs, and with just a basic rig, you can both cut and weld.

Cutting with an oxy-acetylene torch is easy if you don't care about messing up your results, but harder to make precise, clean cuts. The advantage of torch-cutting is that you're not limited to straight lines as with a chop saw, and you can cut thicker materials more easily than with a reciprocating or saber saw. But getting good results from an oxy-acetylene torch takes practice, and the gas can get expensive.

Be careful when considering a deal on gas welding gear. If the bottles are rented or out of date, you can be in for extra expense if the bottles require replacement or recertification. Often it's cheaper to pick a good welding shop near your shop and buy a basic torch kit and rent your bottles from the store. Bear in mind that with rented bottles, you are restricted to having them filled at that shop.

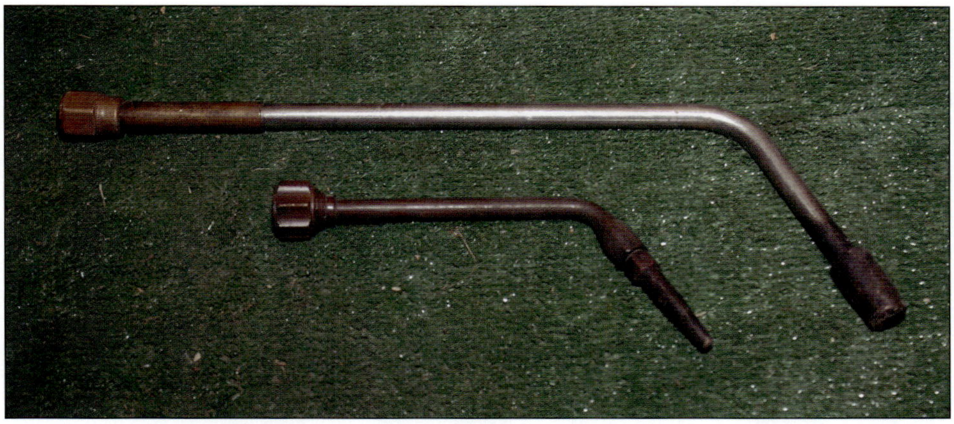

The tool on top is a rosebud flame tip for an oxy-acetylene torch kit. The bottom tip is a standard welding tip for the same kit.

An oxy-acetylene rig like this one requires a set of bottles, regulators and hoses in addition to the welding nozzles. The gas in the bottles must be purchased and can be expensive.

Welding gas bottles must be certified every 10 years. If you buy an older welding kit, be aware that if the bottles may require a recertification before they can be filled. Certification generally costs about $20 per bottle. Welding shops often charge you the $20 and trade your bottle for a new one.

There are many different tips and accessories that go with an oxy-acetylene setup. You will probably buy a kit, or if you go used you will get someone's collection of gas welding gear.

The basic kit includes a pair of regulators that attach to the welding bottles. These allow you to reduce the pressure (up to 3,000 psi) coming from the bottles to just a few PSI. Then there are hoses that connect the regulators to a welding handle. You can screw many kinds of attachments and tips to the welding handle.

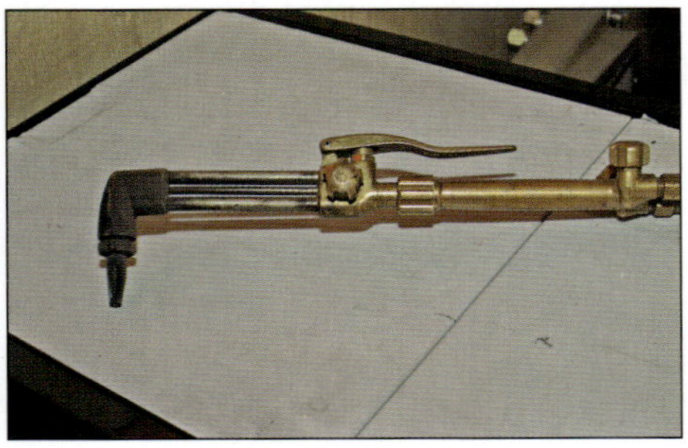

An oxy-acetylene cutting torch attachment. These torches are falling out of favor compared with plasma cutters because of the cost of the gas and the danger of keeping highly pressurized bottles in the workshop.

Welding tips are a basic nozzle that delivers mixed oxygen and acetylene. You set the mixture with valves in the handle. Different sized holes in the welding tips yield different sized flames for more or less heat delivered to your welding point.

A cutting torch attaches to the handle and offers a lever or valve that delivers extra oxygen through the center of a larger flame. This oxygen delivery is used to blow out molten metal and thereby cut through materials. Like welding tips, there are different sizes of cutting tips for larger or smaller jobs.

A rosebud tip is a larger tip with many holes to deliver the oxy-acetylene mixture. This tip is used to heat materials before you work them. Like the other tips, rosebuds come in a variety of shapes and sizes.

It's important to note that the different brands of gas welding tips, handles, and torches may not interchange. Lincoln is the most popular brand on the market today, but older

Soldering has limited utility in automotive metalworking, but it's always good to have a solder/braze kit around, especially if you work with radiators.

This is a basic Lincoln AC stick welder, known in the industry as a buzz box for its distinctive sound when welding. You can buy one of these on the used market for very little money. They last forever and can deliver good welds with practice.

Sears Craftsman gas rigs and other brands often turn up for sale. Before you invest in a gas welding setup, make sure that the brand is compatible with modern supplies, or make sure it has everything you need.

Brazing and Soldering: A close relative of oxy-acetylene gas welding is the process of brazing and soldering. Simply put, brazing and soldering do not melt the pieces of metal being joined, but use low-melting-point metals such as lead, tin, copper, silver, brass, and bronze to glue the pieces together. Except for wiring, automotive brazing and soldering happens with an oxy-acetylene or propane gas torch. For wiring, the best tool is a basic soldering iron.

Stick Welders

Stick welding, technically called shielded metal arc welding (SMAW), is an electrical arc welding process. A traditional basic stick-based arc welder (called a buzz box) is one of the least expensive tools you can buy to get started with arc welding. You can use one of these boxes to do a wide variety of projects. They're not as precise as a wire feed or TIG welder, but with a bit of practice you can get good results on structural pieces. These welders are not generally precise enough for delicate work such as sheetmetal (less than .125-inch thick), although you can get small rods that allow you to work with thin plate.

Stick welders are the most common tools to find in the classified ads. They are inexpensive and sturdy. It takes some skill to get a pretty weld with a stick welder, but the world is held together with stick welds. The most basic stick welders are AC-only and straight polarity. Better models allow you to select both current and polarity. All stick welders allow you set the power level, from about 30 amps up to 225 amps for a basic shop or farm model up to several hundred amps for a top of the line unit.

Wire-Feed Welders

The most common welding technique used in automotive applications is wire-feed or MIG welding. These are also electric arc processes, officially known as flux core arc welding (FCAW) and gas metal arc welding (GMAW). MIG stands for metal inert gas and is so named because the welding gun issues a small cloud of gas such as argon or carbon dioxide to protect the molten steel from oxygen while the weld is taking place. The gun also directs a feed of consumable wire into the weld, taking the place of the electrode or welding rod in other types of welding.

You do not have to use gas to use wire-feed welding. The least expensive welders on the market use flux-core wire to generate the oxygen-free environment required for a good arc weld. This wire has the same sort of material inside that stick welders place on the outside of welding rods. Flux-core wire-feed welding is relatively easy and inexpensive, so it is often used in noncritical applications.

Most wire-feed welders can also function as MIG welders. The difference is that when operating as a MIG, a bottle of inert gas has been connected to the welder and an appropriate spool of wire has been installed. MIG welders are covered later in this chapter. This section covers the use of 110-volt and 220-volt wire-feed welders without gas. For decades, almost all wire-feed welders required 220 volts of AC power, but in the last 20 years, the 110-volt wire feed welder has made wire-feed welding both convenient and inexpensive. Inexpensive wire feed-welders can be purchased new for as little as $150.

Used without gas, a 110-volt wire feed welder delivers AC power and flux-core wire to the weld. The user can adjust the electric power through a dial or switches, and the wire feed speed using a separate dial. Along with the diameter and composition of the wire, these are the only variables you can set on a basic wire-feed welder. A bottle kit to adapt an inexpensive wire feed welder to MIG operation costs about $100 on top of the price of the basic welder. Larger, more expensive MIG welders can cost up to several thousand dollars.

A MIG welder using inert gas to protect the weld area can be operated in AC or DC mode, and with either polarity, depending on the material being welded. Aluminum requires AC operation for best results, while DC straight polarity yields a smoother weld, less splatter, and generally better results on steel.

TIG Welders

TIG welding is also known by the trade name Heliarc welding. Its technical name is gas tungsten arc welding (GTAW). TIG stands for tungsten inert gas. Like MIG welding, the welding gun issues a cloud of inert gas to protect the molten metal from oxidization, but a TIG gun uses a non-consumable tungsten electrode to create the arc, and you use uncoated welding rod similar to that used with an oxy-acetylene welder as feed material in your weld. TIG welding is known for its capability to weld delicate or thin materials. TIG is especially associated with welding aluminum. The gas mixtures used for TIG welding are the same as those used in MIG welding—a mixture of helium, argon, and other inert gases.

This is an inexpensive flux-core wire-feed welder. It operates on household 110VAC current and the wire is inexpensive. The welds tend to be ugly, but it gets the job done. You can add gas to turn this into a lightweight MIG welder.

This is a Miller MIG welder. It costs more than a 110VAC unit, but makes correspondingly better welds. If you buy just one welder, buy a good MIG unit.

Stick welding is a low-cost way to get started in arc welding. Although the falling cost of wire-feed and MIG units is rapidly overtaking stick for automotive applications.

TIG welding shares skills with both stick welding and gas welding, but offers some of the best welds possible for an amateur.

This Lincoln TIG unit allows you to perform stick welding in AC or DC as well as gas-shielded welding of aluminum, stainless steel, and exotic alloys like chrome-moly.

One feature of TIG welders is a foot pedal that controls the amount of electricity supplied to the weld. This allows very fine control, and TIG welding can be used on sheetmetal that would be difficult to weld by gas, stick, or wire feed processes.

The downside of TIG welders is the price. Even a basic TIG setup costs upward of $1,000.

Plasma Cutters

A plasma cutter uses an arc to melt the metal and then a stream of compressed air to blow out the molten material and make the cut. This yields a good precise cut with less skill and lower operating cost than an oxy-acetylene torch. Like a torch, the plasma cutter allows you to make detailed cuts which cannot be achieved with an abrasive or saw.

Plasma cutting is now the tool of choice for most fabricators because of its clean cuts with limited heat damage to delicate alloys. Plasma is also low-cost to use because it cuts with compressed air instead of expensive bottled gases.

A basic plasma cutter like this one is just a few hundred dollars and you don't have to buy expensive oxygen or acetylene to use it.

The price of a plasma cutter has dropped into the amateur's budget in the last decade. A basic plasma cutter now costs about $600 and cuts up to 1/2-inch steel using just ordinary household 110VAC electricity and compressed air. Anyone can get good results with one of these units, and they're rapidly replacing oxy-acetylene rigs.

Spot Welders

If you think you will undertake a lot of work with sheetmetal, a spot welder may be a reasonable investment. Spot welders that are affordable and useful for small shops and home projects look like a large set of pincers. A spot welder passes current from one jaw to the other through thin materials, making a small, round weld. A basic spot welder costs about $600.

Basic Welding

There are dozens of books on the market that describe the welding process. Beyond that resource, there are tutorials and welding instructions freely available online. There's no need to repeat all that information in this book.

Instead, this chapter offers a brief background in commonly used welding supplies and basic settings for common welders. Then we move on to some tips for producing good, strong welds and a few techniques to practice before you commit a weld to your project.

Welding Supplies

Getting the right supplies for your project is critical. You may have seen MacGyver on TV making a weld with a pair of jumper cables and a quarter, but that's really not a recommended technique. The good news is that you're not likely to need everything you can find in a welding shop. A good used MIG welder and a few basic general-purpose selections of wire and gas will get you through almost all projects.

The most important factor in choosing any welding rod (or filler) is to choose a rod made from the same material you are welding. There are different rods and wires for mild steel, stainless, aluminum, and so

Automotive welding is not fundamentally different from other welding, but it tends to require more precision. You want your car to look nice as well as work correctly, so take the time to practice and get good before you weld on your car.

Pick your welding rods by type and diameter, according to the type of welding you plan to perform.

on. Next, choose the diameter of your rod or wire based on the thickness of the metal you plan to weld and the power level you need to use. For most purposes, the smaller range of rods and wires is what you want. Finally, set your welder up with the correct amperage, gas flow, and so on.

We could fill a book with tables of settings to cover all these variables, but the welding supply companies have already solved that problem. When you buy welding rod or wire, ask for the Material Safety Data Sheet. The MSDS, as it is commonly known, contains information about the composition of the welding rod and its flux (if any). It also generally contains a table listing common welder settings and recommended applications for the rod.

MIG and Wire-Feed Supplies

If you plan to use a wire-feed welder on steel, you have two basic choices for welding wire: flux-core and solid metal. Flux-core wire includes its own welding flux—a material that burns and creates the air-free area in the vicinity of the weld. The flux also forms a crust over the surface of the weld that you must chip or brush off as the weld cools. If you try to weld over the crust, some of it will become trapped as a bubble in the weld, which reduces weld strength and looks ugly.

The benefit of flux-core wire is that you don't have to deal with a bottle of gas. You just plug in your welder and start working. The downside is that flux-core wire requires AC operation and produces a lot of smoke and splatter. Flux-core is also

If you use stick welding or flux-core wire, a set of wire brushes and chipping hammers are necessary to clear the crust from the weld for inspection and possible rework.

A good MIG welder like this Miller can be had on the used market for a few hundred dollars. It's easy to use and will help your projects come out better.

not recommended for welding thin (20 gauge or less) materials. With a small bottle of MIG gas (generally a mixture of argon and carbon dioxide) you can work using DC and get a much smoother weld. Common flux-core wire choices for automotive work include Lincoln NR-211 or any wire that meets the AWS (American Welding Society) E71T-GS standard.

For best results in MIG welding, you need the right kind of gas to keep oxygen and nitrogen (98 percent of ordinary air) away from your weld. There's a price range between different welding gases, and of course the better formulations are more expensive. You can use pure carbon dioxide (CO_2) and it works, but you get better results by purchasing a gas with 75 percent or higher argon content. For aluminum or other non-ferrous welding, you want

Flux core wire looks the same as any other welding wire. Always check the label on the spool before you install wire in your welder.

100 percent argon or helium, but these pure gases are not suitable for welding mild steel. To weld stainless steel, a small amount of hydrogen or another reactive gas is added to a basic argon/carbon dioxide mixture. You can also purchase three-way welding gases that include some combination of helium, argon, carbon dioxide, and a small amount of oxygen.

For the vast majority of automotive mild steel welding, an 85 percent argon and 15 percent carbon dioxide gas mixture is a good choice. Your welding shop can make a recommendation about alternate mixtures for specific purposes.

Most mild-steel MIG welding wire is made to the ER70S AWS specification. There are subdivisions—ER70S-3 and ER70S-6 are the most commonly used mild steel MIG welding wires, and the -6 variation is generally considered easier to use. These specifications include elements in the alloy that allow the wire to flow well and create a good, solid weld.

Your welding shop will have a selection of good MIG welding gases available for you. They can advise you on the right mixture for your particular needs.

If you plan to weld aluminum, you absolutely need a bottle of argon or helium gas. Aluminum oxidizes easily and the protective gas is a requirement. You also need aluminum wire and special rollers to push it. The most popular aluminum wire selections are a solid core 4043 or 5356 alloy. The 4043 wire is the most popular and easy to work with. The 5356 alloy is harder, and should be used when you plan to anodize (color) your work, because 4043 weld material does not take the color well.

If you will be welding aluminum regularly, you also should invest in a spool gun. Because 4043 aluminum wire is soft, mounting the wire spool right on the gun allows a shorter wire travel, which is easier on the wire and reduces breakage and wire jams.

If you plan to weld stainless steel, you need stainless steel wire. The most popular alloys for stainless welding are 304, 308, and 316, and you need a special gas formulation as well. Gas for stainless welding includes a small amount of hydrogen or oxygen.

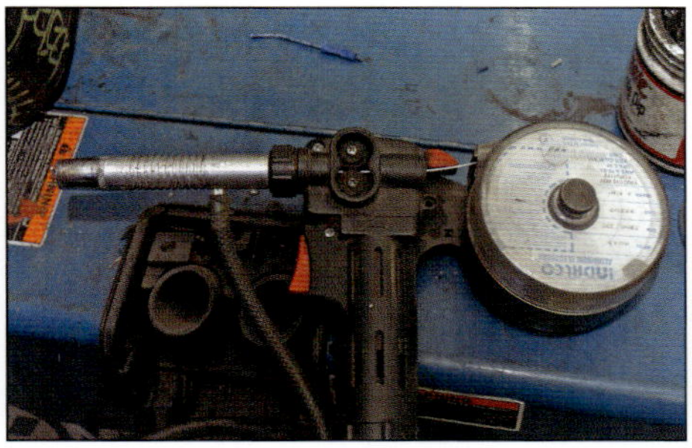

If you plan to MIG weld aluminum, consider investing in a spool gun like this one. Because the spool is right there on the gun, you don't have to feed the wire through a long cable. Also, you can switch the gun easily without having to re-route your welding wire.

TIG Welding Supplies

TIG welding rods are similar to those used in oxy-acetylene welding in that they come in lengths of straight rod in different sizes from 1/16 to 1/8 inch. Like MIG welding wire, TIG rods are available in a variety of alloys based on the material to be welded. There are two main rod formulations for mild steel, known as S6, 70S, and 80S- D2. Steel welding rods have a thin layer of copper plating on their surface to resist rust and promote puddling. Aluminum formulations are not plated and come in 4043 and 5356 alloys, just like MIG wire. Similarly, stainless welding rods are available in 308 and 316 alloys. Most TIG welding is performed using 100 percent argon gas, but mixed gases also work well.

With a TIG welder, you also need to stock a supply of the tungsten points for your welding gun. These points are made primarily of tungsten, but the trace elements included in the manufacturing process

These aluminum TIG welding rods show all four sizes of commonly used rod from 1/16 inch to 1/8 inch. They are sold by the pound and generally come in 4043 and 5356 alloys.

TIG gas is fundamentally the same as MIG gas, but in this setup Russ has added an extra valve to run gas through a plastic tube to flush oxygen out of chrome-moly tubes as he welds.

distinguish several kinds of points. The most common points used are 98 percent tungsten with 2 percent of thorium added. This kind of point has a red tip, and it's a good general-purpose point. You may also want to buy a selection of different tips for various purposes.

TIG tip maintenance is easy. You can create a ball of tungsten at the end of the point by simply making an arc—the ball will develop on its own. For fine work, keep the point sharp with a whetstone or TIG point grinding machine. For high-power work, grind the tip flat for a larger arc point.

Oxy-Acetylene Supplies

There are a tremendous number of choices in oxy-acetylene welding rod. For mild steel, most choose the copper-coated RG45, RG60, and RG65 rods. Each of these has a slightly different formulation, but all work well in an automotive steel context. You can also get a variety of specialty rods made of bronze (for brazing), aluminum, stainless steel and other materials. Many of these rods are flux-cored or flux-coated for brazing.

Gas options center mainly around the combustible fuel. Acetylene is the most common gas used, followed by propane. You can also obtain hydrogen, proprietary MAPP gas, natural gas, or liquid petroleum gas for your torch. In general, acetylene is the fuel of choice. Welding oxygen has been dried to prevent the tanks from rusting. You should never use medical oxygen or other oxygen sources for welding—get your oxygen from a reputable welding shop.

Oxygen bottles are painted green, acetylene bottles are painted red or black. The hoses are also color-matched to the bottles to prevent any hookup errors.

Be sure you always use, transport, and store your welding bottles in an upright position. Acetylene is dissolved in acetone when it's placed in the bottle, and if you put the bottle on its side, the acetone can get into the valve and then into your regulators. If your bottles have been on their sides, stand them up and let them stabilize for an hour or so before you attach your regulators and try to use them.

Stick Welding Supplies

There are a wide variety of stick welding rods available on the market, each optimized for a different kind of welding. Because a stick welder has only a power adjustment, we use different rods to meet various different welding requirements. For example, if you're welding something very easy to work with such as clean new metal, well-fit with no gaps, choose 6013 rod. This formulation is easy to work with, easy to clean, and generally gives good results when everything is in order. If you've got gaps to fill, 6012 is a better choice.

The numbering system on stick welding rods is fairly simple. The first two digits (60 or 70) indicate the tensile strength of the weld at 60,000 or 70,000 psi. The third digit indicates the welding positions approved for the rod—generally 1 for all positions or 2 for flat/horizontal only. The last position describes the electrical current requirements and the composition of the flux coating. Generally speaking, 1 and 5 indicate DC-only, and all other digits indicate AC/DC operation.

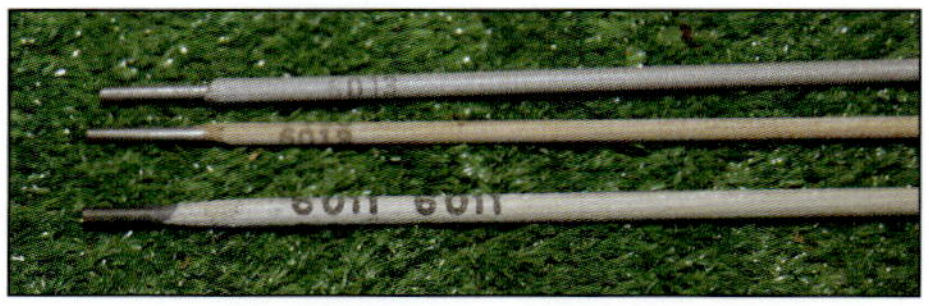

Stick welding rods come in a variety of sizes and compositions. On top are two different brands of 6013 rod, and on the bottom is a larger 6011 rod. Some rods also have color dots and bands to help identify them.

When choosing a rod to use, start with the composition of the material you plan to weld. If you're working with mild steel, the basic rods listed here are good choices. If you're welding stainless, joining unlike materials, or working with other alloys, you should consult your welding shop for a recommendation. Gauge your rod diameter by the thickness of the material you're welding and the amperage you're using. In general, choose smaller rods for lower power settings on your welder. For a rule of thumb, 3/32-inch rods are good to about 75 amps, 1/8-inch rods from 75 to 150, 5/32-inch rods from 100 to 175, and 3/16-inch rods from 150 to 250 amps or above.

Stick Welding Positions: One of the characteristics listed for each kind of stick welding rod is the position in which it is best used. Stick welding makes a distinction between flat (as if the piece is lying on a table and you are standing above and next to it), vertical, and overhead welding. Most modern rods are good in any position, but a few are recommended for use only in the flat or horizontal position.

The table on this page shows the kind of welding indicated for each type of standard rod. The table on page 40 lists the current and polarity settings for the most commonly used stick welding rods.

Stick Welding Rods and Their Uses

Rod	Positions	Best Use
6010	All	Deep penetration, dirty work, splatter, DC only
6011	All	Deep penetration, dirty work, AC/DC, best all-around rod
6012	All	Medium penetration, good gap filler, harder to clean
6013	All	Light penetration, nice looking weld, easier to clean, use with new metal
6014	All	Medium penetration, good filler
7014	All	Light penetration, good filler, use with carbon steel
7016	All	Medium-deep penetration, use with hard to weld alloys
7018	All	Low-hydrogen, medium-deep penetration, often used for building work, needs high power. Always use fresh 7018 rods–they don't keep well
7024	Flat	Used for welding thick plate (above 1/2-inch)
Nickel	All	Used for welding cast iron. Comes in 55 percent and 99 percent Nickel. The 99 percent rods are better if you plan to machine the part afterwards.

Taking Care of Stick Welding Rods: Stick welding rods must be absolutely dry for best results. Rods that have been wet can be identified by their disintegrating flux coating. Like the head of a wooden match that has been dipped in water, the flux dissolves and comes apart easily.

You can buy an oven to store and pre-heat your stick welding rods, or make a simple hot box. A hot box is just an old metal cooler or refrigerator—insulated and sealed—with a light bulb inside to keep the inside warm and dry. The most common solution is simply to purchase a watertight plastic rod case. These are plastic cylinders with gasketed screw-top lids. Put your rods in one of these cases and remove only as many rods as you need. Otherwise, keep the case sealed.

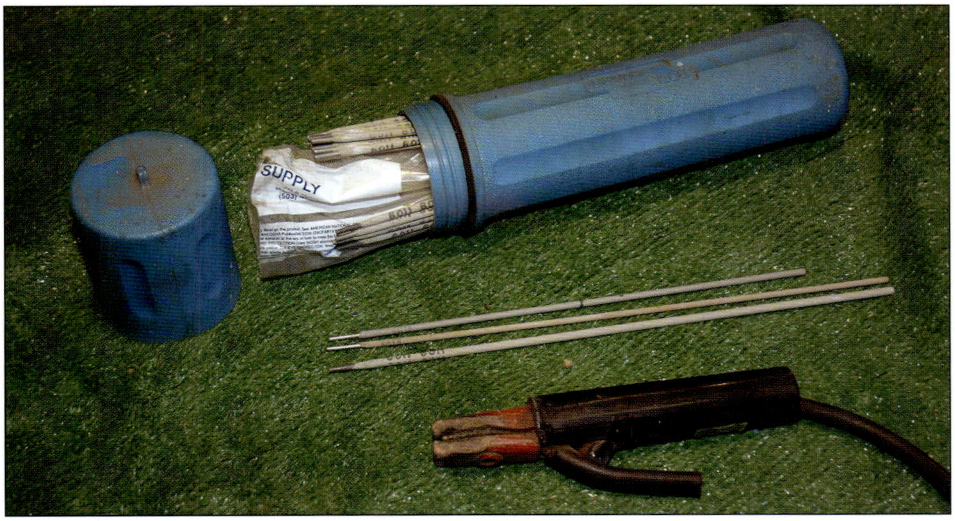

Keeping your stick welding rods dry is as simple as buying a sealed plastic carrying case. You can also build a hot box if you think it's required to keep things dry in your shop.

Preparing to Weld

To create a strong and good-looking weld, you need to have good technique, but it's just as important to prepare your project. The best welder in the world can't get good results if the piece isn't cut, cleaned, and supported properly. Similarly, if the welding machine is not correctly adjusted, it's hard to get good results. Use the sections below to ensure that your weld is set up to succeed before you start.

Getting Good Fit-Up

Good fit-up of the pieces to be welded is the basis for a good result. When you measure and cut your parts, measure carefully and allow for the width of a flame or blade when you make your cuts.

With small parts and tubing, you want to get them right up together

When working with smaller or thinner materials, you can butt the ends together and weld. If you beveled the edges, there might not be enough material to weld into.

If the material is thicker, you get a better weld if you bevel the edges so the weld material has someplace to go.

> **TECH TIP — One Way**
>
> If you're building a three dimensional structure out of square or rectangular tube stock and you are cutting angles for clean corners, make sure you get the angles all going in the correct directions. Nothing's more frustrating that cutting your piece to just the right length and then realizing that you cut the second end in the wrong direction!

for the best results. For thicker materials, you generally bevel the mating edges to give your weld bead a place to go.

Getting the measurements and markings correct is especially important when you're cutting angles. Using a jig, miter box, or locked setting on a chop or band saw is important because a tiny angle error at the weld end is multiplied through the length of a piece and the other end of the bar may end up wildly out of alignment.

As a rule, if you have to estimate a cut, estimate it too long. You can always cut more off a piece of metal, while adding length is very difficult. When cutting a straight angle, estimating a little long allows you to cut or grind the angle again if it's not just right.

Getting angles exactly right is especially important with tube projects, as you may be fitting a fishmouth end around round tube for a weld. Even with a tubing cutter, it takes some practice to get these fitments exactly right.

Cleaning Metal

Cleanliness is critical to a good welding result. Mill scale, oil, grease, dirt, paint, metal filings and other contaminants get into your weld and show up as bubbles, slag, clinker, and porosity. It's ugly and it reduces the strength of your weld.

> **TECH TIP — Aluminum**
>
> If you're preparing aluminum, remember to use files and grinders that are exclusively used with aluminum. Iron or steel filings show up as bubbles full of grit in your aluminum welds.

Start cleaning your work with a good wire-brushing. Grinding and sanding also works to remove paint and adhesives, but can leave its own impurities behind. Brush and grind your work until the metal shines, but don't remove too much of the material. You want plenty of metal to make the weld.

If the metal you're working has previously been coated in paint, oil, grease, cosmolene, or any kind of protectant, you may want to wash it with a cleaning solvent. There are several commercially available cleaning solutions available at your welding shop, such as Ox-Out and Chemclean. These are acidic cleansers that remove oil, grease,

Paint, clearcoat, and any other sealant won't help your weld. This aluminum has been brushed clean before a gusset is welded into place.

mill scale, rust, and other impurities from your working surfaces.

Supporting Your Work

When your metal is fitted properly and cleaned of all scale and impurities, you're ready to position the parts. It's important to get the parts positioned correctly and securely before you start welding. This is when it's handy to have a welding table to prepare your parts.

If your parts are long, you may need additional stands to support them at either end and at one or more places in the middle. You can buy or make variable-height welding stands (sometimes called a dead man) using threaded rod and a tripod stand. You can also use sawhorses, tables, stacks of boxes, or anything else that is available. The important thing is that your parts must be held firmly in the proper orientation. Parts sometimes move when you start to weld, and cutting your pieces apart to try again is extremely tedious.

Don't be afraid to tack-weld your parts to your welding table. If you have a selection of carpenter's squares, protractors, or magnetic angles, measure in every possible way to make sure that your right angles are square and that everything fits and lines up the way you planned.

Making Jigs

If you plan to make multiple copies of a structure, you may find it useful to create a jig. A jig is simply a setup that allows you to make several parts exactly the same way. For example, you might tack-weld some pieces of angle or box stock to your table such that your pieces fit precisely where you want them. If you cut the parts to the same length and use the same jig, you should be able to come up with identical parts every time.

You can make a temporary jig out of scrap pieces of steel to hold parts. Simply cut your scraps to the correct length, tack them onto your table and then tack your part to the supporting piece. When you're all done, break or cut the support loose and grind the tack weld down.

Take the time to observe your parts from every angle and make sure that the fit is correct and everything is aligned properly. Reworking a welded piece is never easy, and you can easily ruin a part (or several) and have to start over. Spending the time now to ensure that everything is right will pay off shortly.

It can be as simple as a sawhorse or as fancy as this tube stand with rollers, but support your work when you're cutting or welding.

TECH TIP — Measure

An indispensable technique for determining squareness in a rectangle is to measure diagonally across the rectangle. You can measure the corners all you want and still end up with a cockeyed rectangle–but when you measure in an X-pattern across the diagonals and the measurements are the same, your corners are well and truly square.

One advantage of a steel welding table is that you can weld pieces to the table to make a jig to hold your work in place. You can even weld your workpiece to the table and cut it loose later.

Preparing Your Environment

It's more difficult to weld in full daylight because the light from the sun gets into your mask and limits your ability to see the weld. Also, you can't see the glowing metal as readily in the full light of day. It's best to weld indoors if you can do so safely, or at least in a shaded area where you can see what you're doing through your mask.

Wind is also your enemy when you're welding. Wind blows away the shielding gases from a MIG or TIG welder, and even from flux-core wire or the flux on a stick welding rod. On the other hand, your welding environment should be well-ventilated to replace the smoke and fumes from welding with fresh air for you to breathe. Once again, indoor welding is best, provided you aren't creating a fire or ventilation hazard.

Get your safety gear together. It's often tempting to just make a tack or run a short bead without your protective gear, but that's precisely when you'll get burned. Keep your safety gear with your welder and it is always close at hand when you're ready to weld.

Make sure you've selected the appropriate grade of lens before you begin to weld. If your helmet is auto-darkening, make sure its settings are appropriate for the type of welding you're about to perform.

Welder Adjustments

Every welding machine is a little different, so getting your welder adjusted correctly is an art. But follow these steps and you should get into the ballpark. Then run some test beads on scrap steel of the same form and thickness as your parts and you can dial in the exact settings you need.

AC, DC and Polarity

Electrical current comes in a variety of forms—120, 240, or 480 volts, it can be single phase or three phase, and it can be delivered as alternating or direct current. In basic terms, alternating current (AC) means that the direction of electrical flow changes about 60 times a second. Direct current (DC) means that the flow of electricity is constant in one direction.

Virtually all wall sockets deliver alternating current. Many welders pass the alternating current through to the weld. However, you may be able to select AC or DC with your welder. A DC setting on the welder converts the incoming electricity to direct current before using it to weld.

Different base materials, welding wire or rods, and welding techniques are suited to AC or DC welding. One is not better or worse than the other. You just have to know when to use each setting with different metals and welders.

Some metals and filler materials weld better under AC and some under DC. Some processes like straight and some like reverse polarity. Get a welder that allows you to select both your current and polarity for maximum flexibility.

Basic Current and Polarity Settings

Welder	Materials	Current	Polarity
Wire Feed	Steel flux core	AC	Straight
Wire Feed	Steel solid core	AC/DC	Straight
MIG	Steel solid core	AC/DC	Straight
MIG	Aluminum 4043/5356 solid core	AC	Straight
TIG	Steel rod	DC	Straight
TIG	Aluminum rod	AC	Straight
Stick	6010	DC	Reverse
Stick	6011	AC/DC	Reverse
Stick	6012	AC/DC	Straight
Stick	6013	AC/DC	Either
Stick	6014	AC/DC	Either
Stick	6020	AC/DC	Straight
Stick	6027	AC/DC	Straight
Stick	7014	AC/DC	Either
Stick	7015	DC	Reverse
Stick	7016	AC/DC	Reverse
Stick	7018	AC/DC	Reverse

In addition to current selection, many welders allow you to select polarity when welding with direct current. DC straight polarity is when the clamp is positive and the welding rod is negative. Reverse polarity has the clamp as the negative side of the circuit and the welding rod as the positive. Polarity is important with some stick welding rods.

Wire-Feed and MIG Settings

For a wire-feed welder, select a power level appropriate to the thickness of your working material. Your welder may have switches or a dial to control the power, but the adjustment process is the same. Start at a lower power than you think you need and run a few test beads. Check for adequate penetration by turning the piece over, and when you can see discoloration from the weld on the back side of the metal, you're working most of the way through the metal.

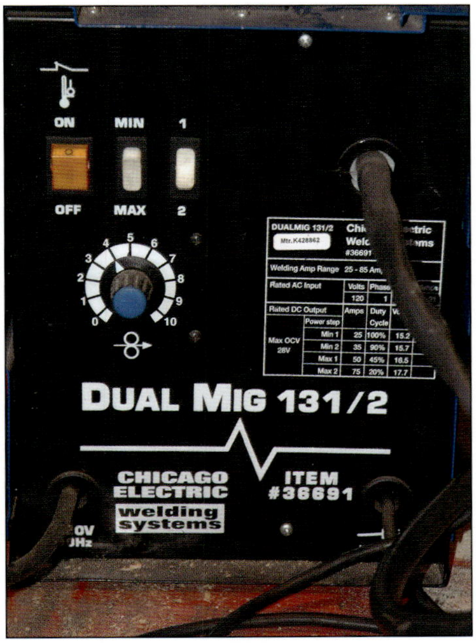

The most basic welders have four power settings selected through two rocker switches. You can also set the wire speed separately.

Baseline Settings for MIG Welders

Material	Current	Wire Gauge	Wire Speed	Gas Flow
1/16-inch (.063) steel	10 Amps	.030	10 fpm	15 cfm
1/8-inch (.125) steel	30 Amps	.035	30 fpm	20 cfm
1/4-inch (.250) steel	50 Amps	.035	50 fpm	25 cfm

Wire speed follows the amount of power you select. If your welder uses a pair of switches to control the welding power, you have 4 power settings to choose from. In general, the more power you use, the faster your wire speed should be.

Set your welder to its lowest power setting and set your wire speed at about 30 percent of its capacity and try a few practice welds. Adjust your wire speed until you get a smooth flow into your weld. If the wire speed is too fast, you will find the wire pushing your welding gun back, or breaking off and leaving short lengths of wire sticking out of the weld. If your wire speed is too slow, the arc will skip and sputter and the weld will be uneven. Adjust the wire speed until you get a good smooth arc and weld bead.

At higher powers, you must increase wire speed somewhat. This introduces more weld metal to your bead and with thin materials, you risk burn-through. See the practice exercises below for more information on setting up your welder.

With the speed set, adjust your wire drive force, or tension. This is achieved at the roller wheels that push the wire through the cable to your welding gun. The rollers must be tight enough to push the wire as it is consumed at the arc point, but not too tight. Set the tension starting from the minimum, so the that wire barely feeds. Then hold the welding gun near a flat, unweldable surface such as concrete. The roller wheels should slip rather than push the wire. Then gently increase pressure until the rollers begin to push the wire out against the test surface. You need only a small amount of force behind the wire.

For a MIG wire-feed welder, you also need to adjust the gas flow. There's no harm in using too much gas—it's just expensive—but you must ensure that there is adequate gas flow to your welding gun. Twenty pounds at the regulator should be plenty for normal (still air) welding conditions, but you need to raise that if you're welding in breezy or windy conditions.

The table above offers a set of baseline settings for a wire feed MIG welder. These settings are simply a place to start your tests, and they are conservative. For full penetration, higher power settings are almost always used.

Oxy-Acetylene Adjustment

With an oxy-acetylene welder, you need to take your welding tip into account. Different welding tips have different aperture sizes to yield a larger or smaller flame. Close the valves on your torch and set your acetylene regulator to about 7 pounds yield to the torch, and your oxygen to about 20 pounds. Then open the acetylene (red hose, typically) valve and light your torch. You should get a smoky flame. Then slowly open the oxygen valve (green hose, typically) on your torch and adjust the flow until you get a small

The gauge closest to the bottle shows the pressure in the bottle. The farther gauge shows the pressure in the hose and at the torch.

pencil-point-sized flare of blue-white flame.

If you open the oxygen too far or too fast, your torch can snap out and lose its flame. If that happens, close the oxygen valve and start over.

Stick Welder Settings

On a basic AC stick welder, the only setting you control is the power. Start low and work your way up until your test welds show good penetration and no burn-through. Be sure you've also selected the right kind of welding rod for the job!

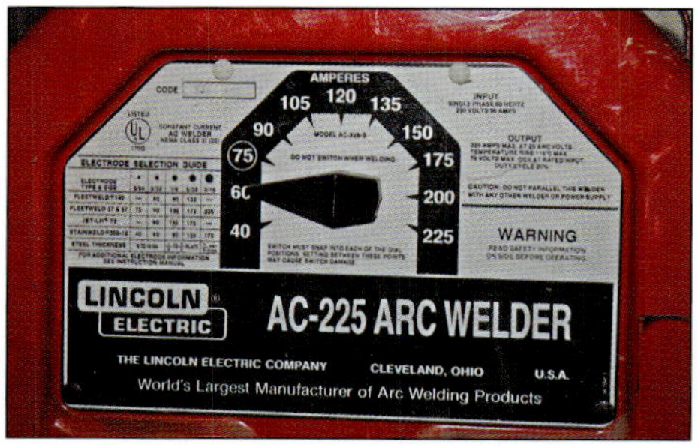

On a basic stick welder, the only thing you can set is the total amperage sent through the stick. Use the lowest possible power for light materials.

TIG Welder Settings

On a TIG welder, you can control the power at the box, or through the use of a foot pedal. The foot pedal is a wonderful tool that allows you to control the amount of energy going to the arc from moment to moment, and this is part of the reason TIG can be used for very fine work such as welding sheetmetal. You can also control the gas flow to the welding gun and as with MIG welding, you need to ensure that there is enough gas to protect the weld.

Another adjustment you make to a TIG welder has to do with the tungsten electrode. The electrode is pointed, like a needle. This allows the TIG welder to create a very small, precise arc. If molten welding rod or other material accumulates on the electrode, the welder's efficiency and accuracy are reduced. Similarly, the tip of the electrode is consumed and blunted over time, so TIG users keep a whetstone close at hand to clean and sharpen the electrode. You can also replace a worn electrode in the gun. Most TIG electrodes are double-ended to get the most use out of the material.

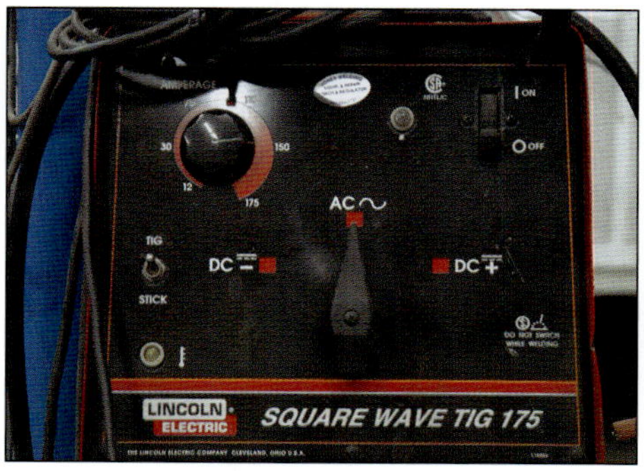

A TIG welder uses only basic controls for the maximum power and current type and polarity. However, most TIG setups use a foot pedal for fine control of welding amperage.

Most TIG welding is done with DC straight through (positive) polarity, except when welding aluminum, which is always performed using AC power.

Basic Beads and Joints

When welders talk about beads and different styles of joint, these are the terms heard most often. The differences between joints can be subtle, and all good welds share most of the same characteristics—good penetration, clean deposition, and even beads.

Generally speaking, a bead is the deposition of molten metal at a joint between two or more pieces being welded. The joint is where the pieces come together, and the type of joint indicates how the pieces come together.

All of the joints listed here benefit from tacking the pieces into place before you try to run a bead.

Look at the light colored metal at the edge of this piece. You can see that the weld on the other side penetrated the underlying metal when you can see an outline of the weld from the back of the piece.

As you weld, try to balance the amount of heat you put into each of the pieces you're welding together. For example, if you're welding a T-joint, the heat from the weld has more area to penetrate in the bisected piece than in the center piece. Therefore, spend more time with the arc on the bisected piece to keep the heat distribution even.

Fillet Bead

A fillet bead is used on a 90-degree joint, on overlapping plates, or on either side of a T-joint. If you cut open a fillet bead, the shape of the weld is roughly triangular. This is a strong bead for connecting structural pieces, and requires good deep penetration. Usually, this bead does not require beveling the edges of the materials being welded. Keep most of your arc directed at the horizontal piece when making a fillet—you're just melting a bit of the vertical piece and letting it flow down into the horizontal part. If you put too much heat on the vertical piece you'll create undercut, which actually leaves the vertical piece thinner than when you started just above the weld bead.

Tacking a T-joint fillet weld on both sides is important because as the first weld bead cools, the thermal contraction can pull the two pieces out of perpendicular alignment. Stitch welding the fillet and alternating stitches on either side of a T-joint also helps prevent misalignment.

A fillet weld has a roughly triangular cross section and can be used when working on an inside angle.

Beveled or Groove Bead

A beveled weld is simply a butt weld where you've ground a slight bevel onto each mating surface of your parts, making a V shape into which you deposit a fillet weld bead. This is generally easier than making a good butt weld and offers generally good results. With thicker materials, beveling becomes even more important to ensure complete penetration of the weld. Depending on the size of the materials, you may need to run several beads to fill a bevel. There are variations on this theme—the U-groove, J-groove, and single-side bevel are examples, but they all mean the same thing: leave some space for your weld bead to flow into.

Inside Angle or Inside Corner Joint

This bead takes place on the inside angle of two pieces of steel. But for an inside angle weld, only the edges of the two pieces are touching. You have to be careful to lay your weld equally on both pieces if they're the same thickness, or correspondingly biased if you're welding a thick to a thin piece. These welds often benefit from multiple passes if the materials are thin and you're worried about burn-through. Make your first pass a light bead and then follow it up with two more beads on top of the first and biased to each piece, so each subsequent bead attaches both to the piece and to the previous beads. Weave the later beads in a wider arc than your initial bead to get good coverage.

TECH TIP

Clean Welds

Any time you make multiple welding passes, be sure to clean all the oxidation scale, slag, and welding crust (if you're using stick or flux-core) from the weld bead before you lay a subsequent bead. Failure to clean the weld area can make your weld porous and weak.

Use your welder's magnet to keep your 90-degree angles constant while you tack your work together.

Inside angle welds are very much like fillets, except the assumption is that only the edges are touching when you start. Often, welders will reinforce inside angle welds by laying two more beads on top of the first, making a larger triangular cross-section.

Outside Angle or Open Corner Joint

This is the opposite of an inside angle bead in that it happens at the outside of a 90-degree joint. Most often, the two pieces are placed with only edges touching, creating a natural area for your weld to fill. Make sure you get even penetration into both parts when creating this weld, and you might want to follow it up with a weld on the inside angle.

Outside angle beads are harder to make because of the lack of welding surface, but as in this case when joining angled tubes, it's not possible to make an inside angle weld on this side of the joint.

Butt Joint

A butt joint is any time you have two flush edges mated together. There's little or no room to place a weld bead into the joint, so you have to melt the two pieces together with complete penetration. A good butt weld takes practice, and most welders prefer to give themselves a little bevel to work with. Also, you need to have both pieces securely clamped when welding a butt joint, or heat distortion will pull your pieces out of position. You can butt weld metals up to about 1/16 inch. Thicker pieces should be beveled. If you cannot bevel a thicker piece for any reason, just leave a small gap between the pieces for the welding rod or wire to fill up with bead. If you leave a gap, plan to run a bead on both sides of the butt weld, if possible.

Butt welds are more difficult to create than a beveled weld. If you have to perform one, be especially careful to get good penetration.

When a butt weld is completed with good penetration, you can see where the weld material comes through the backside.

Stitch Weld

Stitch welding is also known as skip welding or intermittent welding. The technique is useful in controlling the amount of heat distortion you create in a project. By welding a short bead and then skipping a few inches and running another short bead, you can stitch your full weld together while limiting the amount of heat placed into the piece at any given time. After the piece has had a chance to cool, you can return and weld the sections you skipped the first time. A variation on this technique is backstepping, where you start a few inches in from the end of the joint and work backwards to the end, then move farther in and work backwards to the start of your first bead.

You can prevent warping and get a very strong weld by stitching your pieces together. Just weld and skip equal-length sections when working. You can come back and reconnect the sections later if you want a continuous bead.

Rosette Weld

A rosette or plug weld is used to fill a small hole, up to about 1/2 inch in diameter. Use a circular motion to deposit filler rod around the perimeter of the hole until it closes up. The name rosette describes the weld because when you do it right, it looks a bit like a flower. This type of weld is also used to join two pieces of tubing where one tube has been inserted in the other. A hole is made

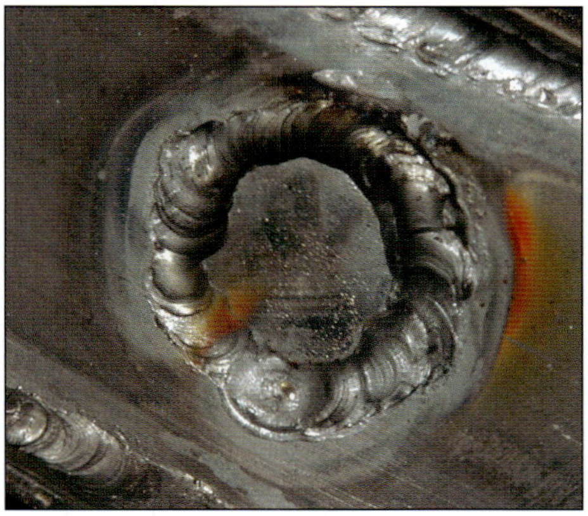

A rosette weld is so-called because it looks like a flower. It's the same stack-of-pennies look, simply executed in a circle around the perimeter of a hole. You can also use this technique to close a small hole.

A plug weld was used here to close up a hole, and then the weld was ground down. A dab of body putty and some more sanding and this hole will be just a memory.

in the outer tube and the weld joins the two pieces of metal.

Welding Practice

When everything is fitted, clean and ready, and you've made some practice beads to warm up, you're ready to commit welds to your project. Get some scrap pieces of steel for your practice sessions. For these initial practice beads, make sure the pieces you're welding are the same thickness and the same material. Welding unlike pieces is an advanced project. Run many beads, until you're confident you can do it right every time. When you're seeing good results, you can try your technique on an actual project.

Follow these steps to get a good result:

1 Securely mount your ground clamp. With any electric welder, you have a ground clamp to connect your welder to your project. This clamp is half of the circuit from the welder to the material you're welding. The other half of the circuit is the cable from the welder to the gun or stick holder. You complete the circuit when you strike your welding arc.

Getting a good connection with your ground clamp is important. With steel, you can clamp to the material you're working or to your welding table, provided you've got good contact between the materials and the table. If you're welding aluminum, you must clamp to the piece you're working. There are a variety of clamps available, including magnetic clamps. If your piece does not provide a convenient clamping location, you might have to weld a bolt or other extra part to your work to provide a ground.

2 Bevel your edges. You need a place to deposit your weld bead and you want to maximize the surface area for your weld, so it's a good idea to grind a small bevel onto the edges you're planning to weld. You don't have to do this, but it helps make cleaner, stronger welds. Just be sure you leave enough material to hold the weld!

Push-Pull Techniques

There are two ways to run a bead. You can push the weld by driving the puddle of molten metal ahead of your flame or arc, or you can pull a weld by dragging your rod, flame, or gun with the puddle trailing behind. If your weld area is getting too hot when you're using the push technique, you can try pulling to help your torch run a little cooler.

Generally speaking, neither way is better than the other, but most welders develop a preference for one or the other. However, you may find that access to the weld site or the structure you're creating dictates which technique you use, so it pays to be proficient at both styles.

It is sufficient to mount the ground clamp of the MIG welder to the steel top of the welding table, because the electrical current travels through the piece to the table. You could also mount it to any part of the structure.

A disc grinder (or belt grinder) is the right tool for putting a consistent bevel on pieces to be welded.

3 Tack your work into place. When you start welding your project together, begin with tack welds to secure everything into place. Your jig and support system is a good start, but by making a whole series of tack welds, you reduce the risk of twisting and warping your work. Welding involves a great deal of heat, and heat expands the metal you're working. If you weld one entire seam without supporting the other seams in your project, the fit-up of your pieces can distort.

A few dots of tack weld are sufficient to hold your project together while you run permanent weld beads. Just point your MIG gun at the joint and pull the trigger momentarily to make a tack.

Making tack welds with a MIG or wire feed welder is easy. Just hold the gun at the tack point and briefly squeeze the trigger. With TIG or oxy-acetylene welders, you need to create a puddle and add a little bit of welding rod to create the tack. Perhaps hardest of all is tack welding with a stick welder, because you must strike the arc and create the tack in the same moment, then simply move the rod away to break the arc. This takes some practice to perform cleanly.

Begin your practice by making several tack welds at every joint you plan to weld. These should be small—no larger than the size of a pea—and they do not need to completely penetrate the material. Make all of your tack welds before running any kind of a bead.

4 Start with a basic push bead. If you're using a MIG or wire-feed welder, position the welding gun at one end of the joint you plan to weld, and squeeze the trigger (or step on the pedal) to start the arc and the wire flow. As the arc strikes, look at the puddle of molten metal created by the arc, the material, and the welding wire you're feeding into the arc. Move the tip of the welding gun in small back-and-forth motions along the welding joint, pushing the puddle along the seam. Keep your motions and your speed of travel even to create a weld bead of uniform thickness. When it cools, your weld should have overlapping edges—something like a deck of cards or a stack of pennies spread out along a table.

If you're using a stick welder, you have to strike your arc with a motion similar to lighting your welding stick

A good weld shows the effect of pushing the molten steel along in its wave pattern. It looks like an overlapping stack of pennies that have been spread out.

Notice how the MIG gun is angled toward the arc point as Russ pushes a weld along a joint.

like a match. Once the arc is created, hold the stick about 1/8 inch from the material and push the puddle in the same way as with a wire feed welder. You need to move your hand closer to the material over time, as the welding stick is consumed. Don't touch the material with the stick, or the arc will stop. Similarly, don't let the gap get too large or your weld quality will suffer and the arc will eventually flame out. When you have used up your rod or finished welding, simply pull the rod away from the material to break the arc.

With most stick welders, the flux covering on the welding rod melts as you work and forms a crust over your weld. Use a welder's chipping hammer and wire brush to clean off the crust and inspect your work. Never give in to the temptation to weld over the crust even for a little bit. Welding over the crust traps the flux material in the weld, creating a porous, weak, and ugly seam.

If you're using a TIG welder, make sure your tungsten needle is sharp and that you have the correct kind of welding rod. Position your welding rod and the welding gun at one end of the joint you plan to weld. Step on your pedal to create the arc and observe the puddle of molten metal. Dip the welding rod into the puddle with small motions. Each time you dip, you leave a small amount of the welding rod melted into the puddle. Push the puddle along the seam with small motions, dipping the rod into the puddle to add material to your weld. Getting a good bead this way requires some coordination, but with a little practice, getting a good bead from a TIG welder is not difficult.

With an oxy-acetylene welder, first get your flame set correctly. Since a gas flame operates at a much lower temperature than an electric arc, it takes more time to create a puddle of molten metal. When you have a small puddle, push it with the flame and dip your welding rod in the puddle to add material as you would with a TIG welder. Gas welding generally takes longer and is more finicky than arc welding, but your results can be just as good. Patience is a virtue with all welding, but especially with oxy-acetylene.

5 When you're comfortable with pushing a bead, you can try pulling a bead. Pulling a weld is a bit more difficult than pushing, but some welders prefer this technique, especially with flux-core wire feed welders.

Using a MIG or wire-feed welder, position the welding gun angled back from the starting point and start the arc and the wire flow. As you weld, observe the puddle of molten metal and pull the tip of the welding gun in small back-and-forth motions along the welding seam. You will leave behind cooling weld.

Making a pull weld, you can see how the MIG gun is angled back from the arc and the weld bead is left behind the gun as it travels.

As with a push bead, keep your motions and your travel speed even. Pull welds with MIG welders on aluminum are not recommended, because the gas cloud tends to dissipate and can result in a porous or dirty weld bead.

With a stick welder, strike your arc and then angle the stick away from the weld. Move the rod in small motions, leaving the puddle behind to cool. Be careful of your arc length, as it's harder to maintain proper distance when pulling a stick weld.

If you're using a TIG welder, pull welding is not recommended. But to try it for yourself, angle the welding

Welding Standards

Many racing sanctioning bodies and government motor vehicle bureaus require welds to meet ASTM standards. These standards generally include 360-degree beads for joining tubes, and plate or tube gussets of a certain size at critical joints, but since the standards books are expensive to purchase, few inspectors and fewer shops have them handy.

If your work must be approved by an inspector before you can take it on track or on the road, you should speak to the inspector about expectations before you begin. Alternately, be prepared to show that your design and execution meets any relevant standards that may be required, but be aware that some inspectors want to see work in progress, and may not approve work that was not inspected as it progressed.

gun away from the start of the weld as you create the arc. Observe your puddle and push the molten material into the arc as you dip the welding rod. Pull the arc along the seam with small motions, coordinating the rod and the gun motions. Again, mind your arc distance closely when pulling a weld.

To pull with an oxy-acetylene welder, work your puddle backwards with the flame and push it with the dipping action with your welding rod. This adds material and pushes the puddle to the area being heated by your flame.

How Not to Warp Your Work

Like most materials, metal expands when it is heated, and it contracts as it cools. If you heat part of a piece during welding and then weld another part as the first part cools, the different rates of expansion and contraction in different parts of the structure will cause the assembly you're making to warp. The problem is more pronounced in smaller, thinner parts because more of the mass of the object is being heated.

Warping happens mainly when too much weld is applied too fast. If you run a long bead on one seam, then try to run a second long bead on another seam, you are at risk of warping your structure.

To help reduce warping, stitch your beads in 1-inch increments at spaces throughout your weld seam. Let each area cool as you weld in another place. Eventually you will join up all your stitches and your piece should have minimal heat distortion. You can also backstitch a project by starting about an inch from the end of the weld and welding to the end. Then start again 2 inches from the end and connect to your previous weld, and so on through the length of the bead.

Backstitching a weld is a good technique when you might be at risk of warping a piece such as this body connector made of mild sheet steel. Start a bit in from the far end and weld to the end. Then back up a bit more and weld up to your last stitch, and continue to work backwards along the joint.

TECH TIP — Ambient Temp

Try to weld an entire project at the same ambient temperature. Don't weld one part in a 40-degree shop first thing in the morning and then come back and weld another part when the metal's been out in the sun all day.

Welding Sheetmetal

Generally speaking, sheet metal is thinner than .125 inch, and referred to more often by its gauge than in terms of inches or millimeters thick. Metal that is .125 inch or greater is generally called plate. Sheetmetal is one of the most challenging materials for an amateur welder. Because it is thin and light, sheetmetal is easily warped, and it's easy to melt it and blow a hole through the material with your welder. Low welding power is required to protect the material, but this can make it hard to start and maintain an arc.

When working with a MIG or wire-feed welder on sheetmetal, tack the materials together in many places to get the positioning established, then run stitch welds carefully. Try to keep your arc focused on the heavier metal if you are welding sheet to heavier stock. Finally, join your welds up into a bead.

If possible, use TIG welding on sheetmetal, because the adjustable foot pedal power delivery makes it easier to start an arc and give it just enough power to make the weld. The fine point of the tungsten electrode also helps focus the arc for precise work.

Gas welders can also be used with success on sheetmetal, but they take more experience and finesse than a TIG unit.

Using a stick welder on sheetmetal is nearly impossible. It can be done by an expert, but it's hard to do without burning holes in the material.

Making a Heavy-Duty Shop Cart or Welding Table

Every shop needs a rolling cart, engine stand, or table, and a welding shop absolutely needs a steel-topped table. This basic structure is strong enough to serve as an engine cradle for a big-block V-8, or add a steel plate to the top to make your own welding table. You can weld on casters if you desire mobility, or keep it as a basic table.

For the purposes of the project, we assume you're using a DC MIG welder with gas and basic mild steel solid core wire. But you can undertake this project with a stick welder, oxy-acetylene, TIG, or wire-feed welder and still get good results.

These instructions provide measurements and dimensions for a small (24 x 48 x 33 inch) structure made of 1.5-inch .095-wall square box steel, but you can easily create a larger model by extending the relevant dimensions. Follow these steps:

1 Get a supply of 1.5-inch .095-wall square box steel. For this project, you need two 8-foot lengths or one 16-foot, and two 10-foot lengths or a 20-foot length. The overall lengths are important to avoid waste. Metal supply yards may have the material in 20-foot lengths, but generally make at least one cut without an extra charge, and this makes the pieces easier to carry home and use.

2 For the basic project, you can make 90-degree cuts. This leaves the ends of the tubes open. For a more advanced project, you can make 45-degree cuts on the pieces that comprise the upper and lower rectangles. This makes a tidier looking finished project. Use your chop saw or hacksaw and cut your steel into the following lengths. Make sure all pieces of a given length are identical:

- Four 48-inch lengths (cut 8-footers in half)
- Five 24-inch lengths (section a 10-foot length)
- Four 30-inch lengths (section a 10-foot length)

3 Clean up your cut ends on a belt or disc sander, and put a slight bevel on the outside edges.

For the basic project, use 90-degree cuts to make the pieces of your table. These are easy to cut and allow the entire structure to come together and stay square. It does result in open ends, but you can cap these with a bit of plate if they bother you.

This helps provide your weld a place to build up without protruding much past the original size of the tube. Give them a nice bevel but don't take too much material off—you need enough remaining to make a solid weld.

4 Arrange your base rectangle on your welding table or another flat surface, such as a solid workbench. Use your welder's magnets, carpenter's square, and tape measure to make sure the rectangle is true. You can check for true in any rectangle by measuring on the diagonals. Both diagonals will measure the same when all your corners are at 90 degrees and the lengths of your pieces are correct. There may be some gap at the joints, but that's less important—you can fill that with weld.

Tack your pieces together once you've got them measured and arranged correctly, then measure again.

5 Carefully tack weld the four pieces together—just enough to hold them in place! Then measure again to make sure you didn't disturb your angles. If all is good, then start running beads. Alternate corners and measure your angles again after each bead. You'll be surprised how much the structure moves as you weld!

When the first parts are tacked correctly and remeasured, run your beads. Make sure to alternate welding areas to avoid heat warping.

6 Repeat steps 4 and 5 for the second rectangle that makes up the top support of your table or cart. Add a third 24-inch piece across the center of this rectangle.

This bead was run a little too hot, and blew a hole through our parts. Go back in at lower power and fill that hole.

7 When you're done, set the second rectangle on top of the first. They should be identical, or nearly identical. Remove the second rectangle and use your welder's magnets and a spirit level to set up one of the four 30-inch pieces vertically on the lower rectangle. Tack weld it and re-measure with your spirit level. Then repeat this step for the other three corners. Remember to tack weld only at this point—no beads!

8 Set the upper rectangle on top of the structure. The structure should be level and the four posts should be square against the corners. If it needs adjustment, a few light blows with a lead or bronze hammer should adjust it. It's OK if you break a tack weld or two—just re-level and re-tack your piece. When you're happy with the structure, tack the top rectangle to the vertical supports.

9 Give your structure one last go-over with your squares, levels, and tape measure. If everything is still good, go around the structure and weld beads on all the appropriate seams. Alternate corners, sides, and so on until all raw edges are welded. Alternating helps stop heat-warping.

10 Now you have a basic box. You can now choose to weld on a plate of steel (use at least 1/4-inch-thick plate) to make it a table or you can fabricate and weld on some supports for an engine or other heavy item. You can also weld on some heavy-duty casters to allow it to roll around.

Tack the top of the table into place and then remeasure with the squares and a spirit level before you run a bead on any piece. In this photo you can see the glow of the weld through the back side of the box steel. This shows us that the weld is making good penetration through the material.

When all the components are joined, you've got the basis for a strong cradle, table, or roll-around cart.

The completed structure is square at all corners, solidly built, and can take a tremendous load. The box steel we used is strong and light, and the basic design will hold hundreds of pounds easily.

The open end at a corner and the completed welds joining the part to the rest of the structure. You can see the good penetration through the material.

If you decide to make a welding table, you may also want to drill some holes in one corner to bolt on a machinist's vise, or weld on some hooks to hang other tools such as your chipping hammer or a wire brush. Other common fitments include a section of tubing that you can use as a holster for your MIG, TIG, or wire feed gun. The attachments you put on your welding table are limited only by available space and your imagination!

Alternate Welding Table Designs

As an alternative design for the welding table top, consider getting some box tube or U-channel steel and spacing them about an inch apart for your table top. The advantage to this design is that it's easy to clamp or bolt parts to the middle of the table. You can also cut with a plasma or gas torch right on the table top, if you position the cut over a gap in the table. You can also fit part of a bent or right-angle piece down in the gap while you work. Many welding tables use a half-and-half design with part of the table made of a solid top and part made in strips. Some tables designed exclusively for cutting use a grid of thin plates on edge.

Bracing Your Welding Table

As an optional extension of this exercise, you can get some more 1.5-inch square stock or 1.5-inch round tube and cut it at 45-degree angles to create braces for your structure. As you cut and prepare, note how the braces must be cut at exactly the right angles to fit well and weld in cleanly. If you extended the size of the project to create a big rack, some bracing is a good idea. If you weld on a top plate to make a table, the plate itself is a strong brace.

Cutting some more steel at a 45-degree angle to create braces for our structure. This will make the basic box even stronger.

Advanced Structural Welding Option: Closed Corners

For a slightly more advanced project, consider cutting the components of your base and top rectangles at 45-degree angles. This eliminates the ugly open ends of the rectangles and gives your project a professional look. But practice on some scrap until you can get consistent 45-degree cuts from your saw—your

If you want to avoid open ends, you can cut your parts at a 45-degree angle and join them up for a 90-degree bend. But be aware that getting these angles correct is harder than it looks!

Once you've got the angles right, tack the pieces together and measure again. If everything is still correct, run a bead to make your corner.

When the bead is run all the way around the piece, you've got a nice professional-looking 90-degree corner.

professional project can look even uglier than open ends if your angles are all wrong, and truing up the angles can be difficult. Also remember that the overall length and width of your rectangles will be the measurement of the longer sides of each bar.

Welding Skills Practice: Thick and Thin Welding

One of the most common automotive welding tasks is to weld mounting tabs onto existing structures. This most often involves welding a thinner tab onto a thicker structural piece. For example, welding a window net mount onto a roll bar, or welding a bodywork mounting tab onto a ladder frame rail.

When you're welding thick and thin pieces together, you must be careful to balance the heat placed in each piece of metal. If one piece is twice as thick as the other, then spend twice as much time with the arc on the thicker piece. Just remember that you have to spend enough time on the thinner side to get that piece up to welding temperature for good penetration.

Follow these steps to weld a basic tab onto a thicker piece of metal.

1 Get the two pieces set up in the orientation you want them. A welder's magnet is generally very useful for holding a smaller piece to a larger piece while you work. Tack your pieces together carefully.

2 Position your welding gun so that the arc starts on the thicker piece, and establish your puddle primarily with the thicker piece and the filler metal you're adding. As you run your bead, gently wave the welding tip side-to-side to attach the thicker piece to the thinner piece. Most of the motion should cover the thicker piece.

As you prepare to weld the thinner material to the thicker, be sure to start your arc on the heavier piece. Your goal is to melt the thicker part into the thinner one. If you start on the thinner piece, there's less material to puddle and join up.

Carefully tack your pieces together, being careful not to overheat the thinner piece.

As you weld, wave the welding tip in small motions to melt the thicker piece into the thinner piece. Be careful not to blow a hole through the thinner piece.

CHAPTER 4

Cutting and Grinding

A large part of any automotive metalworking project involves cutting and shaping the component parts. Sometimes cutting and shaping is the whole project, but more often the initial formation is followed by welding, brazing, or other techniques to create the final product. This chapter looks at the use of standard tools for cutting and shaping metal, and offers some useful projects for practice.

People choose metal as a working material because it can be reshaped and strongly joined far more easily than wood, and is stronger than wood or plastics. You can cut metal into pieces, then weld the pieces back together and grind them smooth so that the cuts are afterwards invisible. And just as important, the piece is as strong or even stronger than it was before you started.

Most metal is sold in basic forms and quantities. Sheetmetal comes in large sheets, tubing and angle iron comes in long sticks, and plates come in a variety of sizes. These forms are almost never exactly right for what you're making, so they have to be cut and shaped. In the past, a blacksmith used a variety of chisels, files, and hammers to separate bulk metal into the required sizes and shapes. Today we have a variety of tools to help us, and we can cut many of our pieces out of cold metal. Still, there's no substitute for cutting iron by melting it, and we have tools for that, too.

Using Abrasive Cutting Tools

For the automotive metalworker on a budget, abrasive cutting tools are the default. You can purchase abrasive blades for any power saw on the market, and a carpenter's table saw is good for straight cuts in metal up to 1/4-inch thick. You can even put an abrasive blade in your 7.25-inch circular saw and get the job done. However, a small investment in a dedicated metal-cutting chop saw makes things substantially easier and safer. The table saw and, especially, the circular saw fling chips and dust all over your shop—and all the hot metal chips seem to find their way to your skin. Plus, when you're moving metal through the table saw or passing the circular saw through the metal, it can get

Welding gets all the glory, but cutting and grinding are the necessary preparation steps before you can build anything fun.

hung up and kick back on you, or the disc can disintegrate, with potentially disastrous consequences.

Chop Saw

A chop saw works by lowering the spinning blade onto the metal being cut. Because you're not moving the metal through as with a table saw, or holding the saw by hand as with a circular saw, a chop saw gives you better and more accurate cuts with a better margin of safety. As with any saw, you have to be careful and observe all manufacturer's safety precautions. Accidents happen all the time with saws, and you don't want them to happen to you.

A proper metal-cutting chop saw works best to make straight cuts in tube and box and small sections of steel plate.

You can buy a saw designed for conventional abrasive blades or for cold cut carbide metal blades. Conventional abrasive blades are made of a composite material that is designed to be consumed rather quickly when cutting. These blades are typically black in color and made from metal oxides, epoxy, and a mesh fabric. They're the same material as a cutoff wheel blade. These blades are generally inexpensive and work well enough that many fabricators need nothing else.

Metal blades for cold-cutting metal are typically designed to run at about 1,300 rpm, which is much lower than the 4,000 rpm used with abrasive blades. The advantage to this kind of saw is primarily a more accurate cut and much less dust and grit released in your shop. But while abrasive blades cost about $6 to $8 apiece, you'll pay over $100 for a 14-inch cold-cutting metal blade. Some saws have adjustable running speeds, so you don't necessarily have to buy two saws to use both kinds of blade. Check the documentation on your saw, or any saw you're considering, and see if it runs at the correct speed for the blades you want to use.

Using a Chop Saw

1. Always follow manufacturer's safety instructions and wear eye protection when using any saw.
2. Make sure the material you're cutting is held firm in the clamp provided with the saw, and if it's long material, make sure your piece is well-supported at either end.
3. When you measure your material, be sure to account for the width of the saw blade when making your cut. Mark your cut line precisely and then cut on the far side of the line for precise results.
4. Let the chop saw work its way through the material. Don't press down on it with great force, especially with a consumable abrasive blade. You can damage your piece with excess heat, and in extreme cases you can break the blade, sending pieces everywhere.
5. When the cut is made, you may need to dress it up on the belt grinder before welding.

Cutoff Wheel

A cutoff wheel is another name for the type of blade used in a chop saw, but the name is generally used to refer to a smaller-diameter wheel

A conventional abrasive chop saw is almost as good as a metal-cutting chop saw. This one costs a lot less, but generates a lot of dust.

As a lower-cost solution, you can put metal cutting blades into a body grinder, or even a circular saw.

that is used in a handheld tool. The blade may be mounted in-line with the tool body (such as a circular saw) or mounted on a body grinder, or mounted perpendicular to the saw body, as is typical with air-powered cutoff wheels.

While chop saws are used to cut long pieces to length, a handheld cutoff wheel is generally used for dress-up work or to remove material from an item too large to fit into a chop saw. For example, you would use a handheld cutoff wheel to remove excess length from a part that is already welded to an automobile body, or from the auto body itself.

As always, to use a cutoff wheel safely, keep the blade shields mounted on the tool and always wear proper safety clothing.

Reciprocating Saw

Sometimes a more traditional saw is the right answer for a cutting problem. This is especially true when you're cutting panels out of a car. If you don't own a plasma cutter, consider a reciprocating saw such as a Sawzall brand for big work, or a basic saber saw such as a Skilsaw for fine control. Both styles of saw offer blades specifically for cutting metals.

To use a reciprocating saw safely and with good results, you need to work slowly and carefully. Especially with a Sawzall-type machine, it's easy to overshoot your mark or get off track. Auto bodies typically have layers of metal, and the in-out motion of a reciprocating saw sometimes hits a hidden interior panel and diverts the saw or worse, bends the blade inside the cut panel.

The old standby hacksaw has a place in every metal shop. Get the best, sturdiest hacksaw you can find.

Bandsaw

When you're working with thin sheetmetal (18 gauge or thinner, or aluminum up to about 1/4-inch thick) you can use a traditional general purpose bandsaw for curved cuts. You need a specific metal-cutting blade, available at most hardware stores and all metalworking supply stores, but no other specialized equipment is required.

A general purpose bandsaw is a good all-around tool to have in a metal shop. Blades are not prohibitively expensive and you can do good work conveniently. Even a novice can cut out complex shapes as long as the design does not require an internal cut. In a pinch, you can weld up the access cut to the internal cut, but this situation is where a tool like a plasma cutter really simplifies matters.

For straight cuts in larger pieces, consider a metal-cutting bandsaw. These saws are generally oriented horizontally and designed to use the weight of the saw to work through the metal. They usually come with clamps and have the adjustability to make angled cuts. Some of them use a water attachment to keep the saw blade and the work piece cool.

Another useful tool option is a handheld bandsaw. These generally have an opening of about 4 inches and are useful for cutting lengths of box section or tube that you cannot maneuver into a conventional bandsaw. Using this tool, you can cut any length of 4x4 box steel quickly and easily.

Hacksaw or Coping Saw

At the bottom of the technology pyramid is the basic hacksaw and coping saw. Although they are inexpensive and labor-intensive, no metalshop should be without these fundamental tools. There are often times when no other tool will do, and this is especially true of the coping saw. You can make delicate internal cuts using a drill to open a hole, and then thread the coping saw blade through the hole to begin your cut. It'll take a bit longer than using a plasma torch, but if you don't own that tool, a coping saw is affordable on every budget.

Always use a blade with at least 32 teeth per inch to cut metal. Also, invest in the best, most solid saw bodies you can find. A weak saw body allows the blade to twist as you cut, giving you an angled cut that must then be ground down. Keep your saw blades tight in the body and work slowly for a clean, straight cut.

Using Shearing Tools

Along with grinding tools, there are many low-cost tools available for shearing sheetmetal and light-gauge plate. Some of these tools are bench-mounted and useful for cutting heavier stock, some are free-standing and used to cut large pieces of sheetmetal. But by far the most common tools are hand shears, and every shop should have a selection. Hand shears allow you to do small cuts and fine adjustment cutting quickly and easily.

Nibbler

Also in the category of shearing tools is the nibbler. These tools are typically pneumatic-powered, but are also available in electric varieties. The nibbler operates by taking a series of small bites out of a piece of sheetmetal. You can use a nibbler to cut many complex shapes from sheetmetal, but the primary tradeoff is the width of the cut. A nibbler makes a wider cut than a traditional shear. A nibbler is also harder to use to achieve square corners.

The other challenge of using a nibbler is that you have to hold it carefully, or it will "eat" off in its own direction. There's quite a bit of vibration as it works, so it can take practice and a steady hand to get precise results with a nibbler.

Cutting a Sheetmetal Gauge Surround with a Nibbler

If you have a nibbler, here's a practice project to create a simple round-cornered under-dashboard gauge panel using a nibbler. Use a hole saw to cut the gauge holes and a brake or basic bench vise to make the single bend, but the overall shape is good and convenient to make with a nibbler.

Soda cans, coffee cans, quarters—anything round can be used as a template if it's got the right radius.

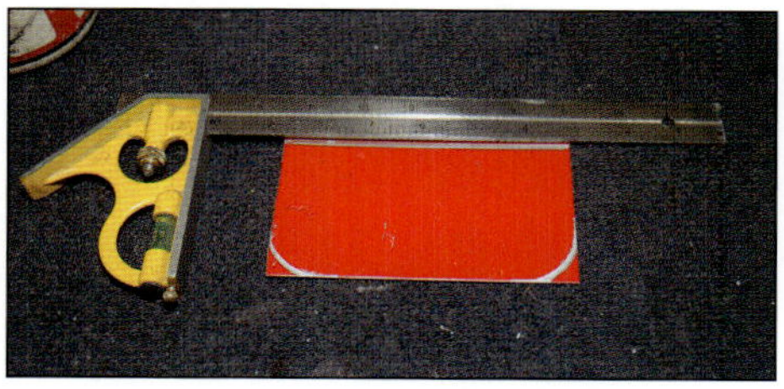

A basic carpenter's sliding square and rule is a valuable tool for marking a line.

1 You can lay out an under-dash hanging gauge panel easily by hand. To fit two standard $2\frac{1}{16}$-inch gauges you need a piece of sheet aluminum that is 5 inches wide by 4 inches tall. Use a soda can to trace 90 degrees of curve on the lower end of the mounting plate and a straightedge to mark an inch from the top for a 90-degree bend.

2 Use your nibbler to trim the rounded edges of the plate. As you cut, note how difficult it would be to get a nice square corner with the nibbler. For that, you need a shear.

3 Dress up the edges of the sheet with your deburring tool, sandpaper, or your belt grinder until they're smooth.

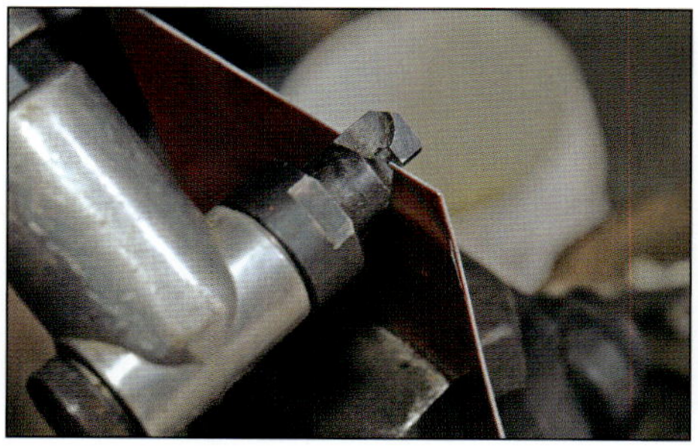

Note how quickly the nibbler works, and how easy it is to slip and nibble right through your project!

Nibblers leave a ragged edge. A deburring tool probably wouldn't be enough to clean this—you'd want to use the belt grinder.

4 Drill two or three mounting holes about 1/2 inch from the top edge. Then place the top inch or so in a sheetmetal brake and give it a 90-degree bend.

5 Now mark your gauge locations on the surface of the plate. If you use the actual gauges as your template, be sure you're not using the outer rim of the bezel. The actual gauge body is smaller.

6 Use your hole saw to cut the holes for your gauges. Alternately, you can drill a hole and use a

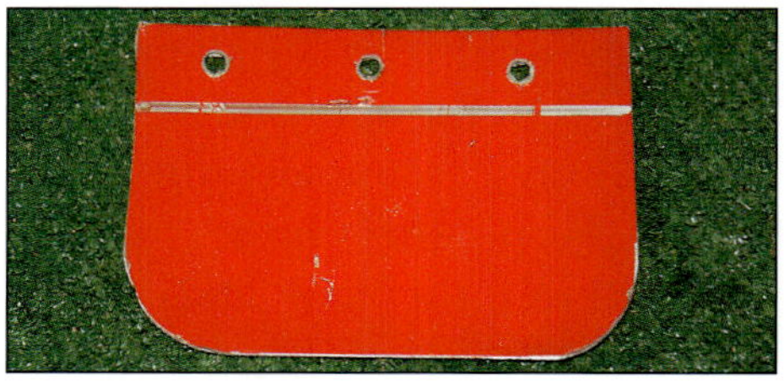

Drill mounting holes while the project is still flat, if you can.

We bent this little piece in the leg vise, just to show that it works well if you're careful.

We used the gauges themselves to mark the locations for the hole saw.

coping saw, but this is time-consuming and the result won't be better than a hole saw cut. For the best fit, use a slightly smaller hole saw than the finish size of the hole. For example, choose a 2-inch hole saw for a $2\frac{1}{16}$-inch finish size and then finish the holes with your deburring tool. Be sure to use the slowest possible speed on your drill press when you're using hole saws, and also be sure to have a stout piece of wood behind the sheetmetal you're cutting. Clamp your sheetmetal to the wood block for best results.

As an alternate process, if you don't have a brake you can still get good results bending a piece of this size in an ordinary bench vise. Carefully insert your piece in the vise with the short end clamped in the jaws. Make sure the bend line is lined up at the lip of the jaws and the piece is all the way to one side or another. Using both hands, and with your thumbs right at the brake point, carefully bend the top about 15 to 20 degrees. Don't go too far! Now loosen the vise jaws and move the piece to the other end. The width of the vise jaws should overlap the previously-bent area. Again, line up the piece carefully along the brake line and bend the part about 20 degrees with your thumbs along the base. Then move the piece back and repeat this process until you've got a nice 90-degree bend all along the brake line. You should end up with a reasonably sharp bend. A couple light blows with a rubber mallet or other dead-blow hammer can tighten up your angle if it's not sharp.

You can get aluminum pre-coated in several colors. This red looks great for car interiors.

As another alternate project, you can lay out a custom-fit gauge panel with a template. Because this panel should be made for your particular car, take a sheet of thin single-layer cardboard and cut it to fit the available space in your dash. Be sure to make some provision for attaching the panel to the dash! For example, older air-cooled Volkswagen Beetles have a panel just to the left of the speedometer that can be removed and replaced with a sheetmetal panel that fits two small $2\frac{1}{16}$-inch gauges for oil pressure and temperature.

Hand and Bench-Mounted Shear

For straight-line cuts, you can't beat a shear. Virtually every metal shop working with sheet uses hand shears of some kind. The most basic are tin snips, and these are just large heavy-duty scissors. You can get good results with a basic set of aircraft style hand shears. Remember that they come in straight-cutting and left/right-biased styles, and it's good to have all three types. This is not to say that you can't cut left or right curves with a straight-cut shear, but it's easier and yields better results to use the right tool for the cut. If you have only left- or right-cut shears, remember that a left cut is a right cut if you start at the other end, or flip the piece over!

> **TECH TIP**
>
> **Panel Trace**
>
> If you want to duplicate a car's existing dash panel, just remove it and use it as your tracing pattern.

The biggest free-standing units handle up to an 8-foot sheet of metal, but limit you to straight-line cuts. More common are the bench-mounted varieties, which can be purchased for as little as $100. The largest of these "throatless" models can handle mild steel up to 3/16-inch thick and with a little practice you can use them to make steady curves in thick sheet metal. Throatless shears work like a very heavy set of hand shears, and work with replaceable blades. The body of the shear also curves upward toward the back to accommodate rotating the sheet metal as you make your cut—this is what allows the throatless shear to cut curves. If you plan to work with heavier sheet and cut curves, this tool is a good investment.

Making a Removable Sheetmetal Panel with a Hand Shear

This is a simple project that can be done in minutes with a set of aircraft shears. If you like, you can use a bead roller to add some fancy touches to your product, or just leave it plain.

1 Make a template of the panel you need. You can draw it right on your sheetmetal, or make a cardboard template and transfer the design to your sheetmetal. Note any bends you might need to make and be sure to leave plenty of overlap (about an inch in every dimension) if you plan to use Dzus fasteners.

2 Working as much as possible with the existing edges of the sheetmetal, cut out your panel shape with your shears. Take your time—

the benefit of aircraft shears is that you can get a good look at your work while you're cutting.

3 Clean up your edges with sandpaper or your belt grinder.

4 Decide where you need to mount your Dzus fasteners. For an ordinary rectangle shape, you can use two or four fasteners. If you use two, position them at diagonally opposite corners of the plate. Drill holes to accommodate the fastener. Generally this means a 5/8-inch hole for the main body of the fastener and two smaller holes for the rivets that mount the fastener to the plate. Drill the main hole first and insert the fastener, then mark and drill the rivet holes. Pop-rivet the fasteners in place.

5 Next, go to the receiving panel and overlay the cover panel. Mark the location of the Dzus fasteners. You can drill a smaller hole

Cutting a nice round corner in thin aluminum is easy with an aircraft shear.

After the plate is cut out and the edges are smooth, install the Dzus fasteners.

Dzus Fasteners

This project also introduces a common device known as a Dzus (pronounced Zeus) fastener. These are spring-loaded fasteners that hold one plate to another. A quarter-turn with a screwdriver, a coin, or a Dzus tool will attach or release them, so they're popular with racers. You have to install a mounting wire to the backing plate, but once installed, Dzus fasteners work well and give your project a professional racing look. Dzus fasteners are available in a variety of depths for different applications. They are usually held to their plates by rivets, but are sometimes brazed or welded in place.

Dzus fasteners hold the world's top race cars together. Get them snug on their spring-wires and they'll stay put until you twist them.

This shows how the Dzus fastener grabs the mounting wire. You need to pop-rivet that wire to the backside of the receiving plate.

in the receiving panel to receive the shaft of the Dzus fastener.

6 Working from the *back side* of the receiving panel, drill smaller holes for the pop rivets to hold the Dzus wires to the panel. Pop rivet the wires into place from the front, however, for a flat, clean, and professional-looking installation. The Dzus wire is generally made of springy material and it stands back from the panel a bit, so the Dzus fastener makes a snug connection.

7 Test fit your panel. The most common mistake is to use a Dzus fastener that is too long, so it fails to get a secure grip on the wire. If that happens, drill out the rivets and get a shorter Dzus fastener or put some gasket material between the cover panel and the receiving panel.

Dzus-fit panels can be any shape or size, and they're easy to remove and replace for ready access to any part of your car. Dzus-fit panels are accepted as bulkheads by virtually all racing organizations.

You have to drill three holes for each Dzus fastener—one big hole for the shaft and two smaller ones to pop rivet the fastener to the plate. Use the fastener itself as your template.

When you have pop-riveted it to the plate, the Dzus fastener sits almost flush with the surface.

This plate will hold tight, and yet you can remove it in seconds with a quarter or a screwdriver. And it looks professional when it's installed.

Using Grinding Tools

No matter how precise your cutting tools may be, you also need metal grinding tools to produce finished products. Every edge cut with a torch or a shear requires sanding or grinding to become smooth and look good.

There is a huge variety of filing, grinding, sanding, and other abrasive tools on the market. We'll cover the most common tools and their uses.

Beyond the usual basic safety precautions such as wearing eye protection, there are specific habits that

Any welding shop or hardware store will have a variety of grinding tools and abrasive supplies to keep them going.

Body grinders are such useful tools, most shops keep a bunch of them around, fitted out with different grinding and cutting abrasives.

should be avoided with grinding tools. Chief among them is the practice of using any part of the abrasive other than the designed grinding face, for example, grinding on the side of a grindstone wheel on a bench grinder. Many bench grinders have lost their protective side covers over time, but grinding on the side of a commercial grindstone can cause it to shatter—and that is dangerous at high RPM when you're standing in the way.

If your body grinder is set up with a grinding face, do not use its edge as a cut off wheel, and don't try to grind with the face of a cut off wheel. They're not made for it. Another common safety problem with body grinders is allowing the cord to get in the way of the work. A metal grinder eats through a power cord in no time at all, creating an electrical shock hazard.

As always, follow the manufacturer's safety instructions with all grinding tools.

Body Grinder and Grindstone

Most body grinders are set up so that the grinding surface faces away from the user. To effectively use a body grinder, use a light touch. If you lean or press into the work, you can gouge the metal more than you intend—it happens in an instant and then you have to fill the hole with weld or body filler. Keep the grinder moving in long, smooth motions and let the grinding face wear down the high spots.

Be aware that using a grindstone, disc, or belt imparts heat to your work, and you can generate enough heat to warp light materials simply with grinding. You can also take the temper out of tool steel and other hardened materials with grinding. In fact, you can get a good look at heat colors by simply holding a bolt against a grindstone. Try it, and you can see the blue, brown, and straw colors that indicate temperature effects on steel.

But you can also produce many useful tools and parts using only a standard bench grinder with a rough stone and a smooth stone. Change one stone to a wire wheel and you can smooth out most of your work. Change the other stone for a buffing wheel and you can polish your work to a mirror finish. The key is patience—using a grinding tool always takes time.

Belt Sander/Grinder

A belt sander with an additional flat grinding face is a key tool in any metalshop. You can quickly dress up or shape any piece with a strong belt grinder. The rounded end produces almost any kind of curve you need, while the flat part of the belt gives you a reliable straight edge. If your grinder includes a round disc, you can also use that face for straight edges. Straight lines are much harder to create with a bench grinder or a body grinder.

Get a variety of belts to go with your grinder. You can get extremely

A belt grinder is useful for cleaning up rough gas and plasma cuts, and shaping parts for welding and direct use.

To set pressure on a regulator, open the valve on the bottle and listen for leaks. The gauge closest to the bottle shows the pressure inside. Turn the valve on the regulator clockwise to increase hose pressure, which reads on the other gauge.

TECH TIP

Straight Cuts

When you want to cut in a straight line with a gas torch, affix a piece of angle iron to the top of the piece you're cutting. Affix it with clamps, magnets, or even tack-weld it on. Position it so that if you hold the cutting head of your torch up against the angle iron, the flame is in just the right position to make the cut. You'll get a straight cut every time!

rough grits for removing lots of material quickly and fine belts down to 400 or 600 grit for polish work. The other secret to good results is to replace your belts frequently. Also, keep separate belts for working with aluminum and steel. You don't want to introduce flecks of either metal into a piece made from another—especially if you're dressing up an edge prior to welding.

A belt grinder is especially useful for creating welding bevels and precise angles such as fishmouth joints in tube steel. As with all grinding tools, bring your patience and use a light touch when grinding.

Cutting with an Oxy-Acetylene Torch

An oxy-acetylene torch is a very familiar sight and a basic symbol of welding. Many movies begin an automotive construction montage sequence with the lighting of a cutting torch. Yet it's important to know that a cutting torch and a welding torch are very different tools even though they both use the same bottle of oxygen and acetylene.

A welding torch uses the basic valves on the oxy-acetylene torch handle to control the mixture and flow of gases. A welding torch produces a comparatively small flame, and is used to gently melt the welding rod and surrounding metal into a small puddle for joining parts together. A cutting torch is a larger tool that includes a lever and an extra valve for additional oxygen flow. When you've got a puddle of molten steel from the basic flame, pressing the lever actuates the increased oxygen flow and literally blows the molten metal out the other side of your piece. If your piece is too thick, you might not be able to cut it all the way through, but thin materials cut very easily.

Note that you cannot use oxy-acetylene to cut very hard stainless steel alloys, and gas cutting generally melts aluminum into a big puddle of slag. Use your oxy-acetylene cutting torch for mild steel and tool steel only. If you need to cut other materials, get a plasma torch. You'll be glad you did.

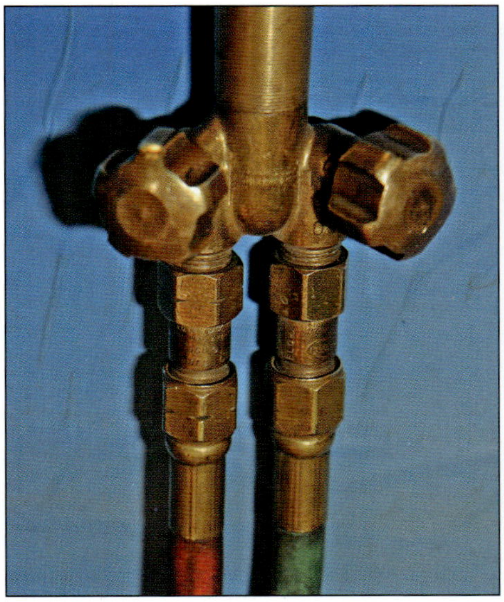

The red hose always leads to the acetylene bottle, and the green to the oxygen bottle. The valves on the handle control the flow to the torch.

When you first strike a flame, you should get a yellow and smoky fire from pure acetylene.

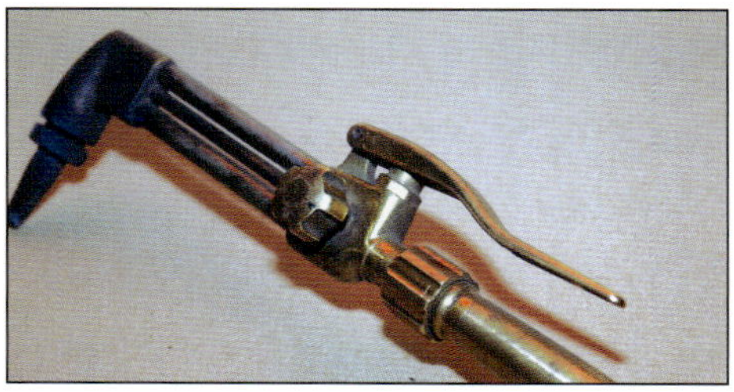

The valve on the handle of a cutting torch controls the constant flow of oxygen. When you press the lever, you get an additional blast of oxygen to cut molten metal.

The best way to learn gas cutting is to try it and practice, so let's get right to the projects.

Cutting Practice with an Oxy-Acetylene Torch

This is a basic project to get you used to cutting with an oxy-acetylene torch. You need your torch kit and some scrap steel. Ideally, you should clamp your scrap metal into a vise on your welding table or workbench. Make sure you've got your gloves and all your safety gear together, and that there's nothing around that's flammable. A fire extinguisher and a bucket of water are good to have close at hand.

Note that the best position for oxy-acetylene cutting is always to lay your piece out flat so you're cutting through from above. This allows the molten metal to drain out the bottom of the cut rather than running down the side of your piece. Obviously, you should never cut from below, or you'll have molten steel raining down on you! Follow these steps:

1 First, close all the valves on your welding torch. You don't want gas leaking out while you're setting things up. Get a piece of scrap steel and put it in your bench vise. It gets hot, so put on your gloves. Select your cutting tip size to match the thickness of the metal you're cutting. Choose a #0 tip for all steel up to .25-inch, #1 for .25 up to .50-inch, #2 for metal up to 1 inch thick. Larger number tips can be used for cutting thicker materials, but are almost never used in automotive applications. In general, select the lowest number (smallest) tip suitable for the metal you're cutting. Your cuts will be more precise and you'll use less gas.

2 Next, set the correct pressures at the regulators attached to your welding bottles. Open the main valves on the top of your bottles. Your regulators have two gauges each. The gauge nearest each bottle shows the pressure in the bottle. You should see at least hundreds of pounds of pressure in each bottle. The gauge on the other side of each regulator shows the gas pressure going to the torch. You adjust the gas pressure at the torch by turning the valves on the regulators. Start out by dialing in about 20 pounds of oxygen and 7 pounds of acetylene pressure for cutting. If you are using a large cutting torch, you might need more pressure.

3 Now find the acetylene valve on your torch. You can tell the acetylene valve because the hose leading to it is red. The hose leading to the oxygen bottle is green. Equipment makers make acetylene bottles with reverse (left-hand) threads so it's hard to get these mixed up if the hoses are already attached to your regulators. Get your torch lighter ready and open the acetylene valve just a little. You can usually hear the gas start to flow. Light it immediately, because you don't want unburned gas to accumulate around you.

4 The fire you get from the torch should be yellow, and it's likely to be smoky. If the first isn't smoky, slowly close the acetylene valve until it starts to produce a little smoke. Then open the oxygen valve on the side of the torch a little bit, and notice that there is no change in the flame. You have to open the valve down by the hose and the valve that is up on the side of the torch in order to flow oxygen into the flame.

5 When oxygen joins the acetylene, the core of the flame turns blue, and there's a set of bright blue flames right at the tip. By adjusting the knob up on the side of the cutting torch, you adjust the constant flow of oxygen into the flame. When the set of blue flames is

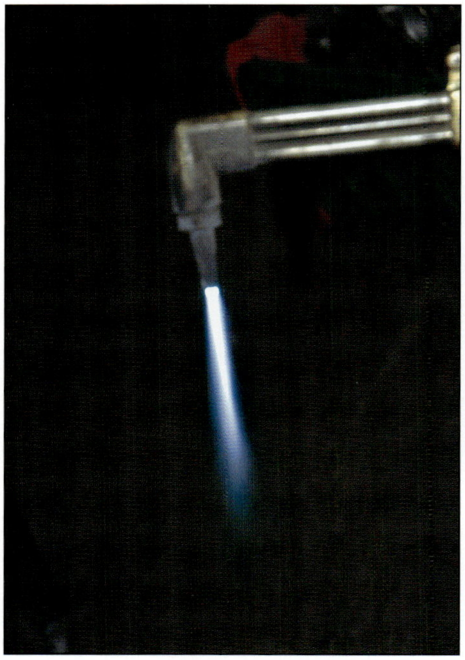

When your oxygen mix is good, you get a short, bright blue flame inside a larger blue flame. Now you're ready to start cutting.

To cut thick material, spend some time preheating the area, then create a puddle before you add oxygen to blow the molten steel out. If you do it right, the oxygen both clears the cut and melts the adjacent metal to continue the cut.

TECH TIP

Gas Cutting

It takes years to get really good with a cutting torch, especially with thick materials. Expert gas-cutters can cut so smoothly it looks as if they used a hot knife, but for most of us, gas-cutting is an inexact and somewhat messy business. So, when you plan your cuts, give yourself some fudge factor and plan to clean up your cuts on a grinder.

small and consistent, try pressing the lever on the torch. The center of your flame should jump out and you should hear the flame increase. If it doesn't do this, open the oxygen valve down by the hose a little more. Pressing the lever releases more oxygen directly from the hose to the center of your flame, and this is crucial for cutting.

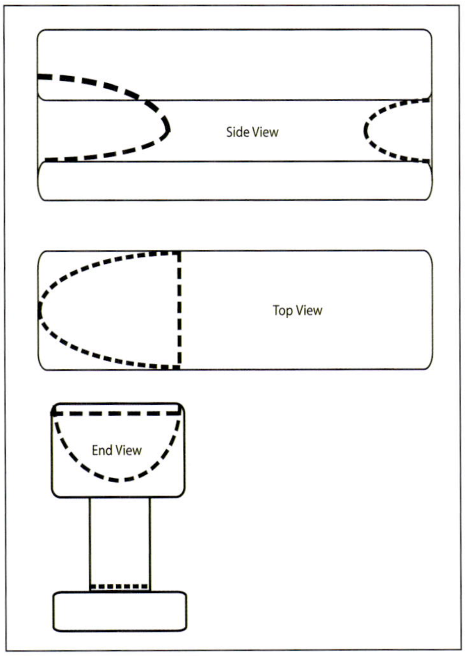

Here's a basic set of cuts to make a traditional anvil shape from a piece of railroad track. There's no need to round the bottom of the horn, unless you want to spend the time doing it.

6 When your flame is set correctly, go to your piece of scrap steel and hold the flame against it. As the steel heats up, it starts to glow and eventually start to spit sparks like a fireworks sparkler. That happens when the steel is at the melting point, and you'll get a puddle of molten steel. Now press your oxygen lever and begin cutting.

7 In a smooth motion, push your puddle forward very slowly. You can gauge how fast you can cut by how fast the metal melts in the path of your flame. If you go too fast, you'll lose your cut. Too slow and you'll melt more than you want to and your cut will be a mess.

Practice your cutting technique on scrap steel until you are comfortable cutting steel of different shapes and sizes. Be very careful about your ventilation whenever you use gas welding. Not only does the flame generate carbon monoxide, but sometimes there are impurities in paint, grease, and other substances on your materials that generate poisonous gases. Galvanized metals and tin in general produce poisonous vapors when heated to welding torch temperatures, and you don't want to breathe any of that.

Making an Anvil from Railroad Track

A good piece of practice with a cutting torch that also makes a useful tool for your shop is to create a small anvil from a piece of scrap railroad track. This low-cost project can be completed in an afternoon with a cutting torch, body grinder, flat mill files, and perhaps a drill.

When done, you have a small anvil suitable for chiseling, light forming, and many other workshop uses. Note that this railroad track is not a hardened steel surface, so you won't be able to beat on it with a 16-pound sledge, but it serves for small work adjustments and light duty forging.

First, you need a length of railroad track. Any piece of track about 12 to 24 inches in length will work. You can use light gauge or full size rail, depending on the size of anvil you want. You can get a piece of track at many iron scrapyards—it's not hard to find. But resist the

Mark your piece of track with the shape you want. You can use a welder's paint pen, a soapstone, or a plain felt-tip marker.

With the track all marked up, we're ready to start cutting. But remember, the shape isn't finalized until you cut.

temptation to go prowling for a chunk of track in a railyard or along train tracks. That's always dangerous and usually illegal.

The thickest cut needed is up to 2 to 3 inches through the bulk of the rail-top to rough out the anvil horn, so you'll need a #4 or #5 tip for those cuts, and a #2 tip for the cuts through thinner portions of the rail. Make sure both your oxygen and acetylene tanks are full before you start, because you're going to use a lot of gas to get this project done.

When you have your piece of railroad track, follow these steps:

1. Design your anvil and mark the design on the metal with a welding marker, soapstone, or paint pen. You probably will not have enough space to plan hardy or pritchel holes. About the only thing you can do is plan a horn or other rounded shape at either end of the piece. Think about the kind of work you plan to do and you can decide on a rounded or flat top, one or two horns (or no horn), and how deep to cut out the throats.

2. Brace up your piece of track on your welding table or some other good surface where you can cut from above. Never cut or weld directly on a concrete floor, because water in the concrete can flash into steam and cause part of the concrete to explode. If you have a vise large enough to hold your piece of track, that works best. Clear all flammable materials away. Pay special attention to what's directly underneath the area you plan to cut.

3. Get out your gas torch and #2 tip and first cut out the throats from the base area. Start with about 3 pounds of acetylene pressure and about 40 pounds of oxygen

We're cutting the throats out of the thin part of the track. We'll clean up our cuts later, and then grind them smooth.

You might have to give the cut piece a tap to get it out, but be careful—it's going to be very hot!

When you've got the throats created, you can cut out the horn. This is thick material and uses a lot of gas. But be patient and a basic torch kit will do it.

In about an hour, we had roughed out the anvil with the torch. Now comes about 2 to 3 hours with the grinder.

available when cutting. Take your time and make your cuts as clean as possible. Follow your marked line carefully and try to keep your cuts straight through the material. Note that the whole anvil gets very hot before you're done cutting. Leave the base of the anvil in place all the way out to the ends of the working surface; it's better for stability.

4 Next, rough out the horn (or horns) you designed. Use the #4 or #5 tip, based on the thickness of the material you're cutting. You want 4 to 5 pounds of acetylene and 45 to 50 pounds of oxygen pressure available. If you want a flat-topped horn, you can just cut straight down from the sides. If you want a round-topped horn, you can try to cut again at an angle to remove a lot of material fast, but unless you're very good at cutting, this is likely to take more work than simply grinding away what you don't need.

The important place to grind smooth is the horn, but we wanted to smooth over our cuts to get a nice looking tool when we're done.

Our anvil is almost done. We spent a long time with mill files getting the top of our horn dead flat. If we had a machinist's mill, we could put the anvil in it and get it really flat along its whole length.

5 Now your anvil has its basic shape. The rest of the process requires harder work. Start by grinding your cuts smooth with an electric body grinder. This takes some time, and if you made any deep mistakes with the torch, you might consider filling them with weld from your MIG welder and then smoothing over with the body grinder. At this time, you should also use the grinder to flatten the top of your anvil if you want it so. If your anvil is long enough, you might consider flattening some of the face and leave some of it curved. If you've got a friend with a machinist's mill, you can also flatten the face easily using that tool.

6 After a couple hours with the body grinder, you probably used up a couple of grinder discs and made a big pile of grinding grit on the floor. But your anvil's looking pretty good by now. You can finish up the detail work with files for the areas you couldn't reach with the grinder. Mill files are also good for checking flatness. If the file wants to rock back and forth on the face, it isn't flat yet. Some people polish their anvils up to a mirror-bright finish, but you can take yours to whatever level you like. It's your tool, after all.

7 Finally, turn your anvil over and drill some holes at the four corners of the base. You can also burn these holes through with your gas torch and the #2 tip. This allows you to bolt the anvil to your workbench or your welding table. Track anvils have also been bolted to truck bumpers, mounted on stumps, and placed on custom-made stands. If you plan to hammer on your anvil, it's best to mount it on a solid piece of wood like a workbench or a section of a log. Hammering on a steel anvil bolted (or welded) to a steel table is extremely noisy!

Optional: If you have access to appropriate equipment or if there's a heat-treating company in your area, you can harden your track anvil somewhat by heating the entire piece to red-hot and placing it in an oil quench. Do not use a water quench or the piece may break. You can also buy some hardfacing rods for your stick welder and build up the top and machine it flat again. But for automotive work, hardening a railroad track anvil is generally not necessary.

Cutting with a Plasma Cutter

Plasma cutters are relatively new tools that use superheated compressed air (or other common arc welding gases) to cut metal. Without getting too much into the physics, gas plasma is what stars are made of. Plasma is also present in the arc of your electric welder, and that's how the plasma cutter works. A plasma cutter (or torch) is an arc welder with a supply of filtered, compressed air. When you actuate the plasma cutter, it creates an arc strong enough to puddle the metal you're cutting. Then the compressed air blows through the arc, which turns it to plasma. The superheated plasma then blows the molten metal out of the cut you're making and melts the metal in its path. A second jet of air or gas does not pass through the arc, and this is used as a shielding gas in the same way that a MIG or TIG welder uses gas.

Modern plasma cutters can be purchased new for less than $1,000. Larger models can cut through steel up to an inch thick, and a plasma cutter can also work stainless steel, aluminum, and other non-ferrous metals easily. The precision and quality of a plasma cut is nothing short of amazing.

There are several plans for plasma cutting tables with waste receptacle trays available on the Internet. These tables feature a grid plan to support your work. The bars of the grid take some abuse from the plasma cutter, but are designed to be replaceable when they become too damaged for further service. Many of these tables also include a chute or tray to catch the slag, dust, and other waste materials from the plasma cutting process. Some of these waste trays are designed to be filled with water, which reduces fire danger and simultaneously helps limit dust distribution.

Plasma is the perfect tool for repairing rusty automotive bodywork because of the narrow cut and the precision of the cut. With a plasma cutters, there is very little oxidization of the surrounding steel in the cutting process. Gas torches—especially in the hands of amateurs, leave a great deal of burned steel behind. The plasma torch passes along the metal so quickly that the heat does not disperse. Thus, there's little or no weakened area left behind. You can cut painted metal without ruining the finish much beyond the place where you cut. Then you can cut out your replacement parts with identical accuracy. If you plan to do automotive bodywork repair, a plasma cutter is almost a requirement in a modern shop. It's a great investment in your work.

TECH TIP

Clear Mark

Make some marks (typically, a series of X letters) in the areas that will be cut out and discarded. If you don't mark your plan clearly, it's easy to get confused and cut out something you wanted to keep when you're in the middle of cutting.

For this project, we found a piece of 1/16-inch aluminum to make a decorative hot rod flame grill. A piece of cardboard sheet about the same size as the metal will make our template.

Cutting Stencil Designs with Plasma

Follow these steps to get started cutting with plasma. Automotive painting stencils such as flames are a good source for practice designs, but if you want to start with an easier cut, consider a basic Chevy bow-tie logo. You can trace virtually any design on thin plate or sheet of steel or aluminum.

1 Make sure you're cutting in a clean, safe environment. Cutting plasma reaches temperatures of about 30,000 degrees, and you can cut right through your welding table or light your workbench on fire very easily. Never use a plasma cutter on concrete, because water that has soaked into the concrete can flash into steam and cause the concrete to explode.

2 Because a plasma cutter is a modified arc welder, there's a ground clamp you need to attach to your workpiece or your welding table, just like an arc welder.

3 Position your piece of plate or sheetmetal and draw or trace a complex shape on it with a felt-tip pen or welding marker. You can use purchased stencils or make your own. For flames, try it yourself. Draw some flames on a sheet of thin cardboard. If you don't like your results, start over with a different color pen or just turn the cardboard over.

4 When you like your design on the template, cut it out with a craft knife or razor and you've got your stencil. Position it on your metal and trace around it to transfer your design to the metal.

5 Before you work on your real project, take a piece of the same material and get your plasma torch set up with the correct power. Use the least power consistent with making smooth cuts when working with aluminum. For sheet-gauge aluminum, this is the minimum power setting on your torch. Ensure that the workspace is clear and that the material is sitting at a comfortable height. In short, make your mistakes here and be ready for smooth work when you cut for keeps.

6 You can start plasma cutting anywhere—the plasma will quickly penetrate aluminum or steel and start your cut. Start in a waste portion of the metal and bring your cut over to your desired cutting line. This prevents you from leaving a large starting hole in the finished piece.

7 Start your cuts at one edge of the piece and cut out your design by alternating sides. This limits the amount of heat transferred into the metal at one time in one area. Sheet aluminum is very prone to warping with just a little heat, so be extra careful with that material. Cuts should begin and end in natural locations and be as smooth as possible. If you need to rest or you're running out of reach, angle your cut into waste material before you stop the torch. You can pick up the line again from another point in the waste material.

8 Try to get a feel for how quickly you can cut the material and still maintain a smooth, clean edge. For best results, hold your cutting tip at the manufacturer's recommended distance from the material and do not exceed the tool's recommended speed as you cut. Your cutter's manual will have this information for you. Master plasma cutters move through their work with smooth, sure motions in long cuts.

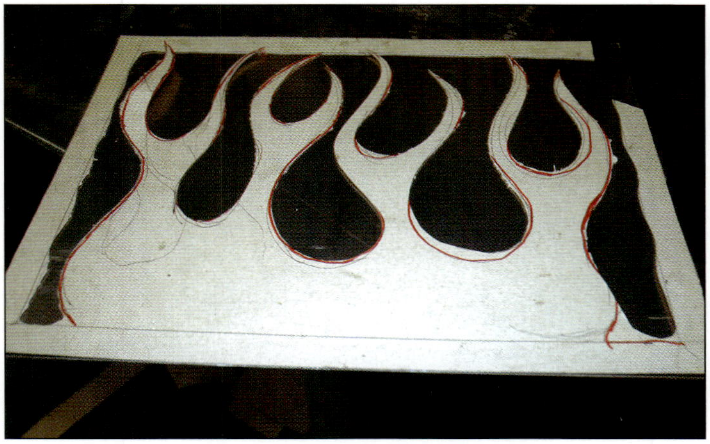

We cut out the template with an X-Acto knife. If we wanted to get fancy, we could even include some writing along the bottom. There's space for it.

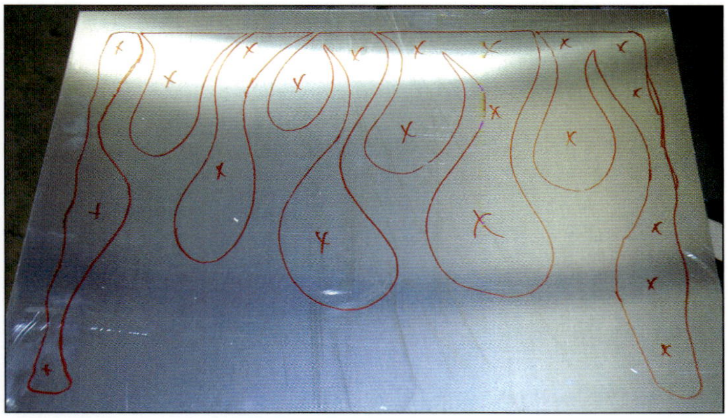

When we transferred the pattern to the metal with a felt-tip marker, we put X marks on the areas to be removed. It's easy to get confused and cut out the wrong piece when you're working!

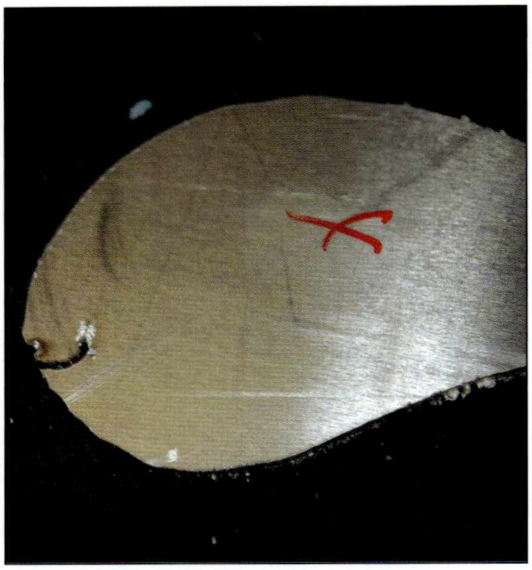

This removed piece shows how we started the cut in the waste area of the aluminum and then moved the plasma jet onto the line we wanted to cut.

9 Work your way through the pattern, discarding waste as you go. You do this by making several cuts so that as much of the leftover metal falls away as soon as possible. This prevents a large weight of hanging scrap metal from moving your piece or making the cutting process more difficult. It also gives your plasma cutter a rest from its duty cycle and allows the tip to cool.

10 Notice how much dust and slag and scrap the cutting process generates. Plasma dust and slag is renowned for getting all over the place, so fabricators have designed special tables strictly for use when cutting with plasma or gas.

Plasma Cutting Roll-Bar Mounting Plates

In Chapter 7 we learn how to make a custom roll bar or roll cage for a car. Your plasma cutter is a good tool for cutting out odd-shaped base mounting plates and gussets you might need to use when mounting a roll structure to a unibody chassis. This procedure is also good for cutting plates to make custom engine or transmission mounts or suspension attachment tabs. However, if your plates or tabs are basic rectangles, choose your chop saw to make those cuts. Note that most sanctioning bodies require roll bar mounting

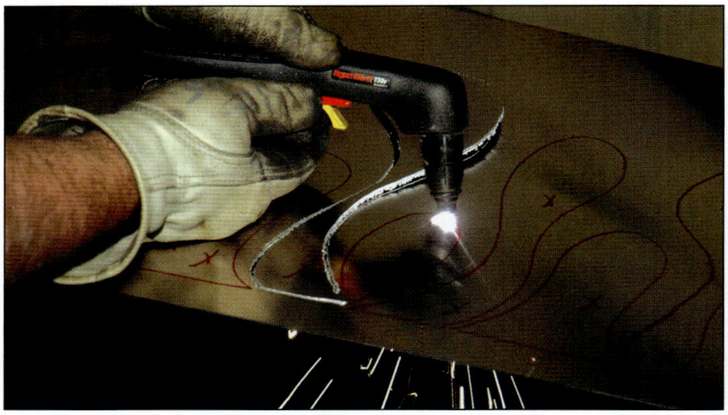

Working steadily, Russ follows the lines we made to cut out the waste sections. Going too slowly can make your line wobbly and warp the metal with too much heat, so go as fast as the torch can comfortably cut.

As each piece is cut out, remove it from the sheet.

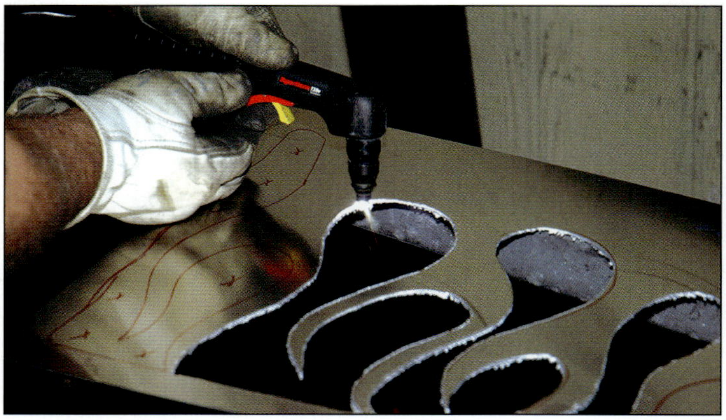

After you have removed a waste piece, you can go back and smooth out any bobbles in your line with the torch.

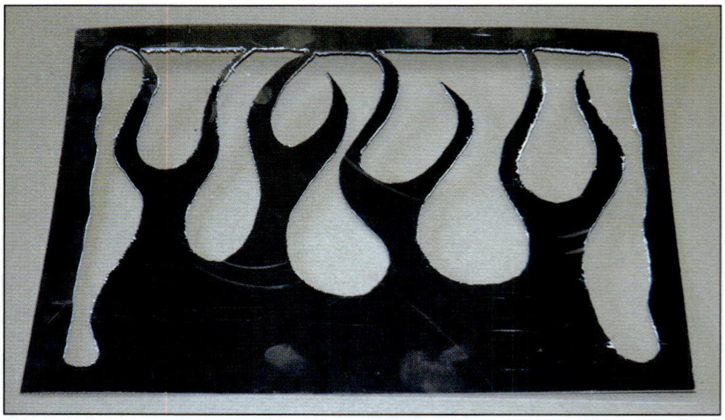

The finished piece looks great. We'll smooth the edges with sandpaper, and we left the tips attached to the frame for support, but this is how all that fancy work gets done on show cars.

plates to be at least 36 square inches of .125 (1/8 inch) mild steel.

Follow these steps to cut out plates, gussets and other custom shapes from steel plate:

1 Create a model for your part in cardboard, or trace an existing piece onto the steel using a felt-tip marker or welding pen. Use existing edges on the material whenever possible.

Plasma cuts steel plate as easily as it cuts sheet aluminum. The temperature of the plasma is about 30,000 degrees.

2 Steel for mounting plates is likely to be thicker and harder to cut than aluminum, so set your plasma cutter correspondingly higher—at least halfway through the range for 3/16- or 1/4-inch mild steel plate. Also, make sure there's nothing flammable under your cutting area, as molten steel will be falling from the plasma cutting process.

3 Make some test cuts in similar materials to make sure your settings and environment are correct before you commit cuts to your real work.

4 It's less critical with most construction parts, but start your cuts at the edge of the material or in a waste section of metal to get the best, cleanest results. Cut as quickly as possible in smooth, long motions. If you're cutting straight lines, consider clamping a piece of angle iron to your work as a torch guide.

5 Molten steel tends to flow and rejoin itself easily, especially if your gas plasma pressure is lower than it should be. You should set the machine with enough power to melt through the material and enough pressure to blow the molten steel out decisively. Still, you might have to run over some small spots twice to free up your pieces as you cut.

6 Knock each piece out as you cut it free. Set it aside or let it drop to cool before you handle it. Dress your cuts up with a grinder, at least at first. Plasma cutting masters can make a cut so smooth that it hardly needs extra work. You can also angle the torch slightly to create your own welding bevels rather than grinding them in later.

One benefit of plasma cutters over gas torches is that there is very little oxidization of the surrounding steel in the cutting process. Gas torches—especially in the hands of amateurs, leave a great deal of burned steel behind. Because the heat is so intense and brief during plasma cutting, oxidization is limited even though the shielding gas is usually just normal air. Thus, there's little or no weakened area left behind.

The bottom line on cutting and grinding is that if you have a body grinder, a belt sander and grinder, a chop saw, and a plasma cutter, there's very little you can't do.

To get a good straight cut, hold or clamp a ruler or even a piece of angle iron to your plate. The plasma jet is in the center of the torch, and you can run the side of the torch against the ruler.

While plates cut with plasma do get hot, they don't get nearly as hot as those cut with gas.

CHAPTER 5

SHEETMETAL WORK

Sheetmetal is at the heart of automotive metalworking. From the most basic flat-sided race car to the most exacting restoration, if you're working with cars you'll soon be working with sheetmetal. Some of the exercises already discussed in this book have involved cutting and bending basic flat sheetmetal. In this chapter, we'll look at shaping and bending sheetmetal into more useful parts.

Basic Sheetmetal Work

Like many skills, working sheetmetal is easy to start and difficult to do well. Yet of all the skills in this book, sheetmetal fabrication is probably the easiest to master. Much of sheetmetal work is accomplished without welding or other heat-related processes. You can undertake a sheetmetal project with nothing more than some aircraft shears and a benchtop brake and get good results. Throw in a hardware store pop-riveter and a manual bead rolling wheel and you're well on your way to professional output.

Materials

Sheetmetal generally comes in three forms—mild steel, aluminum, and stainless steel. Of these, aluminum and mild steel are by far the most commonly used for automotive projects.

Whether you're pounding a dented body panel or fabricating an entire custom interior for a race car, you're bound to work with sheetmetal in the automotive world.

Sheetmetal comes in various materials and thicknesses, but the processes by which you turn a flat sheet into something useful are always more or less the same.

Sheetmetal fabricators prefer aluminum for dashboards, bulkheads, and most other purposes because it is light, soft, and easy to work with. The downside to aluminum is that it tears easily and you really need a TIG or spool gun MIG setup to weld it. But this is a small tradeoff against the light weight and ease of use. Aluminum also polishes up nicely and doesn't oxidize like steel. It can be anodized with color, painted, and even comes pre-coated if you like. The cutting projects from Chapter 4 were executed in sheet aluminum precoated with red paint and covered with a protective plastic sheet so that the blemishes created during the working process peeled right off with the plastic cover.

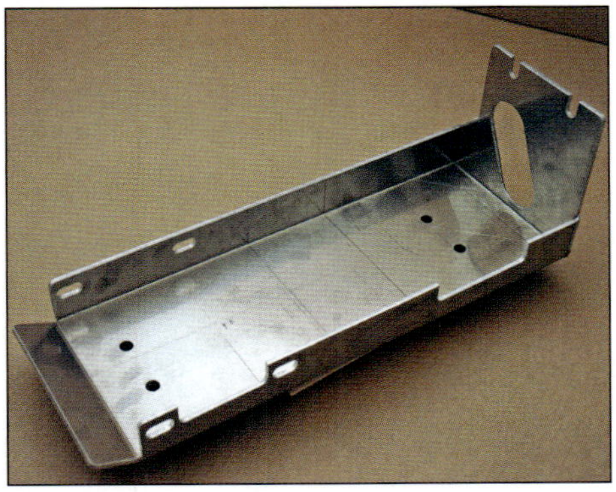

With a little work, a basic sheet becomes a precision part, like this Subaru rear differential skid plate from Primitive Racing.

For fenders, door skins, firewalls, and some critical structures, mild steel is preferred. While it is harder and heavier than aluminum, it's also more forgiving of errors and doesn't work-harden as much. So you're less likely to rip or tear mild steel. Steel is also easier to weld.

Take a look at any project you have in mind and the right material for the job should be obvious. Less obvious is the thickness, or gauge, of sheetmetal to use. For example, sheetmetal of various materials comes in a variety of thicknesses.

Choosing the correct sheetmetal is a function of considering the project you're undertaking and the strength and quality of various materials. Obviously, thin sheetmetal won't do for a car floor that has to hold the weight of a driver in a seat, but in general, you should try to choose the lightest material that will serve your purpose.

For example, for a bulkhead, you generally want at least .063 aluminum, and that assumes that you are using your bead roller to put some shape into the sheet for strength. For a weight-bearing floor, use 14 or 12 gauge steel. Remember that you're always trading off weight against strength when choosing a gauge of sheetmetal to use. Many racing organizations will specify the minimum acceptable gauge for sheet metal in critical applications such as firewalls and protective enclosures.

Measuring Sheetmetal

When you measure a sheetmetal project, remember that you can create an entire 6-sided box from a single piece of flat sheetmetal. It's a matter of knowing which small pieces to snip out and how you will bend it up. For an easy example, disassemble a cardboard box and spread it out. If you separate only those seams that are stapled or glued together, you can see that it started as a flat sheet and was bent to shape with just a few seams joined up. Sheetmetal works the same way.

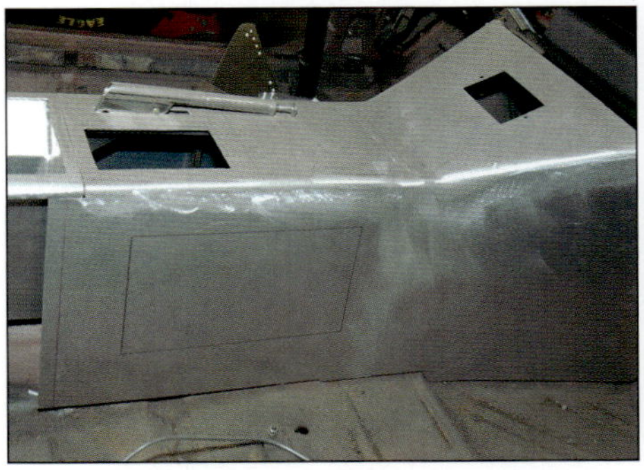

This complex transmission tunnel cover is made of mild steel. The pieces were carefully cut, hand-hammered on a buck, and welded together for an exact fit.

The rule of thumb with sheetmetal is that you need to account for all sides, but because the bends tend to be sharp, you don't have a large extra bend calculation as with tubing. You do have to measure enough, however, to make your attachments. So for an angled corner, it's not enough to bring two raw edges together. Leave a little extra on one side to bend in and have a place to rivet, weld, braze, or otherwise fasten your seam.

Cutting Sheetmetal

Of all the products that automotive fabricators use, sheetmetal is the

It's convenient and fun to use every kind of sheet metal tool such as this full size jump shear, but you can get by nicely with just a set of basic hand shears.

easiest to cut. You don't need expensive tools, but they make your life easier. A large, free-standing sheetmetal shear is great for straight cuts in sheets up to 8 feet long. A smaller bench-mounted shear is useful for most projects. But many fabricators get along just fine using only aircraft shears.

Whatever tool you use, take your time cutting sheetmetal to get good results. Lay out your pattern in felt-tip pen on the metal and be sure to note the side on which you want to cut! You can always trim a little more, but if you cut too small, you have to start over. Sheetmetal never goes as far as it looks like it will when you're handling the big sheet, so give yourself plenty of extra.

Bending Sheetmetal

Getting nice crisp bends in sheetmetal is the mark of the true craftsman. The best and easiest way to do this is with a sheetmetal leaf box and pan brake. But here again, these are large, expensive, free-standing tools. Their weight and size help make perfect, crisp bends. But you can get by and do good work with a simple bench-mount leaf brake.

For boxes and more complex shapes, be sure to get a box and pan brake with adjustable fingers so that you can put a bend in a part that already has a crosswise bend. See the project to create a basic box later in this chapter for details.

For smaller jobs, many fabricators get reasonable results with a machinist's vise. You can make brake jaws from angle aluminum that will help you. Use aluminum, wood, or some other soft metal, however, to avoid damaging your work. Then the trick is just to bend slowly with as much pressure as possible right at the bend. That's how a brake works—it applies even pressure right at the bend.

Bead Rolling

The critical tool that sets a sheetmetal fabricator apart is a bead roller. This tool puts a step or ridge into your sheet work. This allows you to put a little bit of depth into a piece of sheetmetal, increasing the cross-section of the sheetmetal without increasing its real thickness. That cross-section makes the sheetmetal shape more rigid. That's why you see professional jobs that include a number of ribs or raised areas worked into the sheetmetal. This helps stop oil canning, where the body of the sheetmetal panel tends to wobble back and forth.

Russ Nyberg demonstrates making a step in aluminum sheet metal with a bead roller. This inexpensive tool turns flat sheet into custom-fabricated panels.

A bead roller is a simple tool—a wheel or motor operates two matched dies. These dies can create a raised (or recessed) ridge or a single-sided step in sheetmetal when you squeeze the metal and roll it through the dies. The bead roller also includes an adjustment lever that controls the space between the dies. Just place your sheet between the dies, snug down the lever, and give the wheel a turn. The metal is pulled through the die and the shape of the die is transferred directly to your sheet. Once transferred, the shape is called a bead—presumably due to its resemblance to a welding bead.

You can also find dies that make a thin raised line in sheet for embossing, or dies that make an angle bend at the edge of a piece of sheetmetal. This function is different from a brake because a brake makes straight line bends, and the bead roller allows

Russ LaFontaine makes a race car body panel with a box and pan brake.

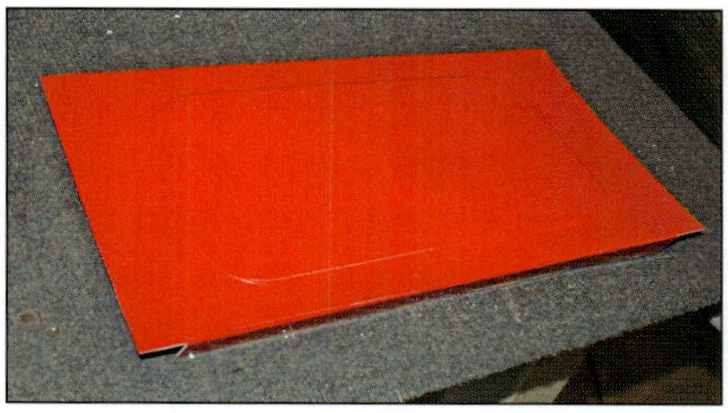

Raising a step in the middle of this panel helps keep it firm, and it looks great, too.

To make a hem in a straight edge, first bend the lip past 90 degrees, then open the brake wide enough to insert the bent lip.

All you have to do is close the brake again to fold over the hem. You get a nice, crisp hem with this technique.

you to follow a curve as you move the sheet through the machine. This is handy if you need to make a lip around a curve.

A manual bead roller with a selection of dies is an inexpensive addition to your shop, and gives your sheetmetal projects a professional look with just a little practice.

Lip-Rolling Sheetmetal

One of the most common requirements is to fold the edge of a piece of sheetmetal over onto itself to create a lip. This is called a hem in sheetmetal work, like making a hem in sewing. If you have a die to put an angle in the edge of a piece of sheet, you can start a hem in your bead roller, but to use a bead roller to make a hem is typically a three-step process with progressive dies. The advantage of this process is that you can make a lip on a curved piece. You have to finish that lip with a bit of hammer work, however.

More often, fabricators make a nice sharp bend past 90 degrees in their brake, then open up the brake and fit the bent edge into the brake and use the closing action of the brake to complete the fold. This technique makes a good clean straight-line hem.

Copying Body Lines

One of the toughest challenges in sheetmetal forming is making a piece that follows a complex curve or cut line in a car's bodywork. Automotive body panels are typically stamped using huge dies, and the whole piece is shaped in just a few steps. If you have to replace a piece of metal with a complex shape, it's likely to require all the tools of the trade.

For making complex curves—that is, curves in more than one direction—you really need an English wheel, or be prepared to spend a lot of time making a model (called a buck) of the shape and hammer-forming the metal on the buck. By moving the sheet within the English wheel and rolling it back and forth, you can gently stretch the metal to create the desired shape.

Custom car door formed entirely from 16 gauge aluminum. Curt Oliver used an English wheel and hammer forming techniques to make this part. Notice how the cut line of the fender follows through the door. Copying lines like this takes real talent and refined skill.

Cut lines are more difficult and require hammer forming. This is where your bead roller comes into play. Find (or make) the correct dies to get the right angle of bend or raised bead in the metal, and then run your sheet through, following the curve of the cut line. This is much more art than science, and depending on the piece you are replicating, could take several attempts.

Yet another tool (there are always more tools to buy!) used to make compound curves in concert with the shot bag is a slapper. This is a modified wooden or metal hammer that looks rather like a spatula. As the name implies, you slap the sheetmetal against the shot bag or buck that you've made. A slapper is usually wrapped in leather to soften the edges of the blow and get smooth results.

When you've got the basic shape, be prepared to do some more massage to get it integrated and welded into your car's bodywork. This can involve hammer forming, hammer welding, and then traditional hammer and dolly bodywork to smooth it into place.

The difficulty of recreating complex bodywork lines is why there's a thriving market in replacement body panels made from the original dies, or dies made to match the original part!

Welding Sheetmetal

Another top challenge for sheetmetal workers is welding sheet. Because the material is so thin, your welder is likely to melt holes straight through the material. Low power is key here—use the lowest power setting available on your welder. If it's not enough to start an arc or penetrate the material, raise the power in the smallest possible increments until you get a good weld. Be sure to test your welder on similar materials before you weld on your project!

TIG welding is popular with sheetmetal because the foot pedal control on a TIG welder allows you very fine power control and the sharp TIG tip allows you to keep the arc very small. At the other end of the spectrum is an AC stick welder—you can try to weld sheet with one of these, but it's nearly impossible to get good results.

In between are the oxy-acetylene, wire-feed, and MIG welders. Of these, MIG is the best, because of its smooth arc and adjustable power. Gas welding sheetmetal takes a light touch, but it can be done and many fabricators like gas welds because they're easier to smooth out and shape into the metal. Inexpensive wire-feed welders tend to make holes in sheetmetal because of their limited adjustability. If you plan to do a lot of sheetmetal construction, it may be worth your investment to purchase a spot welder.

This body mount brace was made from 1/16-inch mild steel sheet, hammer formed, and MIG welded together. The holes remove weight but do not substantially reduce its strength.

This racing seat was TIG welded from 3/16-inch aluminum sheet. Note the simple bends made with a brake to fit the side plate.

Riveting

Rivets are a common fastener solution for semi-permanent installations. Most rivets used now are blind pop rivets. They are called blind because you don't need to have access to the back side of the work to install such a rivet. Just drill a hole, insert the rivet, and use your pop riveter to pull on the shaft until it breaks off.

Traditional rivets required access to the back side of the work, and the rivet was spread by upsetting the rivet shaft between a hammer and dolly. Pop rivets are usually made of aluminum, and occasionally mild steel. They work well for low-stress applications.

If you want to keep something in place forever, weld it. If you want to take it off now and again, use screws or bolts. If you want to take it off at a moment's notice, use Dzus fasteners. But if you want to keep something in place a long time, but make it easy to remove with a little work, rivets are a great choice.

Rivets come in a variety of head and shaft sizes. You can get pop rivets down to 1/16-inch shaft size up to 3/16 inch at your local hardware store. You can also choose a depth for the rivet—if you're just joining two sheets of metal, a shallow depth works best. If you're riveting a thick sheet to a piece of angle iron, you need a deeper rivet.

If you're not working blind—that is, you have access to the back side, you can also get washers designed to add extra grip to your rivets. Put the washer on before you squeeze the rivet and the washer will be held fast on the back side of your work.

To remove a rivet, you simply drill out the center. The back side generally falls away, so if you are using the rivets blind—for example, in a piece of box tube—you'll accumulate a bunch of old rivet bits in your structure. But that's OK—they don't weigh much.

One derivative of rivets that auto fabricators find handy is the riv-nut. These go by a number of trade names, but the design is that when the rivet is set, it provides a threaded hole suitable for a machine screw. A riv-nut requires a special tool for installation, but they're a godsend for making removable panels that must be more solidly affixed than Dzus fasteners allow.

Sheetmetal Projects

The following projects take you through the basic skills of sheetmetal fabrication. It's assumed that you have a brake, bead roller, and some means of cutting the sheetmetal. You can get by with aircraft shears, but larger tools make your job easier.

Making a Box

Our first project is to make a basic box. This involves measuring, marking, cutting, and bending a piece of aluminum sheet. We used 22 gauge aluminum that has red paint on one side and white on the other. The red side is also covered with a protective plastic skin that you remove when you're done with your work. It helps keep the workpiece free from scratches.

1 Consider the drawing on this page. This is the plan for a box. It's drawn as 6 x 8 inches, but you can scale this up or down as needed. But scaling this project down would be hard to do. We scaled it up to 12 x 16 inches for our example photos, and it was still about as small as our big brake could handle. The point is, the drawing works for any 3:4 ratio measurement, such as 15 x 20 or 18 x 24.

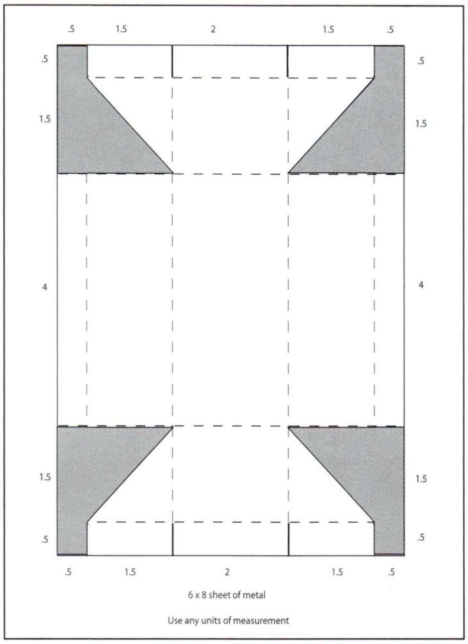

2 We used a basic computer drawing program to lay out our bends and cuts. This allowed us to think through what we wanted to make and how we planned to make it. The bends are noted with dashed lines, and the cuts with solid lines. The shaded areas are to be removed before we bend up the box. Then we

A riv-nut tool allows you to set a rivet that leaves a flush and threaded hole. It's perfect for mounting things onto sheetmetal bulkheads, dashboards, and consoles.

This switch plate is mounted to its console using riv-nuts. The installation is clean and professional-looking. Riv-nut tools are not expensive, and should be in your inventory.

We printed out our design and cut it out as we planned for the metal, then folded it up to make sure our plan would work in the brake.

Here's the paper box all folded up. We're confident the sheet metal will fold in the same way.

printed a copy to test our idea. We cut out the shape and folded the paper to make sure that our idea would work.

3 Next, copy your drawing onto the piece of aluminum you're going to use. Use your carpenter's square and tape measures to get all your measurements and lines right. You can draw it on both sides or just the back. It's convenient to be able to see the plan from both sides, but the back is more important as brakes bend from the back side.

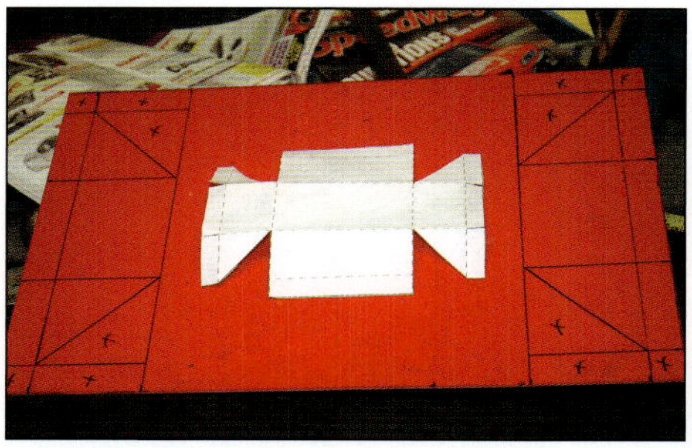

Here's the same drawing, executed on a larger sheet of aluminum. We made the measurements and used our straightedge to draw the lines. We'll cut from this side, but we'll also make the same marks on the white backside for the bending process.

4 Cut away the parts you don't need. We used the big free-standing shear to cut the basic rectangle and then our corner notcher to get rid of the edge pieces. We like the nice sharp cuts the shear and the notcher make, but we used aircraft shears to take out the triangles from the ends of the box and make the end cuts for the riveting tabs. You can do the whole project with shears if that's what you've got.

Most of our cuts are right angles from the edge of the metal, so we were able to use the notching shear. This gave us sharp and accurate cuts.

When the cutting is done, you can see that the aluminum matches the pattern we made. We cut out the triangles with ordinary aircraft shears, and made snips at either end.

5 When you're done cutting, it's time to bend. The order in which you make your bends is critical. Start from the outside and work your way in. First, bend the bottom lip on either side.

Start bending with the long sides at the edge, then bend the end lips up.

6 Next, bend the bottom lip on either end of the box. This is where you made those two cuts on either end. Those cuts have to be able to fold into each other, so press the center one in a little before the next bends.

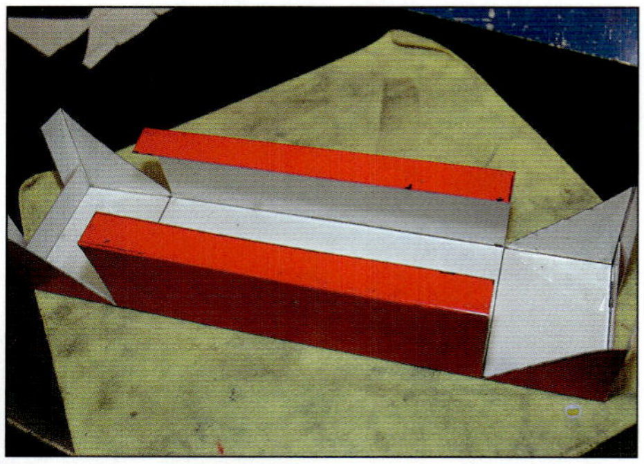

This is where you need to use the moveable fingers on the box and pan brake—you couldn't make these bends without allowing some space for the previous bends to travel through the brake.

7 Now make the two central bends along the long axis of the box. This is where you have to adjust the dies (the teeth) in the brake to allow for the end lip bends you made before. Most adjustable brakes allow you to make space for prior bends. If your brake does not have that capability, you might have to skip step 6 and hand-bend the end lips later with pliers.

8 This step is tricky. You need to re-adjust the brake dies to fit the shorter central end bends, but even with the brake adjusted for the bends, you won't be able to get a full 90 degrees into the sheetmetal. You'll get 45 degrees before you run into your prior bends. Bend both ends as far as possible.

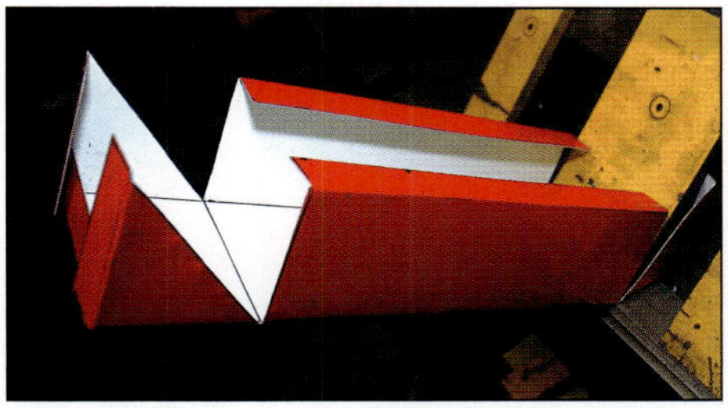

This picture shows the fingers of the brake adjusted for 3-D bending. Even with this adjustment, we'll only be able to make this bend about 45 degrees in the brake.

9 Finish up the bending by pressing the ends in, holding the bend location firmly against your workbench to make a nice crease. You might even be able to get

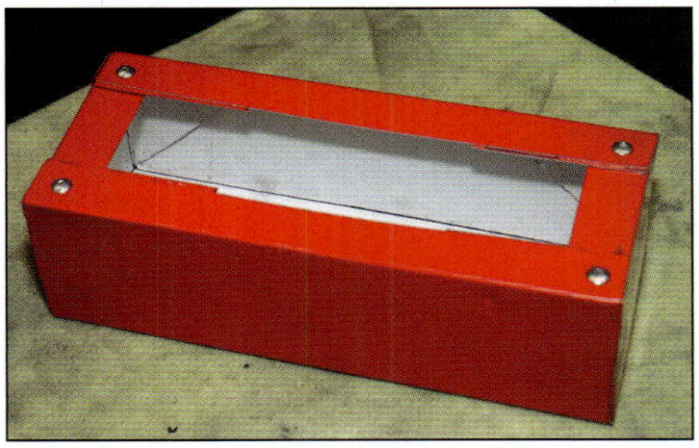

To hold all the bends in place, put a hole in each corner through all the layers stacked up there, and then pop-rivet the joint.

a dolly in there to bend against. You might have to bend open the lips to get everything to fit, but they'll bend back again.

10 Your box is now almost done. Take it over to your drill press and clamp the corners so they're nice and tight and square. Then drill a hole in each corner. It should pass through the three layers of aluminum stacked up there. Put a pop-rivet in each hole and that completes your structure. Make sure your pop-rivet size matches your drill bit!

When you're done, you've got a neat box suitable for a switchplate in a race car or to cover something like a fuel pump in a hot rod or custom. The lines drawn on the surface come off when you peel the protective plastic sheet.

Your box has an open bottom, so it's good for use as a switch box in a hot rod or race car, or to cover something less pretty in the trunk or engine bay. Truthfully, you could make a serviceable box without the diagonal cuts and with one less set of lips—just cut a square out of each corner of the original rectangle. It'll bend up easier. But look at the amount of metal in the corners—you can now weld (carefully!) or braze up those edges, put a lid on the open side, and have a fluid-tight box for an overflow tank.

Optional: If you have a bead roller, why not put some ribs or a raised or recessed step in your box? While it's still a flat piece of aluminum, but after you've got the pattern marked for cutting and bending, go ahead and use your roller to put some shape in the metal. It'll make this strong design even stronger, and it looks good, too!

Making a Bulkhead

Cutting straight lines in sheetmetal can be a challenge without a big shear, but cutting long curved lines has to be done by hand, and you want it to fit well. Bulkheads tend to be large flat or curved sheets with intricate work at the edges to fit whatever installation you're covering.

Most bulkheads that are put into hot rods or race cars are made from aluminum—it's easier to work with, it's lighter, and it shines up nicely. If you're planning to make a firewall, use sheet steel. You want that extra protection.

Follow these steps to make an aluminum bulkhead from 18 or 20 gauge aluminum:

1 Get a supply of thin cardboard from an art supply store. This material generally comes in 24 x 36-inch sheets and costs less than a dollar per sheet. It's perfect for templates because it cuts easily, you can mark on it, and it holds up well enough to use over and over again. Also, get a good heavy-duty pair of paper shears to cut it.

2 Using a felt-tip marker and the cardboard, make a careful template of your bulkhead. Pay special attention to roll bar tubes or other obstructions you'll have to work around. Cut the cardboard to fit perfectly up to all edges. Also,

Fit your cardboard template snugly up to all mating surfaces, especially under windshields.

pay attention to the size of each piece of the bulkhead. This is primarily limited by the size of your brake, if you are planning any bends in the sheet. Also consider your ability to get the shape you want into the sheet with your bead roller.

Don't be afraid to bend the template to work around corners and around obstructions such as roll cage components.

3 If you plan to have a removable access panel, now is the time to plan for it. Leave about 3/8 inch of overlap for all adjoining pieces. This is enough space to rivet, screw, or even weld the pieces together. If your template requires several pieces of cardboard, mark them carefully in relation to each other.

4 Transfer your template to the aluminum with a felt-tip marker. Mark the side of the line where you plan to cut. Check your marks and remeasure the car for perfect fit.

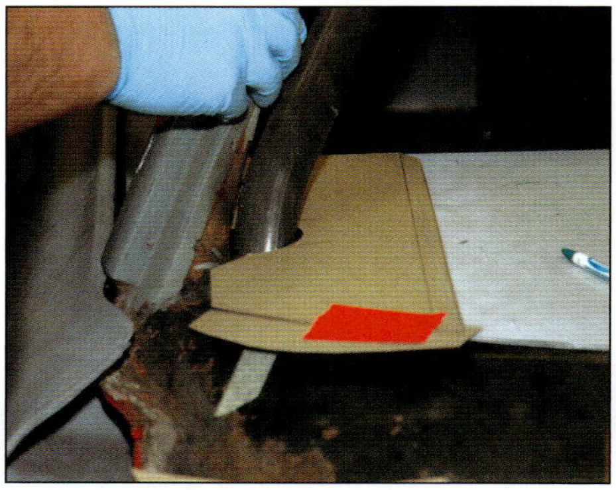

Leave about 3/8 to 1/2 inch for a recessed lip. This allows you to attach two pieces and still have a smooth surface. That's yet another reason to have a bead roller.

When you've got your template just right, transfer your design to the sheetmetal.

5 Cut out your bulkhead pieces and mark your overlaps. Be sure to hit every edge with your deburring tool! Also, mark any shape you plan to put in the metal with the bead roller. Then take each piece to the roller and work the shape into the metal. This adds a professional look to your project and also helps make the bulkhead solid. A perfectly flat sheet wobbles back and forth, sometimes making noise—and it often looks like an amateur job. If you don't have a roller, consider taking your bulkhead pieces to a metalshop and hiring them to do your bead work.

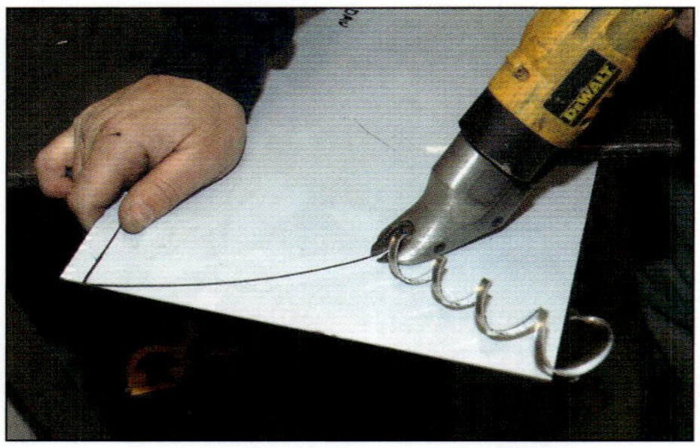

With your design on the sheetmetal you can cut with confidence. If it has a protected side, make sure that you're laying the template for that side to be facing outward.

6 A special case of bead rolling happens on your overlap edges. You want to put a step down

Using a step die with your bead roller allows you to fit bulkhead panels together and still have a flush surface. The lip also gives you a place for rivets, brazing, Dzus fasteners, or screws.

in the back side of each overlap. Make the step the same depth as the thickness of your sheet material. This way, your panels lay flat on each other and fit perfectly. This really enhances the professional look of your project.

7 When the pieces are cut and you've got your shape in the metal, you can make any necessary bends. Put each piece into your brake and bend it as closely as possible to the desired angle. Be sure that your bend lines line up if you're working with multiple pieces that must fit together!

You can bend your bulkhead pieces in the brake before or after you've done your bead roller work, depending on the shape you're working. A ridge will be destroyed by a brake bend, but a step down can be bent on the brake with little damage.

8 Finally, go ahead and install your bulkhead. If you've got nothing to affix the panels to, you might have to design a lip into your panels and attach them to the sides of the space. Alternately, you can cut some strips and bend them in the brake to make your own mounting lips. Rivet or screw the mounting lip to the perimeter of the bulkhead area, then attach the bulkhead to the lip. This is handy if you want to use Dzus fasteners or other removable fasteners to make your panels removable—just remember to overlap about an inch for Dzus fasteners.

This shot shows an installed bulkhead panel held in place with pop rivets. You can see the panels make room for a roll bar brace at the top and share a bead-rolled riser. The panel on the left has a recessed edge to lay flush with the panel on the right, and everything lines up nicely.

Repairing a Rusty Floor

In this project, you'll cut out a rusty patch of steel and cover it and the surrounding area with new steel. This is not a restoration-quality repair, but it will suffice to keep a car on the road. For the specific work, we found an old GMC pickup truck with a rust-perforated area beneath the driver's right heel. We removed just the rustiest part of the steel and then covered the entire area with a new piece of sheetmetal. The material we used was .095-inch mild steel sheet. We corrugated the new metal on the bead roller to give it strength and stitched it into place.

1 Look at the rusty area from both sides to ensure that nothing critical is attached to the area and that no fuel or brake lines run nearby. Cooking your fuel lines while welding is a bad idea.

2 Carefully cut out the weak area. Use some good judgment here—you don't want to cut out too much. You might want to scrub the affected area with naval jelly to remove surface rust or cover it with a product such as POR-15 to seal the rust. But surface rust is not a reason to cut out original structure. Unless you're building a show car or concours restoration, your repair will hold up better with as much of the previous material in place as you can keep.

This floor is in dire need of a repair. The right thing to do would be to cut out the entire floor and make a new one, but the owner just wanted to get back on the road as soon as possible.

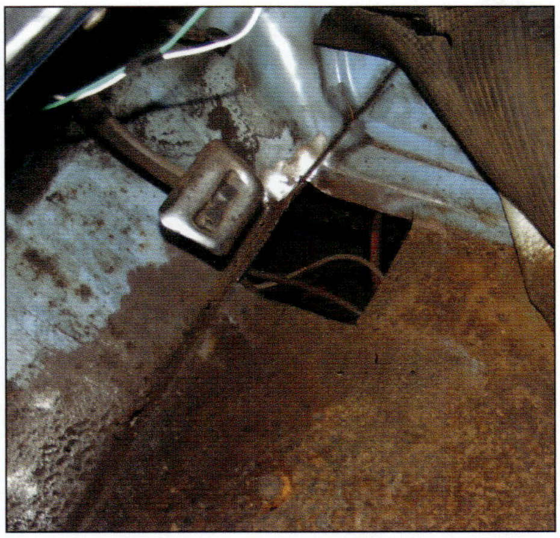

We cut the worst of the rust out of the floor, and we'll cover the rest with new steel. We'll have to work far enough out where there's still good metal to weld up to our new piece.

What's a Cleco?

When you need to hold two or more pieces of metal together temporarily, a Cleco fastener is a popular tool. A Cleco is a metal cylinder with a button on top and an expanding end on the bottom. To use a Cleco, just drill through the metal layers where you want to attach them. Compress the Cleco with the special Cleco pliers and insert the bottom end in the hole. When you release the pliers, the bottom expands and holds the metal tightly in place. Clecos are inexpensive; just about $20 for 25 fasteners and a pair of pliers. This tool is very common in the racing and fabrication industries, and makes a good addition to your tool kit.

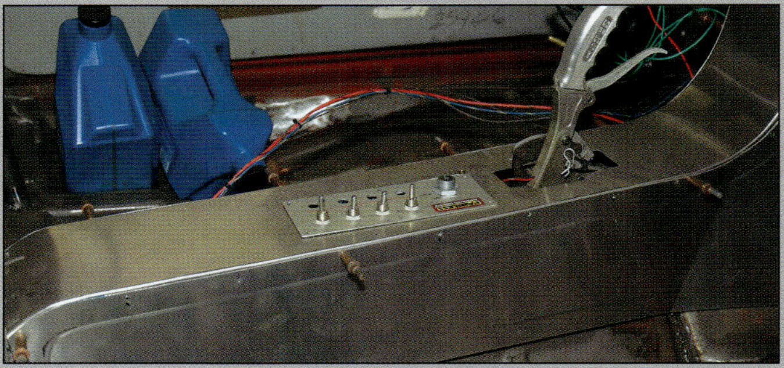

A race car center console under construction. You can see several Cleco fasteners holding the side panel in place.

3 Measure your replacement plates. If you're replacing outer bodywork, cut the new plates exactly to shape. If you're replacing a floor, make the replacement panel big enough to tie in to good sheetmetal away from the rusted area.

4 Because this patch covers parts of two panels that come together at an angle, you can either make one panel and bend it in a sheetmetal brake, or make two panels and weld them together at the joint. We elected to use two pieces for this job because the vertical panel covered a series of complex curves in the original stamping. If your project requires two panels as ours did in this exercise, cut each panel to shape and give it ridges in the bead roller. Then bend the panel to match the surrounding metal.

If you elect to make a single panel, measure the total dimension required and cut the panel to size. Then mark and bend the panel in your sheetmetal brake before you use your bead roller to add structural ridges to the part. Place ridges in both planes of the panel before you weld it in its final location. You may need to work the panel a bit with your rubber mallet or body hammers to get a snug fit around existing curves.

5 Position the panel (or panels) in place and tack-weld them at their corners and in several locations along each edge to hold them in place and prevent warping. If you are using two panels, tack them to each other in several locations at this time.

6 Using the stitch-welding technique, run weld beads around

Russ made the new part in two pieces and used the bead roller to give the panels some shape. Then he tacked them into place and started welding.

Russ uses a stitch welding technique to avoid warping the panels. He welds short stretches and moves around on the project. Eventually, all the seams will be welded.

the perimeter of the new metal, joining it to the surrounding structure. Be sure to skip around the entire perimeter and weld in stitches of about 2 inches. If the piece becomes too hot, take a break and let things cool down before continuing.

7 If you used two pieces for your patch, wait until the perimeter is welded into place before you join the two new pieces together. Use the stitch welding technique for this joint, too.

8 In this project, we had to remove the area where the accelerator pedal is mounted onto the floor. When the new panel was in place, we drilled and re-mounted the pedal.

The final result will keep the driver's feet off the pavement, but doesn't do much to help the rest of that floor.

You can modify this project to fill gaps in bulkheads, replace truck beds, and create new floors and bulkheads for racing and special-purpose cars.

Stretching a Fender

In this project, we'll extend a wheel arch to accommodate larger tires. This is a popular drag racing modification for rear wheels. The subject car is a 1970 Chevrolet Camaro, but the principles apply to any car.

This project involves cutting and welding a car's bodywork, so plan on repainting if you undertake a similar project.

1 Measure how much additional space is present behind and in front of the fender lip inside the wheel well. You don't want to exceed that space, but there's usually quite a bit to work with. Plan how much extension you would like. In the case of this project, we extended the wheel arch by 4 inches.

Cutting a square makes it easy to remove strips from the front and back, and then welding the pieces back together again.

2 Measure and cut the outer fender skin in two squares around the wheel well. Leave a tab hanging down in the middle of the wheel arch so you have the original lines to match as you work. Leave plenty of material at the front and rear of the wheel well to get a good weld and smooth over when you're done. Then cut an additional strip in front of and behind the square you just cut out. Each strip should be half the width of the extension you want.

3 Weld the rear half of the wheel arch to the new rear cut in the fender, then weld the front half into the new front cut. You'll

You can extend a wheel arch as far as the inner structure of the wheel well will allow. This arch was stretched to within an inch of the inner wheel well.

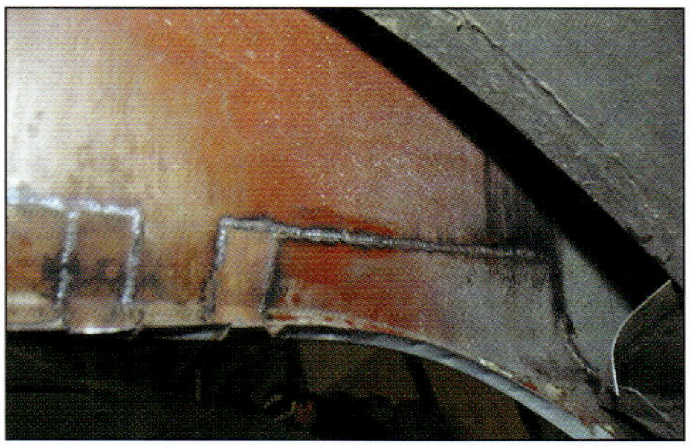

The central tab hanging down as a template. You will weld in new steel here, and it's handy to have a piece of the original as a guide.

have your extension as a gap at the top of the wheel well, with the tab hanging down as your template.

4 Make patch panels to fit the gap at the center of the wheel arch. Make sure you account for the wheel arch lip. Weld the patch into the gap in your fender and grind all your welds smooth.

Larger wheels and tires usually run both to the inside and the outside. This project was undertaken as part of a comprehensive modification plan that included tubbing the rear end of this Camaro to fit huge wheel wells where the rear seat and trunk used to be. The entire rear framework of the car was removed and replaced with a fabricated chassis. However, stretching a wheel well doesn't require all that work. This can be undertaken as a lone modification, working within the confines of the inner wheel well.

You can see how this stretch has brought the wheel's arch almost to the front of the inner wheel well.

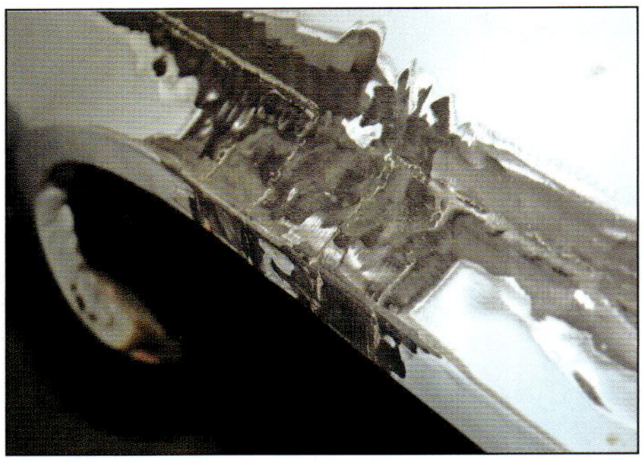

Weld all the parts back in and fill the gaps in the wheel arch with new steel. Bend in the lip, or make a hem if you're planning to roll the lip anyway.

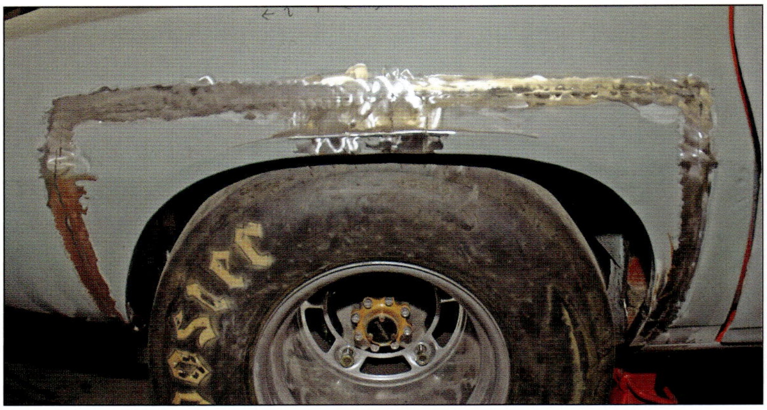

The net effect of this project is that these large drag racing tires fit and look good under this fender.

"Rolling the Bat"

Fender stretching often means rolling and flattening the fender lip to fit slightly larger wheels and tires. You can buy a machine that bolts to your wheel lugs and incorporates a roller for this purpose, or you can just use your hammer and dolly to work down the lip.

But there's also an old school trick for this, and it still works and produces reasonable results. The procedure involves using an old baseball bat as a roller. The bat may be aluminum or wood–it doesn't matter. Just don't use your priceless collectible one-of-a-kind bat signed by Mickey Mantle, because the bat you use is going to get chewed up a bit.

Get a friend to help you and a level piece of pavement with enough room to roll the car forward and back a couple tire rotations. Leave the brake off and take the car out of gear. Working from the front or rear of the tire, pinch the bat between the tire and the wheel arch lip. Now hold the bat in place with tension against the fender lip and roll the car forward or back, as needed. The bat naturally rolls with the tire and pushes against the fender lip. When you're done, the lip is flattened a bit and the fender is pushed out. Repeat as needed until your fender is nicely and evenly flared and the lip completely flattened.

The process is the same as the expensive fender-rolling tool, and you can do it for the price of one garage-sale baseball bat!

Shrinking and Stretching Curves in Sheetmetal

This air-powered planishing setup will put a curve in sheet metal if you work long enough, but is mainly used to smooth light imperfections in sheetmetal. We used it to smooth our fender after hot-shrinking dents.

This is the stretcher side of the same tool. You can see how the second bend is starting to pull the metal away from the machine.

Stretching is just the opposite of shrinking, and it's generally used for creating a curve in metal. There are lots of tools to help you do this, including English wheels, planishing tools, shot bags, and even your basic hammer and anvil. When you're stretching sheetmetal, smoothness is key, and most of these tools are designed to make long, smooth stretches in sheetmetal.

When you stretch a given area of sheetmetal, you make it thinner and larger. You still have the same amount of metal—it's just spread over a greater area. The effect is that the metal wants to curve when you do this, because it's not stretching evenly. You can use this attribute of metal to create just the shape you want.

Because most people don't own an English wheel, we'll use a more conventional shrinker/stretcher tool. Any tool supply store has these for sale. This tool has small jaws that grab the lip of your piece of sheetmetal and press it together or pull it apart a little bit. By repeated application, the

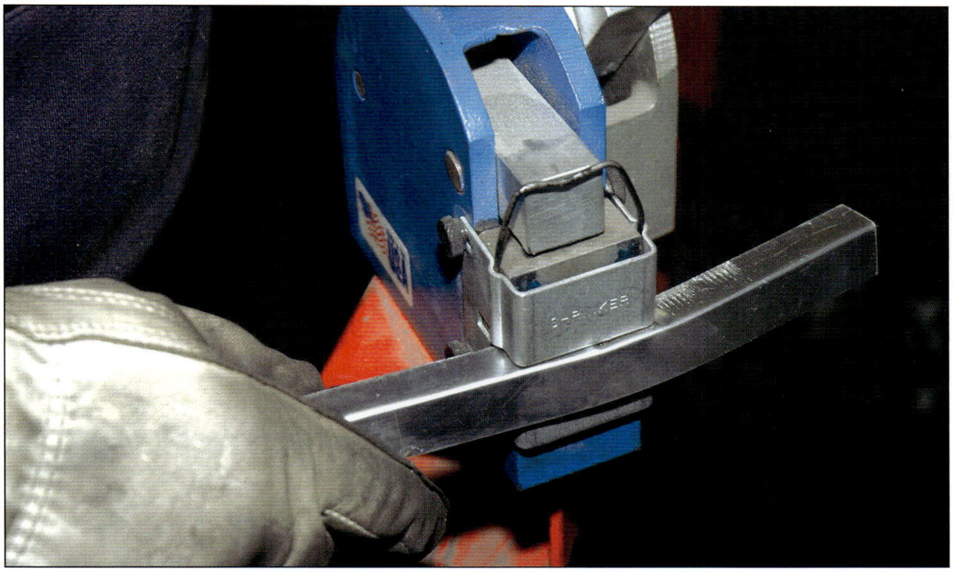

This is the shrinker side of the shrinker/stretcher tool. You can tell because the metal is curving in toward the machine.

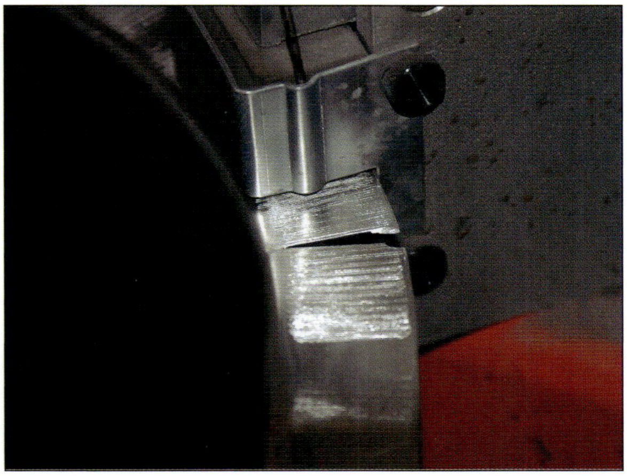

It's easy to rip aluminum with the stretcher. If you've got a choice, use the shrinker side of the tool on this material.

metal starts to curve as the length at the edge is stretched or shrunk. You can use this tool in combination with an English wheel or lead shot bag and the planishing tool for forming fenders, headlight buckets, or any kind of curved shape you need.

If you have a choice, the shrinking application is somewhat safer to use on sheet aluminum. Because sheet aluminum tears easily, it's easy to rip it apart on the stretcher. Mild steel sheetmetal is more forgiving. The shrinker will leave the sheetmetal with a corrugated surface at the shrunk edge, but a quick trip through the planishing tool will smooth this out.

1 As described in Chapter 5, make your flat sheetmetal bulkhead and get it right up to the edge of the bodywork.

2 Make a cardboard template showing the curved edge of the bulkhead to be followed with the stretched and shrunk piece.

3 Get a strip of aluminum or steel and put a 90 degree lengthwise bend in it in your brake. Choose a side that will be mounted to the bodywork and the side that will be the mounting lip for the bulkhead. Assuming that the bulkhead panel is flat, or nearly so, you will stretch and shrink the lip to follow the curve of the template.

4 Use your shrinking die to work concave bends into the metal, and the stretching die to pull the metal for convex bends. Be careful if you're working with steel, and be extra careful with aluminum—aluminum feels nice and soft to work with, but you can easily rip it with the stretcher.

5 Work patiently and evenly, stopping frequently to match your work against the template you created. When it gets close, spend some time with the planishing tool to smooth out the wrinkles made by the shrinking die. You'll lose a little curve, but you can work that back in, and having a smooth surface makes your project look better.

6 When your piece matches the template, match it up to the installation site in the car. You can screw or rivet it into place. The piece will be somewhat damaged by work hardening, so welding it into place is not the best idea, but you can weld it into place if the materials are the same. Using screws or rivets also makes undoing (or redoing) your work easier down the road.

We're stretching this panel to curve around, then we'll fold that lip into a hem on the bead roller.

The finished curved panel with a folded hem. You can create a unique wrap-around dash or other interior curves using this technique.

Here you can see the corrugation left by the shrinking tool. You can work that smooth again with the planishing tool.

Automotive Welding Projects

This chapter details a few projects that are commonly used when working on automotive projects such as restoration, modification for racing, or hot rod construction. The practice welding exercises in Chapter 3 were designed to help you practice the skills needed to undertake these projects, and strong, solid welds are needed any time you're working on a car's frame. The bodywork projects involve working with sheetmetal and require the skills and information described in the previous chapter.

Remember that these projects are critical to the finished product when you're adapting or building your own car. Do not undertake one of these on a car that anyone will drive until you're sure of the quality of your work and the strength of your design.

The chassis is the foundation of an automobile, and it pays to make it straight, true, and as strong as possible. You can reinforce an old frame easily, and keep it straight and level while you work.

Chassis and Frame Projects

The following projects deal with ladder frame and unibody chassis repair and improvement. For all these projects, you should first take the chassis in question to a professional frame and body shop to ensure that it is straight and level. You can measure it yourself, but if adjustments are needed, a professional frame shop is uniquely equipped to make those pulls and get your frame in shape for your project.

On the Square and On the Level

Whenever you work on a ladder frame, and especially when you're welding, you need to be careful not to warp the structure. Many old frames were never completely flat or square from the factory, and most have been hit at some point in their careers. So it's a fair bet that your chassis isn't square or level when you start. But the time to fix those things is now, before your car is assembled. You might choose to invest a small amount of money in a trip to a body and frame shop. But before you do that, you can check it yourself by measuring it on diagonals for squareness and by setting it on a level floor for a basic flatness check.

Once you're confident that you're starting with a square and level chassis, you want to keep it that way while you work. Here's a quick and easy method to ensure that your chassis stays true. When you put your frame up on sawhorses or jackstands, make sure that it's level. A carpenter's spirit level is good enough for most purposes. Then suspend a plumb bob from each corner of the chassis so that the point hangs about 1/16 inch above the floor. You may have to weld a bolt or tab onto each corner to do this. Then, as you weld on the chassis, keep an eye on those plumb bobs. If one or more of the bobs start to rise or fall, the heat and stress from your welding is warping the chassis. Stop what you're doing immediately or you risk permanent damage. Wait for 24 hours and the chassis should return to level. At the worst, if the chassis does not normalize it's an easy pull to get it back to level.

Boxing and Bracing a Vintage Frame

One of the most common automotive projects involves creating a hot rod or custom car out of a vintage domestic street car. These cars use a traditional ladder frame that for most of automotive history was made from C-shaped channel stock. These frames are made from mild steel and at their most basic are just two pieces of channel iron with some crossmembers bolted, riveted, or welded into place. Depending on your make and model, the chassis may be made of hat steel—which is to say, steel that has been shaped into a channel with small lips at the sides. If you look at this material from the end, it looks something like a hat with a brim.

The pieces of channel iron in a traditional frame were shaped to accommodate the spring mounts for the suspension and they were connected with just a few basic crossmembers. One of the first things done to virtually every hot rod is to enclose the channel with more steel to make it a box, and then to add some support to the crossmembers to strengthen the frame structure. If you buy a new hot rod frame, it already has this done.

This example project looks at Rob Zeller's 1937 Chevrolet as it is being prepared for drag racing. It's the same Chevy used for the roll cage project in Chapter 7. In 1937, Chevrolet made their frames out of stamped hat steel with a thin plate spot-welded onto the bottom. That's better than the C-channel that Ford was using at the same time, but not by much. And it's certainly not sufficient to absorb the forces that the drag racing engine will deliver. Amateurs will be

A vintage car like this one, being built up into a period-correct gasser drag racer, will take some serious chassis work before it can handle the forces of a modern racing engine.

pleased to note that Rob completed this frame reinforcement using only a bandsaw, MIG welder, body grinder, and an oxy-acetylene torch.

It's also worth noting again that the roll cage project is an integral part of the chassis reinforcement in this car. The roll cage creates a dome over the ladder frame and helps it resist twisting forces. The cage is attached to six points on the chassis: three points on each side, front to back. If you imagine trying to twist the chassis from any corner, you'd be working against a very strong arch of steel. Even a basic roll bar helps eliminate twist, but a cage is much better.

But there's more to be done, especially if you plan to put a big engine in an older car. The frame must be reinforced in several key areas. Because old frames are stamped, they tend to have nice curving shapes. Use your plasma cutter to carve out matching pieces of plate from 1/8- to 3/16- or even 1/4-inch mild steel. Because these frames are virtually always made from mild steel, your MIG welder is the best choice for this work.

1 Clean the entire frame and make sure it's free of rust and dirt. You can have it sandblasted or blasted with walnut shell, glass, or plastic media, or you can have the chassis dipped in a caustic solution that dissolves rust, paint, grease, and undercoating. It's important that the chassis be clean and that you are able to see any rusty spots. Then have it checked to be sure it's square and level.

Make sure everything is as clean as you can make it before you start. As you can see here, rust gets started working at the same time you do. This will all be cleaned again before it gets painted.

2 For a race car, you must reinforce the front crossmember. In the case of this Chevrolet, the crossmember was originally hot-riveted to the chassis members. Welding up the mating surfaces also helps keep everything in place. The pieces of the crossmember were originally spot-welded together, so grinding and welding the seams helps hold it together under increased stress. On an older car, you can never get all the rust out from between two plates that have been sandwiched together unless you separate the plates, clean them, and then weld them back together.

The rear crossmember was replaced with 2 inch box steel, reinforced with lightened gussets to the frame. The frame rails had already been reinforced, so this is a very strong setup.

You can still see the original hot rivets that held the main engine crossmember into this frame. It's been reinforced with extra plates and welds all around.

3 If you want to keep all the original crossmembers, you can reinforce them. Cover any open channel iron with 3/16 plate to make it a box. If you do not care about maintaining the original components, consider using modern mild steel box tube for mid-chassis and rear crossmembers. This material will be stronger than the reinforced original material, especially if the material had been rusted. On this project, the rearmost crossmember was replaced with basic 2-inch square box steel, with 3/16-inch wall thickness. Plate gussets are also useful for multiplying the stiffening effect of your new crossmembers.

4 The center crossmember is made of larger material and was designed to function as the required driveshaft retainer as well as a structural support on the car. This part was executed in 2-inch by 3-inch .188 wall mild steel. Also attached to this piece are the supports and retainers for the 4-inch exhaust system for the car. Every bit adds to the support for the chassis. Again, gusseting at the connection between the chassis members and the new crossmember adds strength.

This structure serves as an additional crossmember support, as well as the required driveshaft support and mounting point for exhaust supports.

Detail shot of the center crossmember, showing the mounting points for the trailing arms that will locate the rear axle.

5 To reinforce the chassis members themselves, use the plasma torch to cut 3/16-inch plates that match the curve of the chassis and weld them to the inside face of the chassis member. Work by jumping around to weld on different places on the chassis—don't start at one end and work straight through. When it's complete, this reinforcement helps reduce bowing under the weight of the big block engine and under the stresses created when the car transfers weight to the rear under acceleration. These reinforcing plates were cut and installed in a dart style to create a stylish and period-looking effect. You could cut them with straight ends, but it takes just a little extra effort to make your project unique and fun.

These darts in the frame reinforcement are easy to make, they look great, and they're vintage-correct for this type of gasser.

This lightened engine mount connects to the frame reinforcement and shows another of the dart-shaped panels in the frame.

6 In addition to the inside face, the bottom face of the Chevy's longitudinal frame members was originally just a thin piece of sheetmetal. Cut and weld more 3/16-inch plates here to complete the reinforcement. This helps resist the individual chassis members' tendency to flex and also helps resist bowing. As you work, use a lot of C-clamps to hold the parts together. Rob used up to 10 C-clamps at a time to hold the parts in precise alignment while he welded.

This is the rearmost of the plates used to reinforce the bottom of the hat channel frame on the old Chevrolet.

Rob carefully welded this plate with small stitches to recreate the spot welded look of the original parts.

It's a big job to reinforce a frame, but the results are outstanding and the original frames on older cars simply do not stand up to the forces exerted by modern engines, suspensions, and tires. It pays to take your time and get your frame in order.

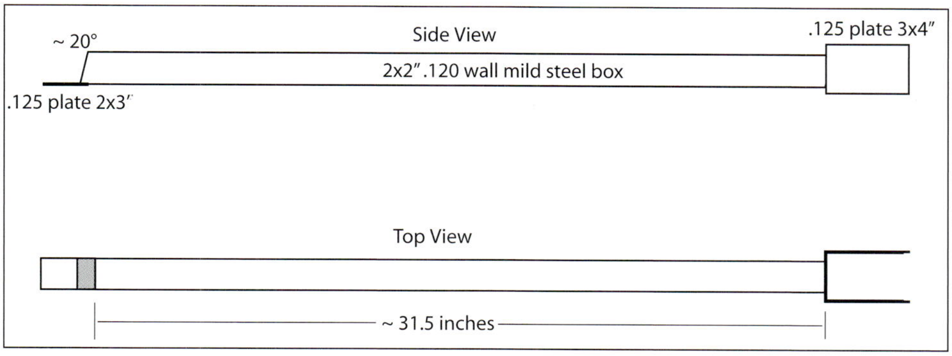

This is a basic drawing of a homebuilt Camaro subframe connector. You need two of these, and they require cutting your floor.

This is the front mount of a commercial bolt-in subframe connector. You can see how it inserts into the front subframe member and drops down to clear the floor.

The rear attachment of this bolt-in subframe connector bolts to the forward perch of the rear leaf spring.

Another view of the rear attachment point of the bolt-in subframe connector.

Making Subframe Connectors for a Partial Unibody

In this project, you'll make subframe connectors for a partial unibody car. Many popular GM muscle cars made since the 1960s, specifically the Nova, Camaro, and Firebird, have used unibody shells for the passenger compartment and then bolted front subframes (also called clips) to that unibody section. The unibody tub on a Chevrolet Camaro is bolted onto the front subframe with rubber pads in between the two metal parts. The rear subframes are integrated with the chassis. Obviously, this is not an optimal design for chassis stiffness! Therefore, subframe connectors and braces are used to turn the factory's design into something like a full-frame car. Connecting the front and rear subframes together approximates a traditional ladder frame and makes a more rigid chassis. A rigid chassis improves structural integrity and handling for all cars, and improves power delivery in high-torque and horsepower applications.

You can buy a set of subframe connectors for about $100 to $200. These can generally be bolted or welded into place. If you choose to make your own subframe connectors, you can use 2-inch by 3-inch .120 wall box steel if you don't mind cutting your floorpan, or slightly bent 1.5-inch .120 wall round tube if you'd rather leave your floor intact.

To make a subframe connector, you need to locate the proper mounting points and create a pair of braces to tie the two sections together under the car. This project was completed on a 1970s Chevrolet Camaro built for drag racing.

On a GM car, the body is mounted on the front subframe using large rubber bushings. Buy some replacement aluminum or polyurethane body bushings and replace these before you begin work on a subframe brace. You also need to strip the seats and carpet out of the car if you plan to cut the floor.

1 The best way to do this job is in a shop with a work pit or on a four-post lift with ramps. This is because there's enough flex in the body and front subframe that the relevant parts will move if you just jack up the car from the usual jack points. Make sure that your car doors open and close normally before you lock things into position with your brace! Whatever you do, always make sure any car is well supported with proper stands before you get under it. Having a car fall on you could be fatal.

2 Once you're under the car, look for the front subframe. They are usually made of rectangular stamped steel sections. In the case of GM models, they are roughly 2.5-inch by 3.5-inch stamped steel. You can make your braces out of round tube or square tube; it really doesn't matter much. Under the driver and passenger footwells, you can see the raw ends of the subframe where they are bolted to the passenger tub. Note the location of the bolts that mount the subframe to the passenger section—you don't want to block those in case you ever have to replace

This is a clean and freshly powder-coated front subframe end. The large hole on top is where the body bushing goes.

Here's what it looks like when you've welded your brace to the rear of the front subframe. Note the extra reinforcing gusset on this installation.

This front subframe end looks more like what you're likely to find in a car. Insert the front end of your brace into this square opening.

Another view of the front subframe connecter installation. You can see that space is left to access the body bushing, in case it needs replacement.

the body. For the Camaro or Firebird, the ends of the front subframe are angled and that angle and an open space in the underside of the subframe provides access to the bolt and bushing, which mounts the subframe to the body. Check to see if the ends of the subframe have been crushed in any way—they often get dented.

3 In the Camaro and Firebird body, next find the forward mount of the rear frame rail on either side. These are stamped steel and are located just inboard of the bolt-on front mount for the leaf springs. To get at this area, you need to remove the rear seat and cut through the sheetmetal. You're looking for four or five spot welds where the stamped frame rail is welded to the tub. These frame rails also terminate at an angle, so you need to cut your brace to match that angle before installation. Also, you can now see that you must cut a strip out of the Camaro's floorpan to fit straight subframe connectors.

Viewed from the underside, this is the rear connection of the subframe connector to the stamped frame rail that is part of the unibody tub of the Camaro. Note that it's located just inboard of the front leaf spring mount.

> **TECH TIP — Other Makes**
>
> For other makes and models, look for a good place to weld a plate to each of the two rear ends of the front subframe and the two front ends of the rear frame rails.

4 Once you can test-fit your brace, carefully measure the distance from the rear of the front subframe to the front of the rear frame rail on each side. Also note anything else in the belly of the car that might interfere with your braces. Convertibles are known to present additional challenges because they have more underbody structure. When you have the overall length you need, you can work on getting the rear angle just right. Different cars are known to be slightly different in overall length, but for 1970s-era Camaros and Firebirds, it's about 31.5 inches. You can cut the front off cleanly at 90 degrees for this project, as you'll be making a fitting for the front subframe.

This is the rear end of the connector viewed from above. You're looking down under the rear seat of the car. This subframe connector is tied into the car's roll bar for extra strength.

5 For the front mount, create two U-shaped sleeves of steel to slip on and bolt or weld to the inner sides of the front subframe piece. These will be 1/8 inch thick, about 4 inches long, 3 inches wide, and 2 inches tall. Measure your particular subframe to get the width dimension correct. Weld a sleeve to the front of each subframe brace. You can add outside gussets for additional strength.

6 Position the front of a subframe brace in its subframe arm, and hold the brace up against the floorpan of the car in line with the front and rear frames and you can mark where you need to cut. It's right under the front seats. Before you cut the floor, make sure that all brake lines, fuel lines, and wires are clear of your work area. When you cut, you will be able to move the brace up until it meets the rear frame rail and lines up correctly with the front subframe.

The subframe connector viewed from underneath the car where it cuts through the floor. Note that where the crossmember was cut, it has been rewelded to the subframe connector.

7 Drill and bolt or weld the front of your brace to the sleeve at the open end of the front subframe. The reason for using a sleeve around the outside of the front is to retain access to the body bolt and mounting bushing. If you don't want to retain that easy access, you can weld additional plates on the bottom for added strength.

10 Repeat steps 1 through 9 for the other side of the car.

As an alternative to this project, if you don't want to weld the subframe brace to your car and you don't want to cut your floor, you can bend 1.5-inch tube slightly to make braces that drop down enough to clear the floorpan, or you can buy a set of bolt-in braces appropriate to your year, make, and model. Installation is easy and requires only basic hand tools and jack stands to suspend the car while you work.

If you make your own braces, you can weld the brace to the rear frame rail or create a flange to integrate the spring perch bolts with the brace for a solid mount. But if you're cutting your floorpan, chances are you're also willing to weld the brace to your rear frame rail.

The original frame on this 1966 Plymouth Fury is pretty beat up, so we'll replace it with something customizable.

Rebuilding a Front Subframe

This is an ambitious project undertaken on a dedicated drag racing car. The car being modified is a 1966 Plymouth Fury III, which uses a full ladder frame. However, the old front end of the frame had been modified, updated, and worked on so much that wholesale replacement was the right answer to accommodate the owner's future plans.

As discussed before, straightness and level are the keys when it comes to frame work. We'll use a jig made right on a steel welding table to get this frame material lined up correctly and the proper tabs welded on for steering, suspension, and engine mounts. When we're done, the front frame is stronger, straighter, and easier to use than the original unit. You can modify this procedure to fit your make and model of car.

1 Carefully measure the existing frame for wheelbase, engine mounts, suspension pickup points, crossmembers, and any other relevant dimensions. Take plenty of pictures of all frame members from all angles because you never know when you might need to precisely locate a mounting bracket or threaded hole! Also pay careful attention to bends in the existing frame. Most frames rise at the front and rear of the car, and you'll want to be able to replicate the bend angles.

Before we cut the frame rails off, we removed the engine crossmember and put in spreader bars to hold everything in the correct relationship while we work.

2 Plan your new frame, paying attention to crossmembers, mounting locations, and structural improvements. If you plan to change the steering, suspension (including sway bars), or any other configuration, be sure that your new plan won't interfere with other systems. Cut and tack-weld a spreader bar between the remaining frame members to keep them in line while you work.

3 Carefully support the frame while you cut the front portion loose. Be sure to give yourself enough material for a solid connection when you install the new parts. We cut down through the body of the frame box section, but left an extension in the bottom side of the frame. This provides us with a place to set and weld the new pieces,

We cut the frame rails off, leaving plenty of supporting material to support the new structure when we weld it on.

Detail shot of the raw frame end after taking off the front section. Note the spreader bar and the lip for reinstallation.

helping us maintain the squareness and level of the new structure and helps improve the strength of the new structure as well.

4 With the old piece cut free, we'll start the new structure by obtaining some 2-inch x 4-inch .125 wall box steel. This is the same basic dimension as the old frame rail, but instead of being a pair of stamped pieces spot-welded together, this is a manufactured piece, welded along its entire edge. The first thing that we'll do is cut the frame pieces to length. We'll measure a little extra to account for the cuts we'll make to replicate the bends in the original frame.

This is the new frame material, marked to take a wedge out to match the bend angle in the original.

5 The old frame rail rose up from underneath the car's body and then bent to become level again. Measure and mark the new frame rails for the bend that brings the frame level with the ground. This bend is expressed as a wedge that must be removed from the new rails. Using a cutoff wheel, we cut the wedge out of each rail, leaving the top side of the rail intact. Then we gently bend each rail to eliminate the gap, creating the bend. After tacking the bend shut and rechecking against the existing parts and the frame remaining on the car, we'll weld the bend into the new frame rails.

Russ uses the cutoff wheel to take the section out of the new frame rail to make the required bend.

The frame rail with the wedge taken out. Russ left the top wall of the rail intact and simply bent the beam over for tack welding.

6 This step is absolutely critical to perform exactly right. Use a welding table to lay out the new frame parts exactly as they will be located on the car. Tack each piece directly to the table in its proper orientation. This step takes multiple tries even for professionals. Measure across the diagonals for squareness and also check your table and the parts to ensure they are level. Check each measurement several times to be absolutely sure.

Tacking support beams into place to ensure that the frame stays square. We've already tacked each frame rail to the welding table after careful measurement.

7 Now we can lay out ancillary parts such as crossmembers and suspension pickup points. Because the parts need to be located in a particular relation to the frame, we'll weld some more pieces to the table to support suspension parts in their proper location. We measure and mount another piece of straight steel perpendicular to the frame rails to line up the suspension mount points. We also weld a support to the table to hold the sway bar at precisely the correct point in space relative to the frame. In short, we're making a complete jig to match the desired structure of the new frame.

Since we've got the frame tacked to the table upside-down, some parts will end up floating in the air in this orientation. So we've created some supports to hold the sway bar mount where it needs to be in relation to the frame.

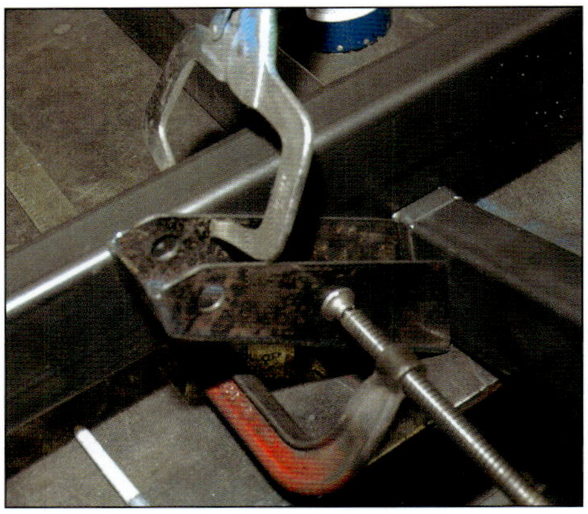

Preparing to tack on a suspension mount point. These were precisely measured and created out of thin plate.

8 When the ancillary parts are all tacked into place, we weld up the new frame and then cut it free of the welding table with confidence that it's built square and true with respect to the measurements we made at the start of the project. Then we'll tack the new frame into place on the car and remeasure just to be sure everything is lined up correctly. Finally, we commit heavy-duty welds to the joint to fix the new frame in place.

9 With the structure welded into place and all the tabs, holes, and support members in place, we're ready to reassemble the front end of this car.

A project like this is also a great chance to add some more support to a car by adding braces to the roll structure, building an arch to protect the radiator, and gusseting the suspension pickup points. If you look at a structure like this and compare it to the original frame, the new work is much more sturdy, and that will help this car on the race track.

Both frame rails are tacked to the welding table and the suspension pickup points are tacked into place. From this supported framework, we'll create the crossmember and add other necessary fittings.

Here's the new frame section being fitted to the car. We have spirit levels on it to make sure it lines up with the rest of the structure, which we've already squared and leveled. We'll also measure from fixed points on the chassis to make sure everything is where it should be before we weld.

Russ has created plates to reinforce the joint with the existing chassis structure. The whole assembly is trued up to the chassis and is ready to be welded into place. We'll stitch weld the connections and use plumb bobs to make sure the structure doesn't warp during welding.

Bodywork Repair Projects

These projects address the most common bodywork tasks that require welding or hot-work. Bodywork is the part of your car that people see first, and most people never look beyond the bodywork, so it pays to take your time and do this work carefully. If you have any doubts, take this kind of work to a professional. However, the satisfaction of performing your own body welding and rust repairs is substantial when others admire the car and ask who did the work. It's easy to find sacrificial body panels to use for practice while you build up your skills!

This hole was welded up with just some filler rod and then ground smooth. The paint preparation process will make it disappear entirely.

Filling Small Body Holes

Holes in the bodywork of a car are one of the most common problems auto metalworkers face. Whether it's repairing bullet holes in a vintage body that you rescued from the woods or removing the telltale holes left by side marker lights or the radio antenna you removed, everyone has some holes to fill.

The first consideration when filling holes is the size of the hole. Large (greater than 1/2 inch) holes should be filled by cutting a plate out of comparable metal and welding it into place as described in Chapter 5. Smaller holes can be filled with welding material. You can use MIG, TIG, or oxy-acetylene welding effectively for this task. Wire-feed and stick welding are not recommended for this type of job.

1 First ensure that there's enough surrounding metal to weld on. If you're filling a rust hole, chances are that the surrounding metal has also been rusted thin. If you try to weld on that, you'll shortly have a larger hole. In that case, cut out the rusted portion and use a patch panel. After all, the rust is probably still eating your car from the back side, right?

2 Get some heat shielding putty from your welding supply shop. This is simple stuff that is designed to be used wet. It surrounds your work area and soaks up residual heat. This is handy if you don't want to repaint a whole panel just to weld up a small hole. Spread the putty thickly around the hole with about 1/4 inch of metal showing.

3 Use a circular motion to deposit filler rod at the edge of the hole until it closes up. This is another use of the rosette weld technique. If possible, use the hammer welding technique to smooth your work as you go. When the weld has closed the hole, you can grind, file, or sand it smooth. For very small holes, a simple dab of filler rod is often enough.

Shrinking Small Fender Dents

One set of techniques that is indispensable in automotive sheetmetalworking is shrinking a dent. When you have door dings and other small dents in sheetmetal, you don't want to simply fill them or grind them down. With a gas torch and some gentle work, you can actually repair these dents as if they never existed.

When it is heated to bright red, mild steel is actually malleable like moist clay. It can be shaped with a variety of presses, hammers, and anvils. Auto bodyworkers have a specific set of hammers and handheld anvils (called dollies) for fixing dents. If you don't have a set of auto body tools, they're not expensive and when it comes to sheetmetal, nothing else really works as well.

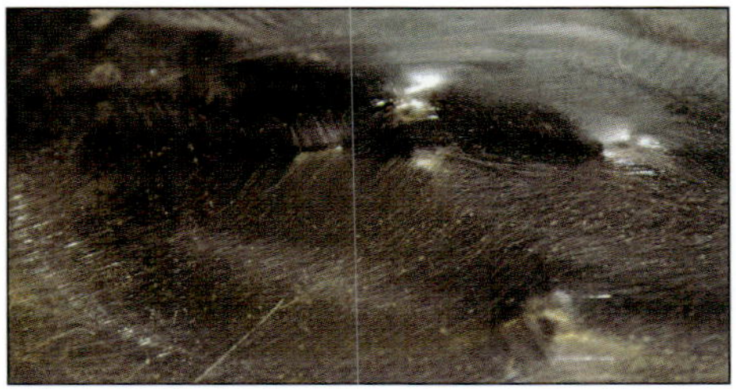

We used a chipping hammer to put some big dimples in a sample fender to practice our hot shrinking technique. We'll get rid of these in a matter of minutes.

1 To shrink a dent, you work it from the convex side—that is, the raised side. First, pound out the dent as smooth as you can with a hammer and dolly. Notice that no matter how careful you are, the hammer leaves small dents in the material. These are actually places where the hammering action on the cold steel has stretched the sheetmetal. If you look at the back side of the sheetmetal, those dents appear as little pimples on the surface.

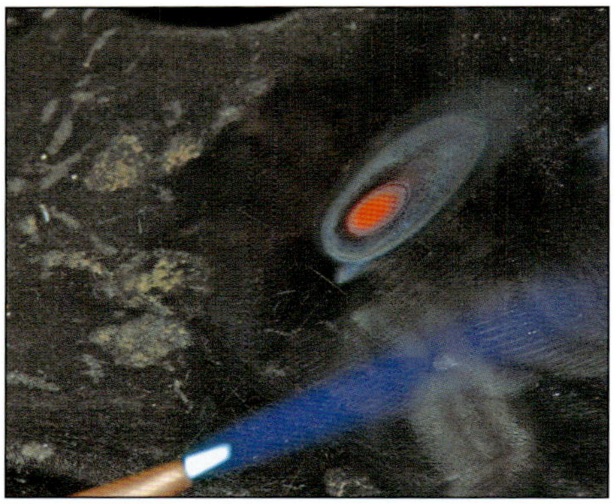

Keep the heat from your oxy-acetylene torch focused on the dent, but don't let it create a puddle. You just want a bright glowing red spot.

2 To shrink those dents flat again, use a fine welding tip and get a small, precise welding flame going on your oxy-acetylene torch. Heat up the pimple of metal just until it glows red, but keep the heat focused right on the raised bit so the surrounding metal stays cool. Then gently tap down the high point with a light hammer from your bodywork kit while backing up the dented place with a smooth dolly. The hot metal is melted just enough to become malleable, and as it is pressed down and outward, it thickens where it hits the surrounding cool metal.

Strike while the iron is hot! You need to gently tap down the dent.

3 Take a wet rag and cool the hot spot as quickly as possible. The result is that the high point of the dent is gone and the metal is now much smoother, but you didn't create a thin spot by grinding it down! You might need to repeat this process a few times, and as always, practice improves your results.

All auto body work takes time and practice to master, but that's the fundamental trick for eliminating door dings. Obviously, using this technique means having to repaint when you're done. The heat from the torch burns your paint right off for about an inch around the dent.

The perfect shrinking flame—just a little blue tip for precise heat placement in your dent. Have your hammer ready to go, because that heat won't last.

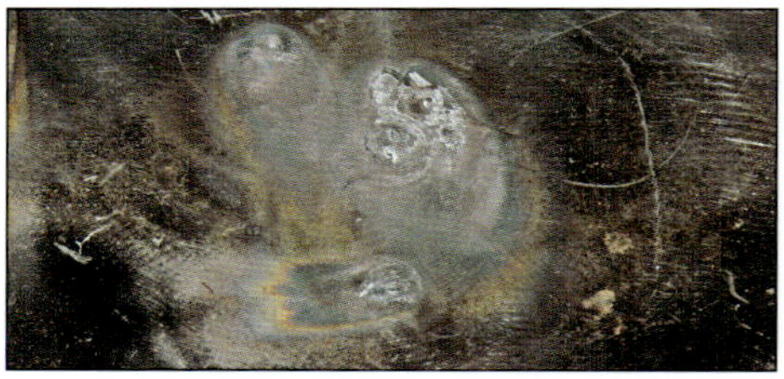

The same piece of fender a few minutes later. It's not perfect yet, but a little work with a file and sander will make it so.

Repairing Rust

One of the common problems that plagues restorers and customizers alike is rust. Rust attacks almost every car at some point, and it needs to be repaired in every restoration, race car build, and often just to keep a car on the road safely.

If you happen to have a popular model of car, you're in luck. Companies are now making panels stamped to match the bottoms of body panels, fenders, and doors. These panels are made specifically for rust repair purposes and they cover the areas where rust strikes. Cars as diverse as the Ford Model A, 1957 Chevrolet Bel Air, Porsche 356 and MGB all have panels readily available. Check your parts supplier to see if rust panels are available for your car.

If rust panels are not available for your car, you must create new parts

> **TECH TIP**
> ### Holes
> If the hole is smaller than a nickel and you're working with good, thick steel, welding up the hole is probably easier than patching. You can cut patches as small as a dime if you think the results will be better than working with weld.

Here's a familiar sight. There are small holes to be filled with weld, dents to be hammered out, and rust along the bottom of the fender. The best way to deal with this kind of rust is to cut away the rotten metal and replace it with a patch panel. Sometimes you can buy the panels premade, but more often you need to make your own.

by shaping basic sheetmetal to match the old fender or door skin. Rust usually strikes below the belt—that is, at the bottom of a body, fender, or door panel. This area is usually flat or at least simply curved with a lip or roll under at the base.

We'll look at a common problem—a fender with a rusty corner. We'll use the plasma cutter to cut a corner out of our sample fender and replace it with a piece of flat 20-gauge mild steel.

1 Determine the extent of the rusty area. After cleaning off paint, body filler, and any other covering on the steel, probe the area around the actual rust hole with a scratch awl or other sharp steel implement. Dark spots on the metal can indicate very thin areas that are prone to rust-through in the near future. Poke around with the awl and see if it pokes through in any location.

2 Cut the rusty piece out in a square, if possible. This makes your fabrication task a little easier. Make sure you're cutting into good metal—you need as much thickness as possible to weld in your patch.

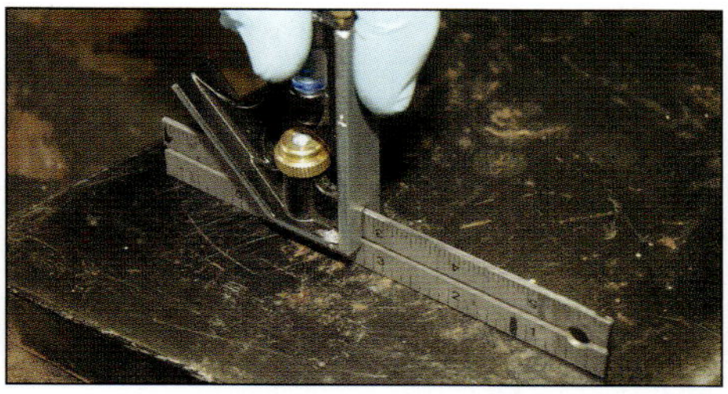

We're working with our sample fender again. Here we're checking the curvature of the fender to see if we will need to do some shot bag or anvil work on our patch piece before we match it up.

Corners are among the most challenging pieces to patch because they require a double lip and are often on a compound surface curve as well.

Here's the fender with the bad spot cut out. We're making a template to create our replacement piece.

3 Cut a template out of your sheet cardboard to match the shape, plus any lip or shape that you'll have to put into the metal. Also include about 1/4 inch around the mating sides of the patch for a recessed lip behind the surrounding metal.

The template, with space marked for the two lips and with space behind the fender for two recessed attachment lips. We'll create those four lips using the bead roller and the brake.

4 Transfer your template shape to a piece of sheetmetal of the same gauge as the receiving panel and use your plasma cutter, band saw, hacksaw, hole saw, or bench shear to cut the shape. Any accurate cutting tool works. If you use a hole saw to cut a circle, fill the pilot hole when you're done putting in the patch.

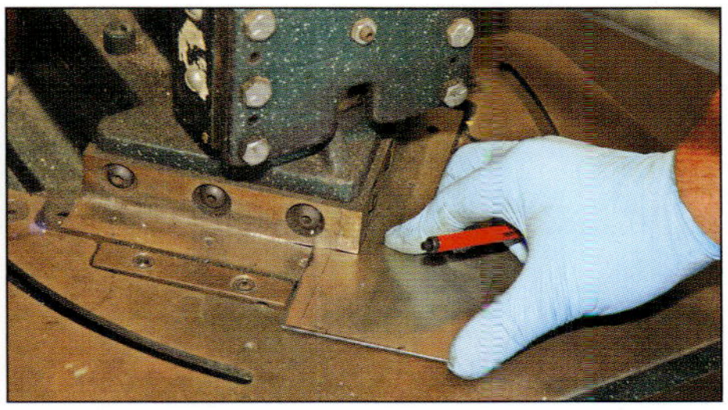

We cut out our patch on the notching tool because of its great precision and clean cuts. With thick steel, getting a good cut with hand shears could be a challenge.

5 Use your bead roller to make a step a little greater than the thickness of the sheetmetal on the extra material around the mating edges of the patch. This is so you can insert the patch and have the front surfaces match up nicely. If your patch has a lip, as ours does, use your brake to make any necessary bends.

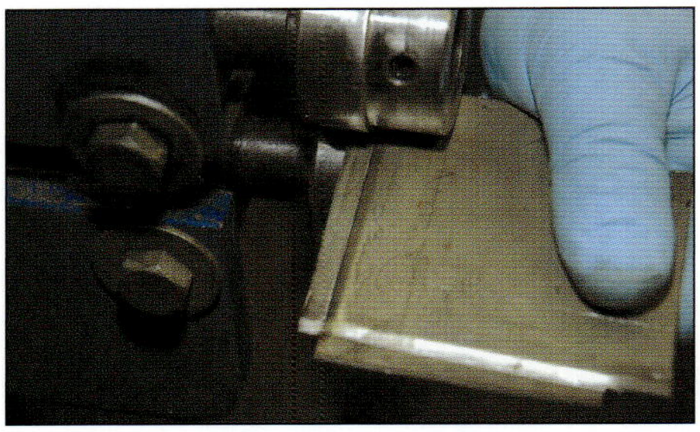

Putting a recessed lip on the patch with the bead roller will let us weld it to the fender with good backing and still keep the surfaces flush.

Finally, we finish our patch by bending the lips crisply in the box and pan brake. Now we'll see if it fits as well as our template.

Here's the piece, ready for fitting. You can see the recessed lip for welding. That will really help make this a strong repair.

Test-fit the piece and hold it in place with clamps. We could have matched that bottom lip a little better, but overall the fit is excellent because we used a template.

6 Clean the paint, rust, and body filler from your patch so you get a nice clean weld, free of ash, slag, or other impurities.

Cleaning the paint, scale, and any dirt from the welding area is always a good idea. This little disc sander is just right for the job.

7 Insert the patch from the back side and use your welder's magnet or clamps to hold the patch in place. You might need to work with the metal a bit to follow any gentle curves—it's rare that an automotive panel is ever truly flat!

8 Make a few tack welds to hold the patch in place. If the curve of the patch is not exactly right, you can tack one end and then flex the patch into place and make more tacks along its length to get the curve just right. Once the piece is tacked, move the magnet or clamps before you weld all the way around. Keep the welding heat as much as possible on the patch piece rather than the surrounding metal, because it's likely to be thicker.

As always, tack your work into place before you commit any welding beads. Remember, this is sheetmetal, so use low power and let the work cool between stitches.

9 Stitch-weld the rest of your patch perimeter. Be careful about getting too much heat in the piece and warping it. You may want to use a moist rag to cool your welds. You may also want to do some hammer welding to keep the weld bead as flat as possible.

Stitch-weld in short strokes of less than an inch to prevent the metal from warping, but weld the entire perimeter of the patch.

10 When you're done welding, grind the surface welds down with your body grinder. For the final touch, use your files and a sanding block to bring the weld down to the level of the surrounding metal. Afterwards, you can work further with hammer and dolly, or just fill any low spots with lead or body filler, then file and sand it smooth and level with the surrounding metal. If you choose lead for authenticity, however, be sure to wear a respirator when sanding!

Here you can see the stitches Russ made, and you can see the excellent penetration of the weld into the recessed tabs we made. This is a solid weld that will hold up under bodyworking.

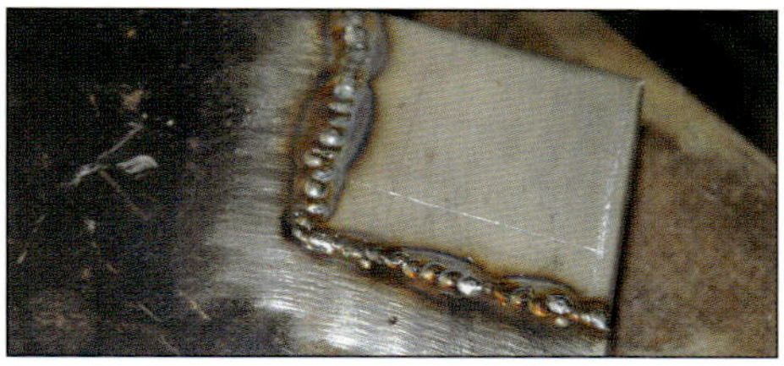

The front of the weld isn't very smooth, but we'll work it with the disc sander to bring that down to level with the rest of the metal.

This was one of the more challenging pieces in that there is a lip to work with, but comparatively easy in that the panel is nearly flat. Some rusty spots happen on compound curves and creating a patch panel requires extensive English wheel or shot bag planishing work to match up.

Making a Patch Panel

Many automotive suspension and chassis components are made from thicker pieces of stamped sheetmetal, welded together into strong structures. Still, over time and especially if placed under greater stress than the manufacturer intended, these parts can crack and break.

This project reinforces a lower suspension control arm from a 1967 Austin-Healy Sprite, modified for vintage racing. The original part was designed for the stresses made by a 60-horsepower engine, a tiny front anti-roll bar and a hard, narrow tire. The part is now over 40 years old and subject to about 100 horsepower and hard cornering with a fat, sticky racing tire and a stiff anti-roll bar. No wonder it cracked!

When you're faced with a situation like this, you can repair a part over and over until it fails catastrophically, or you can really get on top of the situation and make the part as stout as it needs to be. Some builders would throw away the original part and make a new one from tube steel, and they wouldn't be wrong to do so. But since this is a vintage car, we wanted to make an old school repair and improvement to keep this car appropriately authentic for competition.

Our solution was to make a patch panel to cover the stressed area of the control arm. This reinforces the arm and repairs any cracks already present in the part. We decided to perforate the patch to allow access to existing mounting holes and to lighten the part, as this control arm counts as unsprung weight.

1 Take the control arm (or any part) off the car and clean it thoroughly. This arm had been powder coated, so getting it clean took a long time with the wire wheel

After grinding down the welds, things are looking pretty good. There's still some hammer and dolly work and maybe even a bit of body putty in our future, but the rust is gone and replaced with shiny new metal.

Hammer Welding

Hammer welding is a specific technique used widely in automotive bodywork. The technique is simple to explain, yet tricky to do well. You do it like this: As you weld, have a hammer and dolly handy. When you've welded a stitch, place the dolly behind the weld and use the hammer to pound it smooth while it's still red hot. This smooths out the weld and reduces the amount of grinding, filing, and sanding you have to do afterwards. You might even get a helper to do the hammer and dolly work–it goes faster that way.

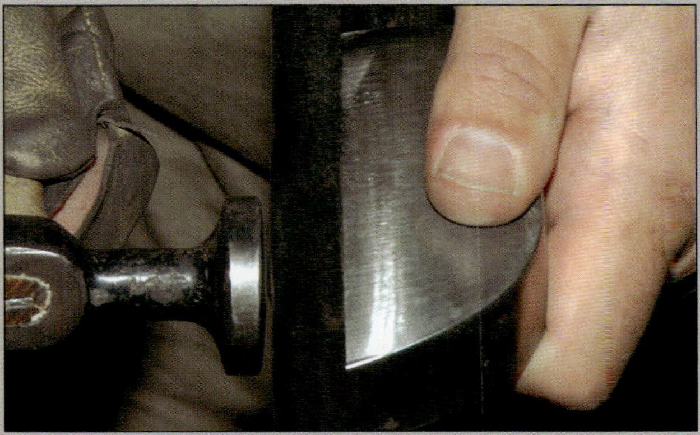

If you've got a friend to help, hammer welding is a good technique to use when patching bodywork. Get the hammer and dolly in there while the weld is still glowing and you can work things toward smooth and save yourself some grinding.

2 Make a cardboard template for the patch piece. In this case, the patch needed a slight curve, and needed to wrap around the kingpin pinion receiver at the outer end. That receiver is the focal point of the stress on this part, so it was important to support that point.

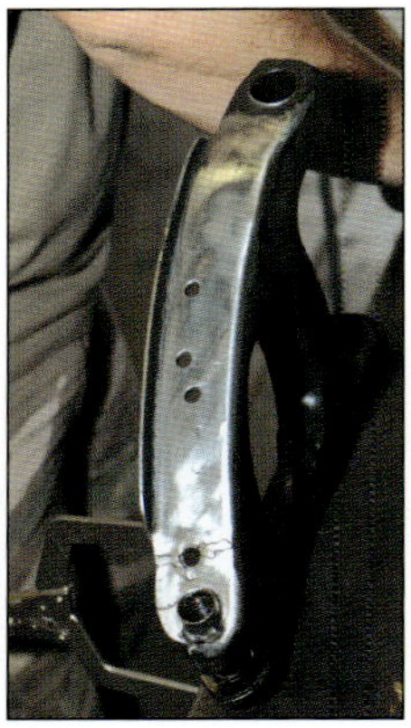

With the A-arm cleaned up, you can see the crack and a previous repair down at the bottom of the picture. We'll put a strap along this side of the arm for reinforcement.

This template will be more challenging to cut out because it curves to match the stamping of the A-arm.

3 We used the heavy duty aircraft shears to cut the repair piece out of 16-gauge mild steel, then a step bit to cut the 3/4-inch holes to lighten the repair piece. We refined the shape and cleaned up the cut on the belt sander.

We cut the curve for this piece with a set of heavy-duty aircraft shears. The piece was small enough that the plasma cutter would have been overkill.

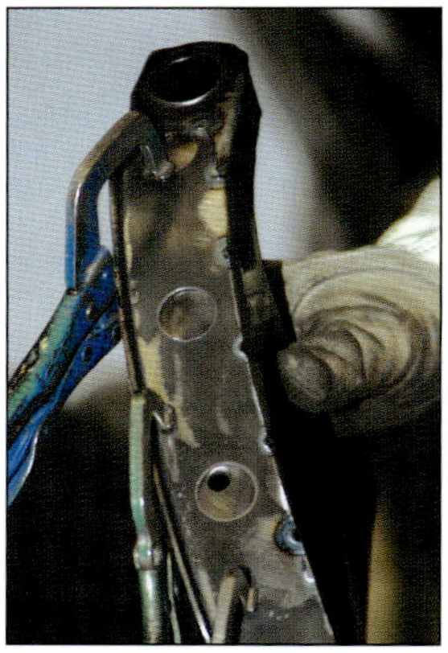

Tack welds with the TIG welder let us be sure that we had the strap positioned correctly.

4 After some test-fitting and adjustment, the piece was ready to weld. We used the TIG welder to tack the piece to the control arm in several locations. Using clamps to keep the repair form-fitted to the part, we stitch-welded the perimeter. As always, we alternated the stitching areas to allow the welds to cool and normalize so as not to warp the repair piece or the original stamping.

5 We finished up with some rosette welds inside the holes in the repair piece. This helps the reinforcement by creating additional points of attachment to the original stamping. We paid extra attention to the cracked area around the kingpin pinion receiver, making sure we welded up the original crack as we put on the reinforcement.

6 The TIG welder offered us great control and penetration for this project. Almost no grinding was required. We'll do the same repair on the other side of the car after racing season is over.

With this reinforcement, this piece is not likely to crack again. However, we should have left the locating bolt in place at the outer end, because the heat from the welding warped the arm just enough to make reassembly a challenge. Live and learn!

Painting, Plating and Powder Coating

When you're working with steel parts, it's a good idea to get something on the part to help prevent rust. The usual choices, in increasing order of expense, are paint, powder coat, and plating.

Paint is a good solution, and if a part cracks, you'll know about it right away because the paint will crack along with it. Powder coat is a lovely covering—watertight and beautiful, but it sometimes hides a crack for a while. Still, powder cracks too and shows you the break.

If you choose plating for a stressed part, consider nickel-plating rather than chrome. Chrome plating often hides a crack where nickel does not, and the nickel looks almost as shiny. Plus, it's a little different and that's cool. Many race car drivers have come to grief when their chrome-plated axles or suspension components failed with a crack that had been developing for some time.

Tube Steel Projects

A hollow tube is not as strong as a solid cylinder of the same *diameter*, but it is stronger than a solid cylinder of the same *weight*. This is why tube steel is used to build race car frames, roll structures, and high-stress parts such as sway bars and suspension components. Tube is also used for exhaust pipes and occasionally, intake manifolds as well. It's a near-universal material in the automotive hobby.

Most tube-shaped mild steel used for automotive roll structures is between 1.25 and 2 inches in diameter and has a wall thickness of between .095 and .125 inch. Thinner tubing is used for exhaust systems or decorative light bars but for structural strength, .095- or .120-wall tube steel is generally required. Never use exhaust tubing or other inappropriate materials for structural work—it fails when you need it most. If your car is entered in any event that requires technical inspection, they'll drill a small hole in the bar or use an ultrasonic tester and measure the wall thickness anyway.

Virtually every competition car in the world is required to run a roll bar or cage in the modern era, and countless convertibles and other street cars also use roll bars to protect their occupants in case of rollover. Roll bars also provide a sturdy mounting point for competition seat belts and fire extinguishers, and with a little extra work can include seat mounting rails as well.

Russ works on a complex tube roll structure. It takes good materials, good design, and good welding to produce a cage good enough to protect the lives of the people inside the car. If you doubt your ability to deliver all three aspects, it's best to take this project to a professional.

The tube on the left is .120- wall 1.5-inch DOM suitable for a roll bar. The piece on the right is .063-wall 3-inch ERW exhaust tubing. When selecting a piece of tube for a project, you must consider the material, the manufacturing process, the diameter, and the wall thickness.

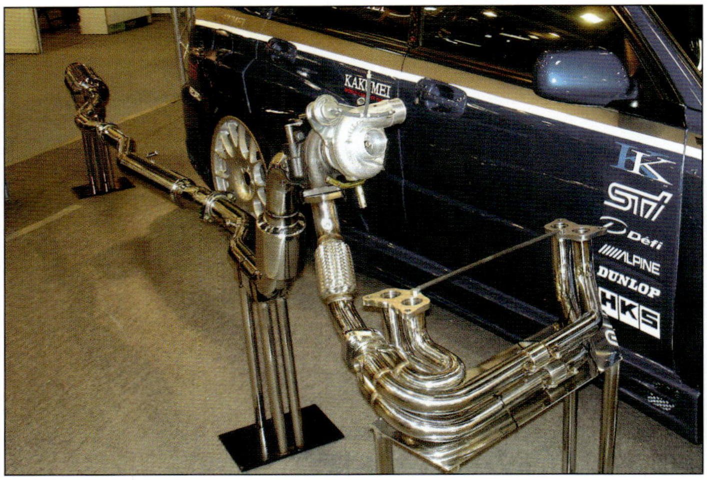

This Kakumei stainless steel exhaust system is precisely bent and carefully welded and polished to look great as well as flow well.

A roll cage has to be built to the specifications of the car's racing organization. NHRA, SCCA, CORR, and NASCAR all have good, proven designs for you to use.

In this chapter we'll look at what it takes to put a roll bar into a car, how to make a custom exhaust pipe, and how to make a subframe brace out of tube metal. Other common projects include driving light bars, tube bumpers, radiator protection, and utility structures for pickup trucks. You can build an entire race car or dune buggy chassis or even an airplane out of tube steel, but such projects require an entire book to themselves. The skills and experience necessary to undertake more extensive projects are all contained in these basic exercises.

Working with Tube Steel

There are three kinds of tubing commonly used for structural automotive fabrication. The first is ERW, which stands for Electronic Resistance Welding. This is a flat piece of steel that has been wrapped around a buck and then welded to form a tube. The entire seam is welded along the length of the tube by a machine that is similar in operation to a spot welder.

Some organizations allow ERW tubing to be used for structures, and if you're working with ERW in a structural context, remember that the weld (visible as a bluish line on the tube) is usually placed on the inside of a bend. Some builders place the weld at the side of the bend. But if you try to stretch the weld on the outside of a bend, the welded area will weaken and possibly crack or break during bending, or worse, after you have installed it in the car.

The second type of tubing is called DOM, which stands for Drawn Over Mandrel. DOM tubing is also welded from a flat sheet, but after welding, the tube is reheated and formed around a mandrel to precise specifications. DOM tubing is

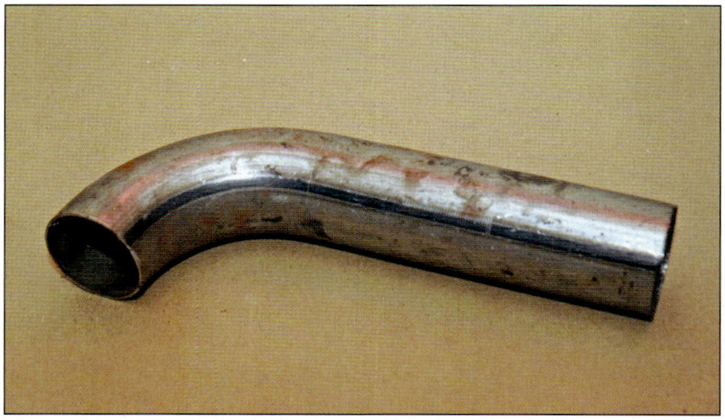

You can easily see the blue stripe on this piece of exhaust tube that marks it as ERW construction. Notice that the bender has placed the blue stripe to the inside of the bend.

DOM tube lacks the blue stripe to tell you what it is, but there are usually markings on the tube. If you're in doubt about the materials or construction of a tube, don't use it for a critical application like a roll bar.

significantly more expensive than ERW, but also stronger. It does not have an obvious blue stripe.

Seamless tubing is extruded from a single mass of molten steel and formed on a mandrel, but this material has no welds. It's very strong, but also very expensive.

Cutting Tubing

To join up roll cage bars, you also need a fishmouth tubing cutter. This is a hole saw connected to a mount that can hold a piece of tube at any angle. This allows you to measure and mark an intersecting piece and then cut the tube for a perfect fit. You can also cut and grind to get a proper fit, but this is far more labor intensive. The shop that does your bending probably has a fishmouth cutter, and if you have measured your angles, they can cut your support pieces as well.

For straight cuts in tube steel, a chop saw, metal-cutting band saw or a hacksaw works best. Don't use a gas

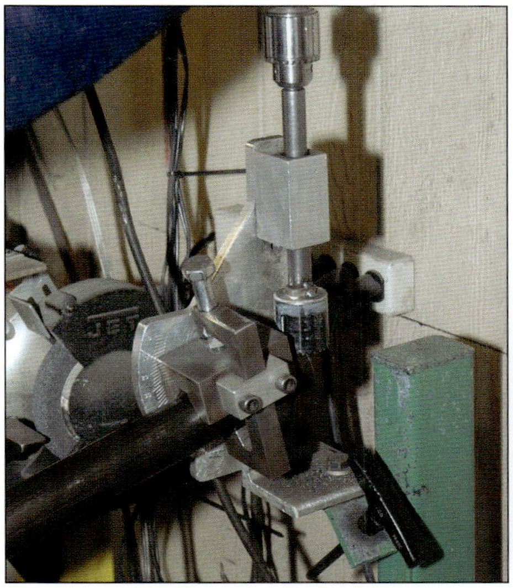

A fishmouth cutter with a protractor to indicate the angle of the cut is essential for almost all tube structures. The alternative is hours and hours of difficult and exacting work with a grinder.

The result of a good fishmouth cut is a tube that's ready to weld into place with no gaps. Just make sure that you get the length measured correctly. It's easy to make a fishmouth a little too short.

A Word About Chrome-Moly

Most structural specifications are written for mild steel tubing, and specifies DOM or ERW–and possibly have different size and wall thickness specifications for each. There is usually a different specification for 4130 Chrome-Molybdenum alloy tubing. This material goes by a number of common trade names–4130, CM, Cro-moly, Chrome-Moly, and so on, but it all refers to the same material.

Generally, chrome-moly tubing is stronger than mild steel and so structural regulations allow a smaller diameter and thinner wall thickness to be used. This reduces overall weight, which is highly desired by racers. But there are tradeoffs to using chrome-moly. For example, chrome-moly requires TIG welding materials and techniques. Consult your material supplier or welding supply store for current information about the correct welding rod or wire for your project. If chrome-moly is not worked properly, it can become brittle.

Base plates and flat gussets for chrome-moly can be made of mild steel, as long as the welding process used is approved for the chrome-moly portion of the piece.

You can't identify chrome-moly just by looking at it, but like DOM, it usually has markings somewhere on the tube that identify the material for you.

If you choose to invest in chrome-moly, you may want to protect your investment by hiring a specialist to work with the material to ensure maximum structural integrity.

This sand car chassis is made entirely of custom-bent and welded tube. The structure is both light and strong, and also inexpensive to produce.

cutting torch if you can avoid it, as it burns the steel at the cut.

Bending Tubing

The first thing to say about bending and welding tube is that it's as much an art as a science. You can calculate everything to the millimeter, but each bending machine and bending die is a little different from every other one. It's important to know how your particular equipment works and how much fudge factor you have to allow. The only way to know that is through experience, and you're likely to waste a lot of tubing on the learning curve.

One trick as you're getting to know your bender is to make a few test bends to find out exactly where the bend curve begins. Then you can use a long protractor or angle finder to keep track of the bend progress.

Getting the Right Bender

The shape of tube steel presents certain special challenges for the fabricator. While it is possible to make smooth bends in tube steel, it is not easy. Improper bending technique will crimp, kink, or collapse the tube, destroying its structural integrity. Special tube-bending equipment is required to bend tubing accurately without reducing its strength too much. The inexpensive kind of tube benders that press upward with a bottle jack are absolutely not appropriate for creating roll bars,

A powered free-standing rotary tube bender costs a few thousand dollars. Make sure it comes with a good supply of dies for different size tubes and different radius bends.

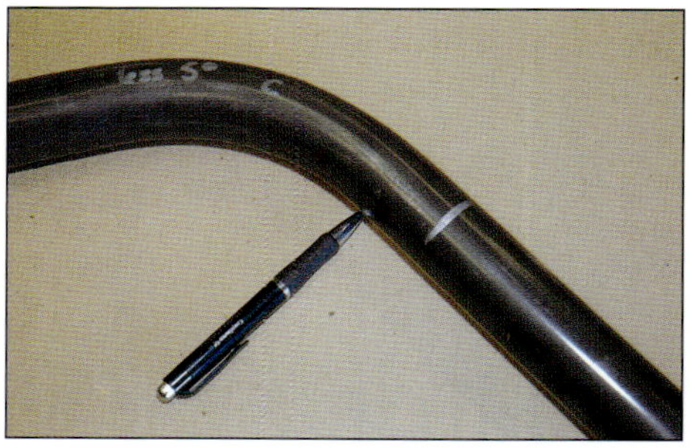

On a rotary tube bender, the paint mark on the tube marks the end of the die on which this bend was made. The pen marks the point where the metal actually begins to bend. The difference is about 1/2 the tubing diameter.

The Lowdown on Bending Tube

Many amateur roll bar and cage builders find it economical and effective to hire a professional racing shop to bend their tubes. These shops typically have a professional computer program indexed to their powered tubing benders. If you simply provide the basic dimensions and the rules that govern your roll bar or cage design, the shop can accurately cut, bend, and test-fit your parts for you.

In almost every case, it costs far less than buying a bender and doing the work yourself. Tubing benders cost hundreds of dollars used (if you can find one) and up to thousands if you buy new. If you're not going into the roll bar business, the cost of a bender just doesn't pencil out. Plus, if you buy your tube from the shop that does the bending, you might even get the first few bends included in the purchase price.

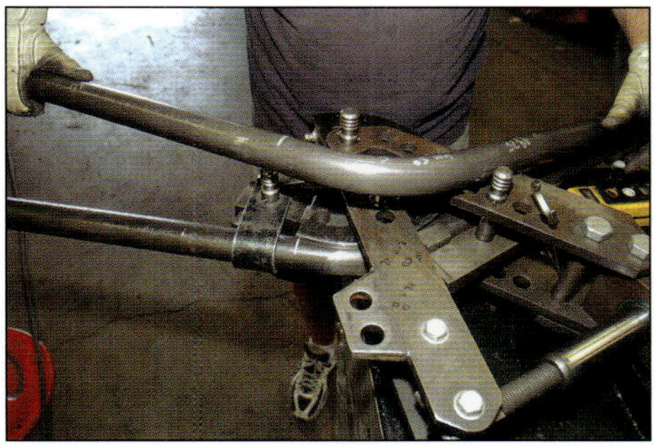

Don't rely on your protractor to make identical bends in matched pieces. Hold the original part over the bender and confirm the bend with your own eyes. It's far easier to get it right the first time than to have to put it back in the machine for a little more bend.

tube-frame chassis, or other critical components. They stretch the metal far too much and will tend to crimp materials in significant bends.

For roll cage and chassis work, you need a mandrel or a rotary tube bender, and these are expensive tools. You can purchase hand-powered benders, but these require a very strong installation base because of the long levers required to put enough torque on the tube to bend it. Powered mandrel and rotary tube benders can be free-standing, but are even more expensive yet.

Whatever bender you choose, it's critical that you make your bender installation absolutely level. Any errors in your bends because the system isn't level will be doubled every time you flip the tube around to bend the other side! If you think you have an error factor in your bender, see if you can work the tube from one end to the other, as opposed to working outwards from the middle.

Bending is Forever

Tube steel hardens a little when you bend it. Because the steel on the outer side of the bend has been stretched, it becomes more brittle. Therefore, most organizations that specify roll structures have specific rules about the number of bends, the maximum number of degrees of each bend and total bend, and the inner radius of each bend in a piece of tubing. The purpose of these rules is to limit the amount of work hardening that can be introduced to a piece of tube through bending.

Bending a piece of tubing properly requires a manual or hydraulic mandrel or rotary tube bending machine. In the past, people bent steel tube by filling the tube with dry sand and welding the ends shut, then heating the bend area in a forge and bending the tube around a buck of the desired radius. This worked well to avoid crimping, but is work-intensive and much less accurate than using a bender.

The most important fact to remember is that bending is forever—once bent, you can't unbend a piece of tubing. If you bend it wrong, it's done.

Planning Your Roll Structure Project

A good tube steel project begins with careful planning. A roll bar or cage takes more material and more work than it looks like in the results. Moreover, each bend and cut must be precisely correct—even a small gap is difficult to weld over and shows in the final product.

The first part of planning your project is to design the bar or cage you want. The design should fit well with your car and require a minimum of alteration to the surrounding interior panels and bodywork. But if you are building a roll structure to use in a racing or off-road vehicle, you must also plan to meet the requirements of at least one sanctioning body or insurer.

Judd Weld of Grindesigns in Bend, Oregon, built this rally cage for a Subaru WRX. A rally cage is about as tough as they come, and well-designed with plenty of supporting braces.

The Sports Car Club of America website (www.scca.com) allows anyone to download their General Competition Rules. Section 9 of these rules includes detailed drawings of a variety of roll structures. Cages built to SCCA rules are accepted by most track racing organizations worldwide. For drag racing cage rules, you can consult the National Hot Rod Association (NHRA) Tech Faq on www.nhra.com. Performance rally has some of the most involved cage rules in motorsports, and the rules are standardized by the Federation Internationale de l'Automobile (FIA). Pictures of FIA-approved roll structures are available at www.rally-america.com.

In general, most sanctioning bodies for racing or other organized automotive activities have common or very similar standards. A good roll bar design works for drag racing as well as drifting or autocross. There are some variations, however, and not all organizations let you overbuild your roll structure—because a roll structure also enhances your car's frame stiffness. Vintage racing organizations in particular are picky about overbuilding a car's roll structure.

A good rollbar design generally starts with one main hoop made of one uninterrupted piece of DOM mild steel or chrome-moly tube. That tube will have a total of about 180 degrees (plus or minus 10 degrees) of bend along its length. It should not mushroom like a pickup truck light bar, which is to say that there should not be reverse bends in the main hoop.

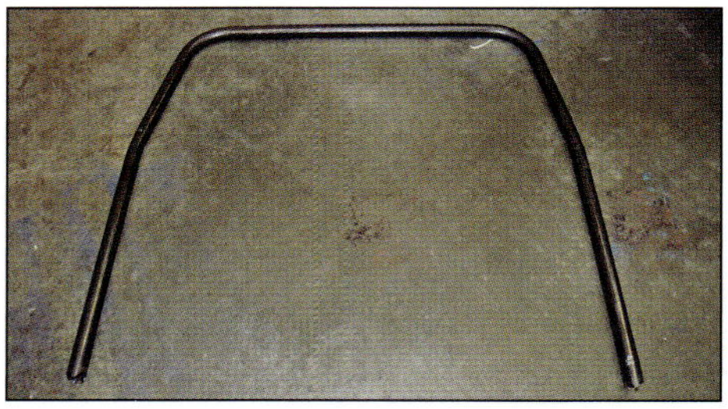

A basic main hoop, with four bends. The first shallow bends allow the hoop to follow the car's body lines, then the main bends are slightly less than 90 degrees to create the top of the bar.

A good roll bar design uses strong rear braces and cross braces. Generally this means that the rear braces attach along the top or within 6 inches of the top of the main hoop and proceed without bends back to a solid mounting point. These braces should be at least 30 degrees away from parallel to the main hoop for good fore and aft support.

Here Russ has a nylon tie-down showing where the second cross-brace will go in a roll cage for a 1958 Chevy Bel Air. You can use string, tape, or anything that makes a straight line.

Most rules for roll bars and cages require that your welds meet ASTM (American Society for Testing and Materials) standards. Those standards call for a 360-degree weld for the supporting bars that connect to your main hoop. If you cannot weld all the way around, you may be able to use supporting gussets to reinforce the joint. Check your rulebook before you begin!

Always plan to make your tube welds all the way around the joint. If you cannot get in to weld all the way, ask and find out if a gusset is an acceptable substitute.

Most rules also require that you place the main hoop as close to the inner roof as you can. But be aware that when you weld in the rearward supports, you might burn your headliner. Many roll bar builders make the top welds before moving the bar into its final mounting place. This also allows you to conveniently paint the cage.

Depending on your car, you may have to pass bars through one or more bulkheads to meet the angle and attachment requirements in a given set of rules. Cars such as the Porsche 914 and Toyota MR2 almost always require some holes in body-work and the rear windows to accommodate a roll structure. Figure this into your plans because you can't change supporting bar angles or attachments too far and still expect to pass technical inspection.

If you are building a roll bar for your own use and have no need to meet any particular specification, you should still consult at least one reputable racing rule book because the designs they specify are proven, safe, and generally very well documented. You don't want to get too creative when your safety is on the line.

While you design your cage, you should also be preparing your car. You need to remove carpet and seats and other material and objects in or around the mounting locations. Pick strong locations such as reinforced corners and add mounting plates there if your car is a unibody design, or cut through the floor and tie your roll bar to the ladder frame if your car has one.

Once you have settled on a design, it's time to figure out what

TECH TIP

Strings

You can use string or tape to plan and measure your support braces. A piece of twine taped into place along the centerline of a planned brace tube gives you a nice visual representation of the finished cage. You can see where the tube will fit, how long it needs to be, and approximately what the angle will be at each joint. Strings are also easy to intersect to plan and measure X-shapes and diagonals. Any straight line can be represented with string!

Removing the seats, carpet, sound deadening material, and maybe even the headliner is a good start to a roll bar project. You need space to work and you'll be making a lot of heat in the car.

supplies you need. Measure all the basic dimensions for your roll structure and add 10 to 20 percent for wastage, bends, and fitment. Some roll structure specifications allow you to use a lighter grade of tube for supporting bars, but in general it's best to make the entire structure out of the same size and grade of material.

Calculating Bends in Tube Steel

Before you cut or weld any tubing, you have some homework to do. Measure the dimensions of your project carefully, and get a friend to repeat your measurements to be sure. As a rule of thumb, cut your tubing parts a little long, because you can always shave a little off, but adding a few inches is hard to do.

Calculating the length of tubing required for a bent roll hoop is more tricky than it looks. It's not enough to add the vertical and horizontal requirements, and if you get it wrong your roll bar will be wrong in some dimension. Here is a basic equation to help you calculate the length of tubing (in inches) required to make a bend:

Total Length =
(Center Line Radius x .01745) x
(Bend in Degrees)

Below is a simple graphic representation of the relevant measurements. For the rest of the example, you can assume that the tubing being bent is .120 wall and 1.75 inches Outside Diameter (OD) and that the Center Line Radius (CLR) of the bending die being used is 6 inches.

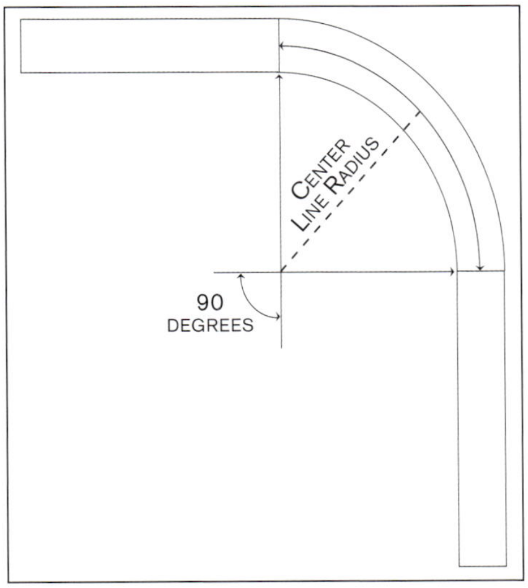

Let's break the equation down:

6.0 CLR x .01745 =
.1047 inches per degree of bend
.1047 x 90 degrees of bend =
9.423 inches total length

So with a CLR of 6 inches and a 90-degree bend, 9.423 inches of tube are used in the example bend.

But there's another calculation you need to perform, and that's to find out how tall your roll hoop will be once you've made your bend. Again, it's not obvious.

To find the total height of your 90-degree bend, take the CLR of the die and add half the OD of the tube. This is because the CLR takes you from the start of the die to the *center* of the tube, not the top! Then add another half of the tube's OD to account for a little fudge factor caused by the tendency of steel to stay straight a little way past the starting point on the die. The math for the height calculation is shown here:

1.75/2 = .875
.875 + .875 + 6 =
7.75 inches from the start of the bend
to the top of the tube

Of course, on the legs of your hoop it's easier to just cut the tube a little long and measure from the center of the bar. Measure outwards from the center and make your bends, then trim the legs to the desired height, measured from the top of the mounting plate to the top of the hoop. Where these equations really come in handy is when you have to measure the distance along the top of your roll hoop between the two bends. So they're really used more for calculating the total width of a roll hoop.

For example, if we want our roll hoop to have a total distance of 36 inches from the outside edge to the outside edge, we must subtract the 7.75 inches of bend length from each end of the top of the hoop. That makes the distance between bend start points along the top of the hoop just 20.5 inches for a 36-inch-wide 1.75-inch OD roll hoop with a 6-inch CLR.

But not all bends are an even 90 degrees, so you have to be able to calculate the length of tubing used in a bend of any number of degrees. The table below shows the length of tubing (in inches) used for a 1-degree bend at a number of common CLR measurements. To find the length of tubing used, simply multiply the relevant figure for your die's CLR by the number of degrees in the bend you're making.

Using the figures in the table below, if your CLR is 6.5 and you're making a 35-degree bend, you will use 3.969875 inches of tube in the bend.

Alternate Method: Working It Out on The Floor

With all the computer programs and equations, calculating your tubing bends can be an intimidating proposition. However, there is another way: Just draw your structure on the floor!

Actually, you can draw on anything big enough to make a 1:1 scale drawing of your roll bar, but a flat concrete floor works best, and most people have easy access to one of those. You still need a tubing bender, but for a simple roll bar, this procedure should yield good results. You need a carpenter's square, a tape measure, and a felt-tip marker. Then get some chalk or paint markers and follow these steps.

1 Measure your car for the size of roll bar you need. That is, the overall height from the base plate or frame rail to your headliner, or however tall you want the bar to be. Then measure the width of the hoop at the top and between the base plates or frame rails.

2 Use carpentry tools and your chalk to draw a square or rectangle on the floor that is as large in every dimension as your roll bar. For example, if your bar is 36 inches tall and 40 inches wide, that's the size of your rectangle. Measure it carefully and make sure it's square by measuring along the diagonals. When the diagonal measurements are the same, the box is square. Make a vertical line down the exact center of the box so you know the location of your centerline. That's 20 inches from either side in this case.

3 Get a piece of tube that is somewhat longer than you really need. This is critical because you're going to start in the middle and make the bar, then trim it to length by cutting off the ends. For example, in our project, we've got 40 inches of width and 36 inches on each leg. So you need at least 112 inches, plus your fudge factor. A 144-inch bar would be more than enough. Mark your piece of tube in the exact center, at 72 inches in this case.

4 Line up the centerlines of your tube and your box, so the tube is on top of the box and sticks out to either side.

5 Grab a piece of scrap tubing of the same size as your bar material and give it a 90-degree bend in your bender. Make sure you've got enough material to leave at least six inches hanging off of either end of your bend. Place the bent tube in one upper corner of your square, just alongside of the roll bar tube. You can see the point where the bend ends on your scrap tubing. Mark that same spot on the roll bar tube. Then repeat this step on the other side. Now you know where to start your 90-degree bends to maintain your 40 inch total width.

6 Bend one end of your hoop and then lay it down inside your diagram to make sure you got an exact 90-degree bend. You might have to overbend just slightly to achieve the perfect 90 when the bar is removed from the bender. Then make the second bend, keeping the piece perfectly level with the first bend so it lays flat.

7 When the second bend is done, lay the bar back onto your diagram. It should sit perfectly flat and contained within the width, with the centerlines lined up. The legs, however, will stick out beyond the height you need. Mark them according to the bottom of the diagram and cut them off with your chop saw or hacksaw.

By adding lines inside your basic box using a protractor, carpenter's bevel, and a long carpenter's level, you can figure arbitrary degree measurements with this method. For example, to make two 45-degree bends instead of a single 90 you can cut off the top corner of the box with the protractor and level and then bend your tube to follow that

Tube Length Use Per Degree of Bend

Center Line Radius	Length of Tube Per Degree
3.0	.05235
3.5	.061075
4.0	.0698
4.5	.078525
5.0	.08725
5.5	.095975
6.0	.1047
6.5	.113425
7.0	.12215
7.5	.130875
8.0	.1396

contour. The more complex the design, the harder it is to implement. But it can be done because all your measurements derive from that square box that matches the overall dimensions of the hoop. The trick is to center your piece of tubing on the centerline of the box, then work outward from the center.

Fishmouth Cuts

Fishmouth ends are among the most challenging joints to create. A good fishmouth tube cutter makes this job possible, if not easy. A fishmouth cutter is a modified hole saw and a vise that holds the tube at a desired angle while the hole saw cuts the shape of the receiving bar. You can also do this with a good vise mounted on a drill press, but a fishmouth cutter is easier. Without some kind of fishmouth cutter, be prepared to spend hours at your bench grinder.

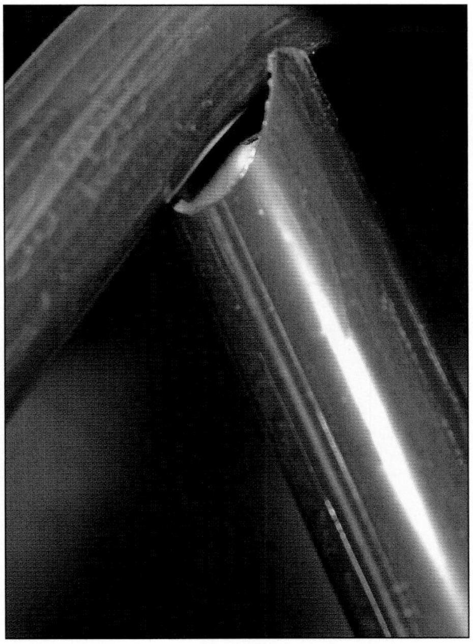

Getting a tight fishmouth may require a few tries, especially at first. But you need to get those angles and cuts just right for a good weld and a strong cage.

For a simple example, consider welding a straight horizontal bar between the vertical posts of a basic hoop 40 inches wide. Each end of the bar needs to wrap around the outside diameter of the vertical posts. At its shortest point, that bar must be 40 inches long, but the outer edges may be over an inch longer. To create this bar, calculate the length between the centerlines of the two posts and cut your bar to that length. The measurement will be the distance between the insides of the posts plus one tube diameter, or the outer distance minus one tube diameter. If you're using 1.75-inch tube, that's 38.25 inches in our 40-inch example.

To cut a 90-degree fishmouth, you can use a hole saw of the same outer diameter as the tubing and clamp the tube into your drill press. Make sure you've got some wood under the tube! Bring the hole saw down so that it cuts a semicircle out of the end of the tube. Then swap ends and make sure that you line up the second cut the same as the first! You may have to grind a little to get the length just right, but if your hole saw matches your receiving tube diameter, your fishmouth should line up cleanly.

Cutting a fishmouth at an arbitrary angle is harder. This is where a dedicated fishmouth cutter comes in handy. You can set an angle for the base plate on most drill presses, but more care is required to get the cut just right. Always measure the shortest and the longest lengths required in any bar. Some very complex bars may require the fishmouths to be cut at different angles or with the two ends cut along a different bias, and you must measure those individually.

Welding Tube Parts Into Your Car

When you go to weld tubes into your car, you typically have two types of weld to run. First are straight cuts where you mount the tube to a flat surface such as a mounting plate or frame rail. You also have fishmouth cuts where you mount the tube to the side of another tube and must cut the open end to wrap around the body of the second tube.

To weld flat ends (and angle-cut ends that are otherwise flat), make sure that your entire tube is positioned correctly and that both ends of the tube fit flush against their mounts. You can bevel the edges a little bit for a strong weld. Begin as always by tacking your work into place and rechecking all your measurements. When you're satisfied that everything is in its correct place, go ahead and complete your welds. Make sure all your welds go a full 360 degrees around the tube and achieve

If possible, the best place to attach a roll bar is straight to the box frame of the car. If you have a unibody car, you need to make base plates of at least 36 square inches.

Hydraulic Press

If you have access to a porta-power hydraulic press, you can use this tool to make minor adjustments in your bends and to push stubborn pieces into place for welding. Think of it as a third hand for holding everything together—when you're happy with the positioning, you can go ahead and tack things into place.

good penetration all the way through the base plate. Unless you're working with 4130 chrome-moly, MIG welding is generally the best way to attach tubes to base plates.

More Projects

The first question to answer with any roll bar or chassis project is purpose of the project, and the rules (if there are such) that must be satisfied. Those factors generally dictate the design you must use. Typical rule-based roll bar design requirements are tubing size and thickness, base plate size or tie to the frame, and then the overall design—usually the number of supports, minimum distance above the driver's head, seating the driver within or near to the plane of the main hoop, and the number, angle, and configuration of the supports. Also, the minimum and maximum radius of the bends is often specified.

Chassis requirements are even more complex. Most organizations have approved homologated designs that they prefer. These are proven designs and you should use them unless you've got a very good reason to try something else. Organizations such as SCCA require new tube chassis designs to be submitted to engineering analysis before they can be used in competition.

Usually there are chassis and roll structure diagrams in every organization's rule book, and those designs must be followed. The insurance companies that cover motorsports in the modern age require these standards. Alternately, you can ask your local officials to suggest a good local car to use as a model. There are also cage kits you can purchase that meet common rule sets such as NASCAR, NHRA, or SCCA.

Making a Basic Drag Racing Roll Cage

This project involves creating a basic rear-supported roll bar, with forward braces and a driver's side door bar, made to NHRA specifications for a car that runs 8.5 second or higher quarter-mile times. The rules and diagrams are downloadable from www.NHRA.com.

Street Roll Bars

Roll bars and roll cages in race cars are required because of the greater danger of rollovers and other impacts faced by racing drivers. Race cars are also built with integral seat mounts connected to the roll cage and heavy-duty seatbelt mounts. Finally, racing drivers wear crash helmets and arm restraints to protect themselves in an impact.

A roll bar in your street car can be very dangerous if your head can hit the bar in an impact. Also, street bars tend to be shorter than racing roll bars, to accommodate the factory soft or hard tops on a convertible. Thus, street roll bars are often shorter than head level for a tall person, providing no protection at all. Also, in a race car, the driver is held tightly a supportive seat with a 6-point seat belt harness. In a street car, your stock shoulder belt does little to stop your body when the car is upside down. Roll bars look great and sporty on a street car—especially a convertible, but don't believe that they offer protection in a rollover.

This roll bar is lower than the tops of the passengers' heads and is unpadded. It probably poses more of a danger to them than a rollover accident.

1 Remove the seats and carpet from the car. You need a completely accessible work area, and carpet or seats are in your way, plus they pose a fire hazard. If possible, you might want to remove the headliner, but it is difficult or impossible to replace the liner after you've completed your roll bar.

The best possible environment for installing a roll cage is a completely bare-metal chassis. There's nothing to catch on fire or get in your way while you work.

2 Measure the main hoop dimensions. If you are tying the plate to a mounting plate in a unibody car, measure from the floor (less the thickness of your plate), but if you are tying to a traditional ladder frame, go ahead and cut the holes in the body floor above the frame and measure down to the frame. Measure your dimensions so that the top of the roll bar is as close to the headliner or roof metal as you can make it.

You also need to measure the width of the roll hoop at the top of the hoop and at the bases. Most rules (and good structural design) want about 180 degrees (plus or minus 10 degrees) of total bend in your hoop. Mushroom-shaped designs such as those used in light bars for pickup trucks are not as sturdy, which is one reason those bars specifically disclaim protection in rollover accidents.

Use clamps to hold everything in place while you measure and make adjustments. You can also use racheting tie-downs as a low-cost come-along to move and hold pieces in place.

3 Take rough measurements for your supporting bars. In general, these are straight pieces. You're just looking for approximate lengths at this time, and you'll remeasure, cut, and install the supporting bars after the main hoop is in place.

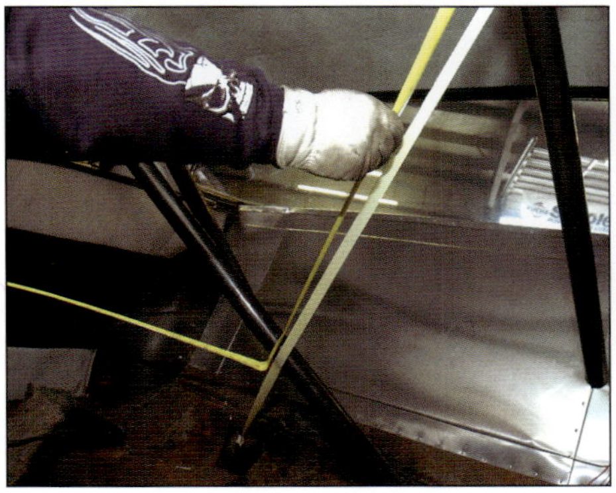

Russ measures the distance for a supporting brace. You have to wait until you get the main hoop in place to get the exact lengths, but you can get a rough estimate of your total tubing needs before you bend or install any tube.

4 Calculate your bends using the formulas and procedures given above. Now you know the total length of tube you need for your main hoop and where the bends go, and about how much extra tube you need for supporting braces. Now you can buy your tube and have the main hoop bent to your specifications. As always, cutting the arms a little long is better than a little short.

5 Purchase some steel plate and make your base plates if you're installing your bar in any kind of unibody (stamped sheetmetal) car. You want to use large base plates to spread the load in a rollover. As a general rule, most sanctioning bodies demand plates of at least 6 inches square (36 square inches) and 1/8-inch (.125) thick. Weld the plates into the base area you measured for your roll bar. You may need to spend some time with the wire brush or other tools cleaning the base metal before you weld. As always, tack first, then form the metal to the mounting place, and finally fill in the welds all around your base plates.

In this installation, the main hoop mounts to a gusset-supported extension of the frame. This is almost as strong as attaching to the frame itself.

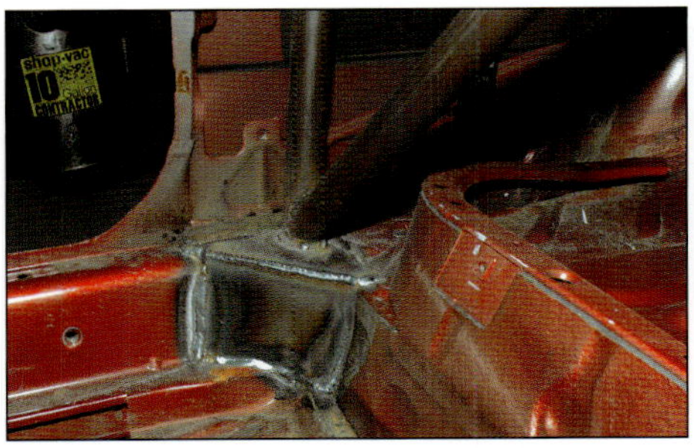

Here's a base plate formed around a corner using two plates. It still meets the 36-square-inch rule and makes a very strong installation.

6 Make final adjustments to your main hoop and tack it to the base plates. Tack the hoop securely, but don't weld it all the way around yet. You want to make sure everything fits right before you make that commitment.

7 Make and weld in your supporting tube mounting plates. If a mounting plate must fit around a curve, you can cold-forge it (beat it with a hammer) around an anvil horn of the same size or ask the same shop that's bending your tube to bend the plate for you. Either way, you will likely have to do some hammer-adjusting when you install the plate. You want a nice flush fit to your mounting point, so you can securely tack the plate into place, then work it with the hammer to finish the fit before you weld.

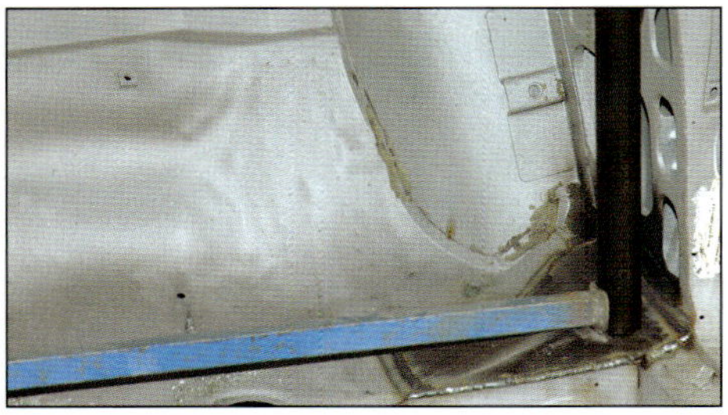

Under the spreader bar holding this main hoop in place, you can see the hammer-formed base plate welded to an already strong point on this unibody chassis.

This base plate was formed around a front strut tower on a 1985 VW Golf rally car. This will really strengthen the chassis when this point is tied into the roll cage. It will also help keep the strut tower from failing under increased stress.

8 Remeasure your supporting braces from the main hoop to your mounting plates, and use a protractor or carpenter's angle finder to get the correct angles. Remember to allow a little length for the fishmouth, because the ends of your supporting braces need to fit around the curve of the tubing. Mark the places where your braces attach.

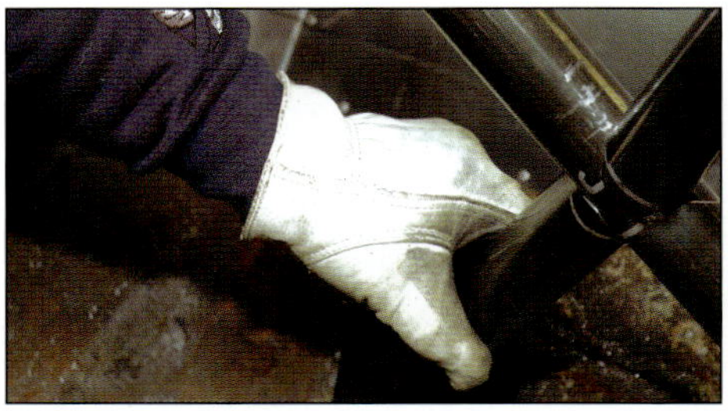

Test-fitting a support brace to make sure the length and fishmouth angles are just right. This brace will go through that hole in the floor and mount straight up to the car's frame.

Cutting and finishing your braces may be the most time-consuming part of the project. But it is absolutely critical to a quality result that these pieces fit perfectly with minimal gaps. You must bridge any gaps with weld, and the closer everything fits, the easier that will be.

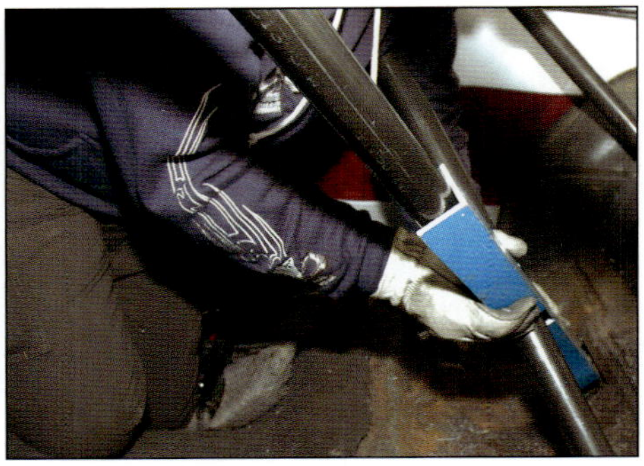

Here Russ uses a piece of angle iron to hold the divided half of an X-shape in perfect alignment with its mate while he tacks the piece into place.

If you're creating an X-shape in the braces, make one diagonal brace full-length, then make the second bar out of two pieces. Use a piece of angle iron with a notch cut out of the middle to keep the second bar of your X straight when you tack it into place.

9 Tack your support braces into place. You may have to make a few attempts at this before everything lines up just right. Once the supports are all tacked, you can start welding everything into place. If you

A practice weld of a piece of tube to a base plate. You can see that Russ got good penetration into the base plate from the weld all the way around the tube. Chances are you won't be able to check your work like this, but practice and check your results beforehand.

have welds near the headliner or other interior panels, use an aluminum plate or other non-weldable, non-flammable material to protect the parts you don't want burned. Note that you might not be entirely successful in that goal. If possible, you may want to pre-assemble the parts and then move them into place.

10 Note where your driver-side door bar is required to mount for your car and measure to that point. In a unibody car, you need to add a mounting plate of .125-inch mild steel just like you used for your main hoop and support braces. Cut the plate-mounted end at an angle and fishmouth the end that attaches to the main hoop. Be sure of your measurements because the bar is required to intersect the main hoop at a minimum distance from the floor. Technical inspectors are very strict, so don't yield to the temptation to move that bar to a more convenient angle. You can buy kits that make the door bar removable, and these kits are worth the investment if you're concerned about day-to-day use of your car.

This is the upper end of the removable door bar. We used a removable pin for this end because this bar is designed to swing out to allow easy entry to the car.

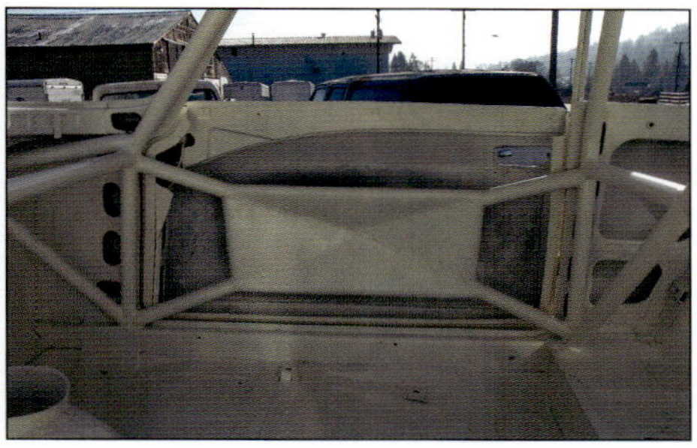

Mild steel cages start rusting as soon as you stop welding. So it's best to get a coat of paint on them as soon as possible. The best way to do this is to put your cage in a fully stripped car and then send the whole thing off to the paint booth.

Clean up your welds, mask off your car, and paint your roll bar. Mild steel rusts quickly and your project looks best with a fresh coat of paint applied as soon as you're done.

Creating a Tubular Chassis Brace

All performance cars benefit from stiffening their chassis. This is equally true for modern unibody designs, older half-tub designs such as GM's Camaro and Firebird, and full-frame designs on vintage and antique cars.

To begin with the oldest designs, early mass-produced cars such as the Ford Model A had frames made from stamped channel steel, welded and riveted together into a ladder structure. As we discussed in Chapter 6, enclosing the fourth side of the frame is known as boxing the frame and by itself improves chassis rigidity. This modification has been part of the hot rodder's art since the beginning. Later cars went to a central unibody tub with bolt-on subframes at the front and rear. A roll cage further adds to the stiffness by connecting the sides and the

This little kit allows you to weld in a removable door bar. You weld two of these tabs to your main hoop and forward A-pillar brace, and then weld the clevis ends into a length of tube. The clevis ends can be pinned or bolted into place.

This is the bottom end of the door bar. It's bolted, but will still function as a hinge. Make sure you get the tabs welded in at just the right angles or your bar won't fit right!

A-Pillar Bar Measuring Jig

Building a full roll cage is just an extension of the same process described for making a roll bar. You need to add a halo bar from the top of the main hoop around to the top of the windshield and then legs down along the A-pillar to the floor. Or you can make two legs that come forward along the roofline and down the A-pillar from the main hoop, and then join them with a bar along the top of the windshield. Either way, you need to bend some bars to follow the contours of your car.

To get those bars bent accurately, follow the basic steps for measuring and calculating bends. One tool that experienced cage builders use is a template jig. This is simply a set of short tubes pre-bent at various angles. These bends have set screws in their ends and you mate them up with straight tubes of varying lengths. By slip-fitting and choosing different angles, you can make a model of the A-pillar bar you need.

Once you have welded your halo and A-pillar structure into place, you can add door bars, bars forward to the firewall or into the engine bay, a Petty bar, or other supports for your roll cage. As always, following proven designs as specified by racing organizations is always the best practice.

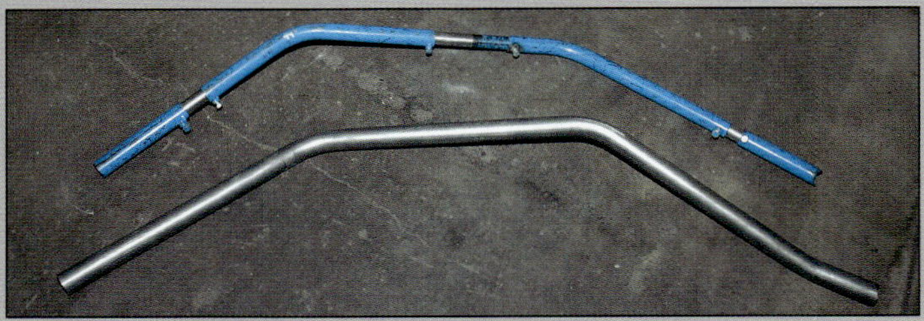

This adjustable A-pillar bar can be configured to fit virtually any car using different bends and straight lengths of tube.

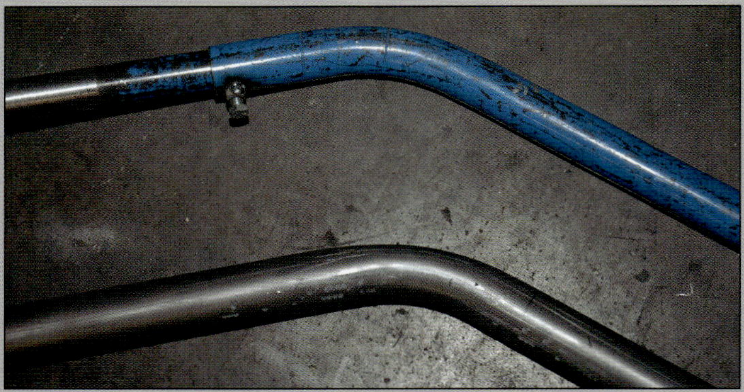

Detail view shows the slip joint construction that allows the user to test-fit the template and then recreate the correct shape in tube.

diagonal corners under a modified dome.

Finally, modern unibody cars benefit from tying together the suspension mounting points in several places. This reduces chassis flex during cornering and during acceleration for high-powered cars.

Frame and subframe braces work best when welded into place, but many are designed to be bolted into place, and these offer a good fraction of the benefit of a weld-in brace, and are removable to return the car to stock configuration. The same design can often be used for both welded and bolted braces, and the only difference is the fastening method.

This project creates a bolt-in subframe brace for a unibody car. The goal is to reduce front-end flex in hard cornering. This design fits a 1990–1997 Mazda Miata, but you can adapt the particular design and dimensions to your own purpose. We made this part with about $5 worth of supplies from the metal scrapyard and about 3 hours of work with the plasma cutter, tubing bender, drill press, and TIG welder.

1 The Miata has two box-section parts in its undercarriage that support the lower A-arms of the front suspension and two transmission support mount points. These form the rectangle of the frame brace. Other models of car have different undercarriage configurations but it is

The mount point for one side of our Miata chassis brace. The box section with three holes holds the lower front control arm, and we'll slip a mounting plate in there. The loosened bolt in the picture will be our other control point.

generally possible to find four (or more) points to conveniently bolt on some kind of brace. If your car has a ladder frame, you can weld tabs to the frame to mount a brace.

2 Measure the distances between each of the four holes and draw your rectangle on a piece of scrap cardboard, plywood, or on the floor of your shop. Check and recheck your measurements to make sure they're accurate. But remember that depending on the car you're working with, the convenient mount holes may not define a perfect rectangle! That's OK, as long as your finished piece lines up with the mounting holes.

3 Based on your rectangle, design a basic brace that relies on arches or triangles for support. We decided to create a lightweight brace with one arched and one straight beam, tied together with a lightened and stressed skin. Some cars with more places to anchor a brace can use more complicated bracing. Do some research for your particular make and model and see what others have done before you design your own part.

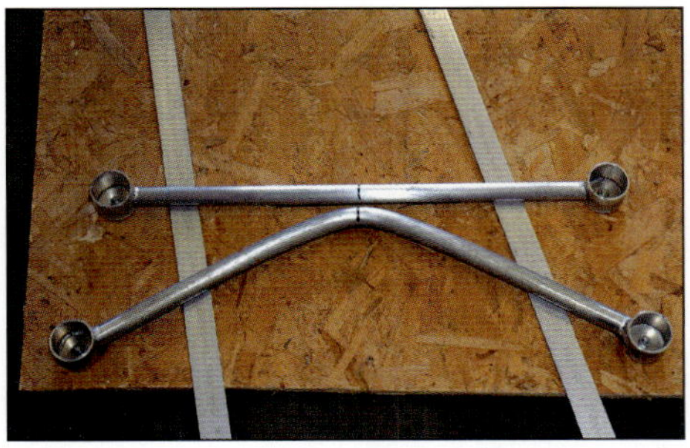

We laid out the jig for our chassis brace on this piece of plywood. We wanted a light, strong brace, so we borrowed a roll cage trick and brought a bent tube up next to a straight one, making three strong triangles. We'll tie the pieces together with a stressed skin.

4 You may want to create a jig when you begin welding. Depending on the materials and method you choose, warping and shrinking may bend your brace out of true. One way to create a good brace jig is to draw your base rectangle on a sheet of thick plywood and drill holes at the locations of the mounting points. Then attach your first pieces to the plywood as you tack your work together. As you weld each part into place, the plywood template holds the dimensions for you. If you plan to produce several pieces, create your jig out of steel and you can weld right on it without fear of lighting it on fire.

5 Start with large pieces for the mount points. We used 2-inch lengths of 1.75-inch .120 wall aluminum tube. Then we cut some discs with a 1.875-inch hole saw to make cups out of our short sections of tube. Weld the discs to the ends of the tubes and then bolt the resulting cups to your template. We used the TIG welder at 110 amps with 1/16-inch aluminum rod for this part, using the foot pedal to modulate welding power.

A mounting cup made from larger aluminum tubing with a plug of aluminum plate welded in. This is large enough in every dimension to accommodate the tube and to allow us some fudge factor when we install the part.

6 Now measure your distances and cut your aluminum tubes. We used 7/8-inch .120-wall aluminum tube that we picked up from the scrap bin at the metal yard. Make one brace straight and bend the other one on your bender to make a pointed arch. The two pieces may touch in the middle, and you may choose to weld them together, but you don't have to. Weld the tubes to the cups all the way around. Aluminum warps very easily, so keep the cups bolted to the template to hold everything in place. We left the TIG welder at 110 amps and continued to use 1/16-inch aluminum rod.

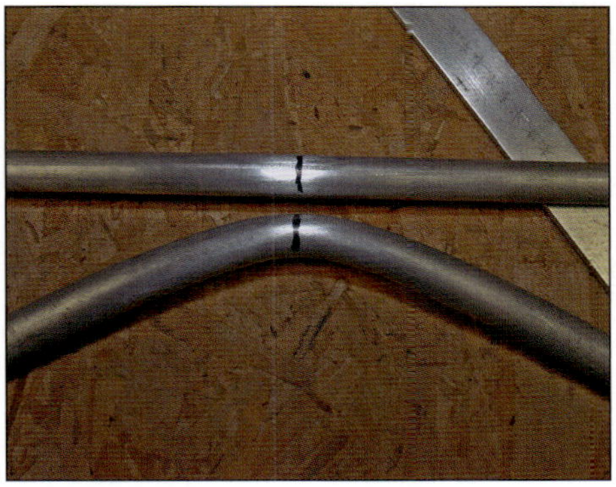

Keep the centerlines of your tubes lined up. This will help you keep the whole piece accurately placed on your template.

Keep your TIG heat low and you can get good penetration without burning through the aluminum.

7 When the tubes are welded to their cups all the way around, use some cardboard to make a template for the skin. You can cut one piece and form it around the straight tube, but it works just as well to cut two sides. We used .095 sheet aluminum for this material.

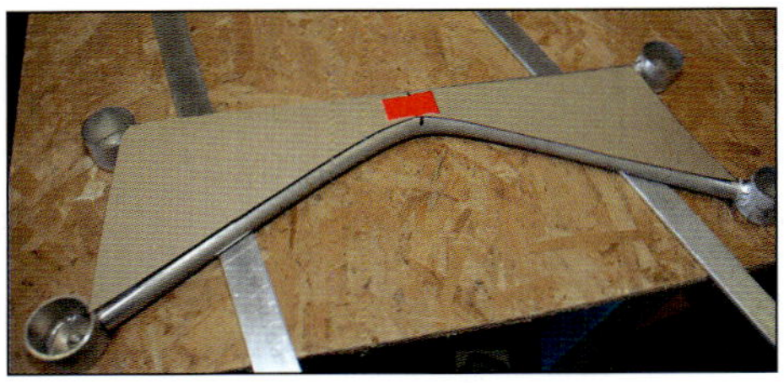

As always, our trusty cardboard makes a good template for the stressed skin of our chassis brace.

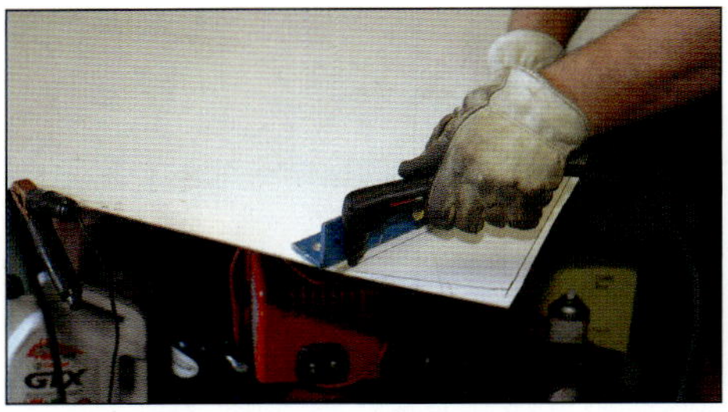

Russ uses a piece of angle iron to get a straight cut in the aluminum sheet with his plasma cutter.

8 If you choose, you can use your hole saw and lighten the skin by taking a few holes out of it.

Taking out these holes doesn't reduce the skin's strength, but it makes it a little lighter. You can see the hole on the left has already been recessed, and we're about to do the one on the right.

This is already a very lightweight piece, but the holes give it a very sporting look. We also recessed the holes with a special clamp made just for the purpose. These are available through metalworking supply houses.

9 Weld the skins to each side of the brace using a stitch pattern. We switched to 1/8-inch rod for this part of the process, as it requires more filler material. The stitch pattern helps avoid warping the part and is almost as strong under tension as an uninterrupted bead. Keep the piece bolted to the template as you install the first skin, then unbolt the piece and clamp it to the table as you weld on the second skin. When you're done, try to flex it—you'll find that it's strong!

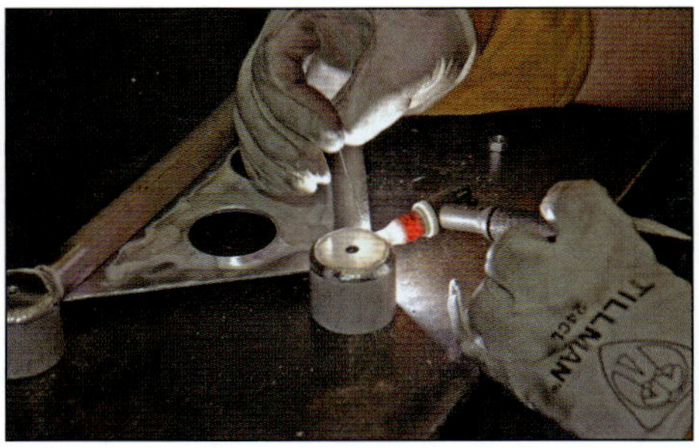

First tack the skin into place, then work in short stitches with plenty of cooling time to keep the brace from warping. Keep the brace bolted to the jig as much as possible.

You can see where Russ has marked off regular intervals on the piece for his stitch welds. He's stitching the skin to the tube in short increments. Aluminum sheet warps very easily, so take your time on this step.

10 Mounting your brace to the Miata's A-arm support boxes requires backing plates and we decided to weld a nut to the backing plate with the MIG welder. For the Miata, the plates must be 2-inch square, 1/8-inch steel. If you can't

Drill a 3/8-inch hole in a 2-inch square mild steel plate. Three good, solid tack welds are all it takes to affix this nut to the plate.

Installing the brace takes a little more work with a drill to enlarge the holes in the cup. Despite our best efforts, our measurements were a little off. That's why you allow a bit of fudge factor.

Detail shot of one corner of the brace. Our plate with the nut welded on is up in the box section behind this cup.

get a backing plate into the mounting area, you may have to weld a nut to a solid location (such as a frame rail) to bolt up your brace. Don't weld a nut to thin sheetmetal floors, or you'll just rip the sheetmetal as the brace takes up the chassis flex loads.

You may also want to create a strut tower brace. Look in the engine bay of most modern cars and at either side you'll see the strut towers where the shock absorber and spring are bolted on. When the suspension compresses, these towers have a tendency to flex inwards toward the centerline of the car. A strut brace resists that tendency and keeps your chassis in its designed shape. A basic strut brace mounts to the top of each strut tower and places a firmly held bar between them. The brace may also connect to the firewall bulkhead for additional support. Commercial strut braces don't cost much, but if you want to create your own or none are available for your make and model, they're easy to design and build.

This V-8 header is tacked together and ready to weld. The mating surface with the cylinder head and the 4-into-1 collector at the other end are purchased pieces, but the bends are made up of short sections that can be adjusted before they're welded.

Making a Custom Exhaust Pipe

One of the most common tasks when creating a custom car is to create a modified exhaust pipe. Some of these are complex creations with 4-into-1 collectors and delicate routing around underbody components, and some are little more than straight pipes. Many builders also add features such as sidepipes and lake pipes or dump pipes that bypass the muffler when you remove a plate or even just pull a lever. It's not hard to fabricate these add-ons and the results can be very effective.

One hard truth about exhausts is that you cannot make custom pipes using the inexpensive jack-based tubing benders. If you crimp an exhaust tube, it's not the end of the world, but it's the end of a good high-performance exhaust. An exhaust pipe only allows as much gas flow as at its narrowest point, and if you kink it you just made that part!

To do a good job on exhaust pipe bends requires a very specialized mandrel-based tubing bender. Your best alternative is to buy pre-made bends, cut them as needed, and then weld them together. If you do this job well, you can get a smooth exhaust path and a good-looking part.

Exhaust tubing has very thin walls, and for this reason, low-power MIG or TIG welding is ideal. TIG is generally considered to be overkill for exhaust systems. You can also weld exhaust tubing with gas and flux-core wire, but that takes more finesse. Stick welding exhaust tube is very difficult because of the tendency to burn through the material.

For this project, we re-create an existing exhaust system that is rusted out. We'll replace a muffler along the

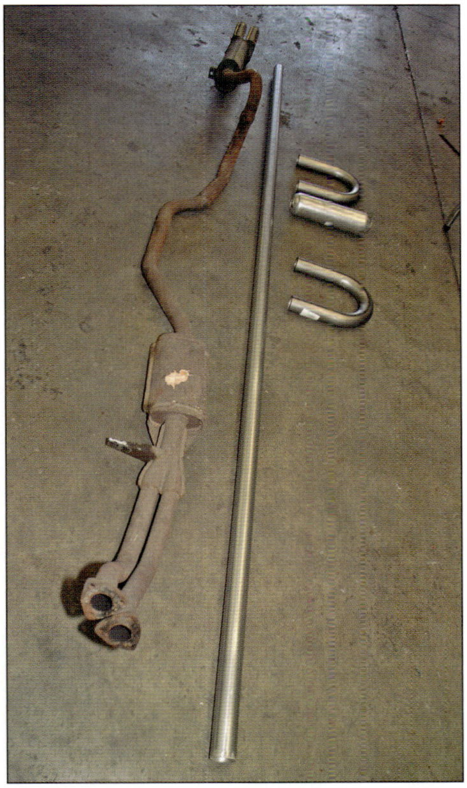

The old exhaust is laid out next to the new components. We've got a stick of 2-inch tube, two 180-degree bends, and a resonator. We'll reuse the muffler and the input Y-pipe from the old system.

way, keep some good parts from the old unit, and smooth out the flow for better performance. When we're done, the new product will fit just like the old one. This particular exhaust is made for a 1965–1974 Alfa Romeo GTV coupe.

Before you begin, you should decide if you're going to increase the size of the pipe. An exhaust system can only flow as much gas as its narrowest point allows, so look for restrictive areas in the original design. It does you no good to put a 3-inch tailpipe on a system that has a 2-inch segment somewhere along its line. You should also check with your engine builder or mechanic and find out if your engine requires a certain amount of resistance (called back pressure) to stay healthy and happy. Some engines also require a resonator or balance pipe to work properly.

1 Lay out the old pipe (or as much of it as you've got) on the floor and measure it to see how much tube you're going to need. Buy some extra pipe in case you make some mistakes. Also, obtain the mufflers, catalytic converters, resonators, or other parts you need for the project. If you're going to install any bungs for exhaust gas temperature or oxygen sensors, have those on hand as well. On our project, we smoothed out some unnecessary bends in the old system, but we still needed to build an arch over the rear axle.

Welding the new resonator onto the old Y-pipe. We had brushed off as much of the surface rust as possible and had dressed up the edges of the Y-pipe on the belt sander.

2 Look at the design of the original pipe to see if there are logical places to cut the pipe and create the new one in sections. This makes fabrication, installation, maintenance, and modification all easier. Look for welds on the old pipe where sections were joined, or just identify places where the pipe could be sectioned. An exhaust tube expander costs less than ten dollars and allows you to make slip-joint fittings with ease. If you're concerned about keeping the pieces together, exhaust clamps are readily available at any auto parts store. Working in sections, build up the new pipe to match the original part.

3 We completed our project with just two 180-degree bend pieces and a 10-foot stick of straight tube. By measuring carefully and cutting the pre-bent pieces, we were able to use those 360 degrees of bend to create a couple of complex bends.

Cutting loose the Y-pipe from the rusted-out resonator chamber. We used a cutoff wheel for accuracy and found that the original Y-pipe piece was made of stainless steel and in very good condition under a light patina of rust.

If you get a supply of U-bends, you can cut as much or as little curve as you need out of them to match any existing bend. You might have to cut short sections, however.

Matching up sections of bend cut from our 180-degree bent pieces to the original muffler, which is fairly new and in good shape.

You can tack the new parts right up to the old to make sure you're getting the bends and the angles matched up exactly right.

4 If you have identified places where you can smooth out the pipe and improve flow, make those sections as you designed them. You may also need to fabricate and weld on tabs or spears to suspend the new exhaust on the existing hangers. You may also need to weld or bolt the resonator, catalyst, or muffler into the system. If the part uses a mounting flange, you can purchase a matching flange and a gasket at a muffler shop and weld that flange onto your pipe. See the exercise in Chapter 3 about welding thick and thin parts together for the proper technique.

5 Add in any new design features you planned to include in your project. If you need a 4-into-1 collector or other complex part, these can be purchased pre-made if they're beyond your current skill level to make. Simple items like dump pipes are a good way to start practicing your custom fabrication skills, or they can be purchased in pre-made segments.

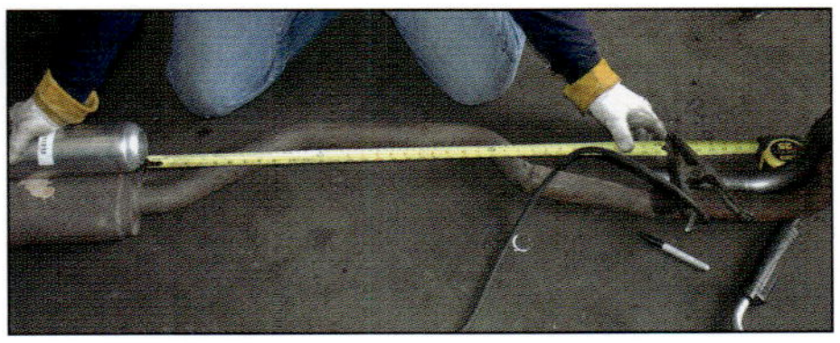

Measuring the overall length of the pipe. We're going to eliminate that bend in the middle of the pipe. The bend was originally designed to skirt a bulge in the body pan, but since this exhaust will be installed on a race car, we don't have to worry so much about it, and we'd rather have a straight pipe.

When you match a section of curve, tack weld it to the original in its desired location. You can build up the whole exhaust this way and be sure that it matches the old one.

Building up the precise curve that we want to clear the rear axle. We'll tack the pieces into place and then complete our welds when we know this design is what we want.

Welding the resonator to the new pipe. With this done, we'll break our tack welds and commit to the rest of the welds in this new system.

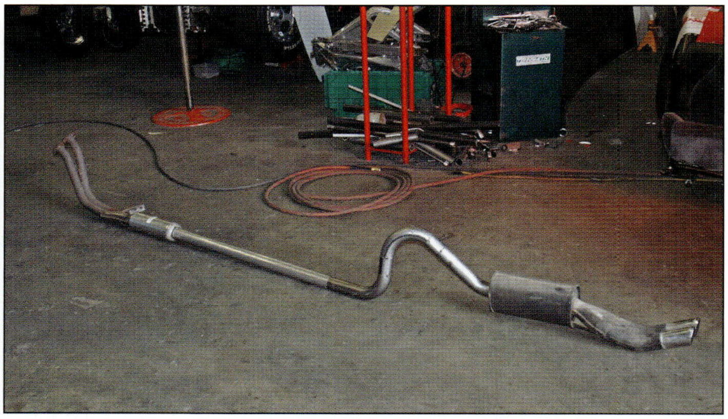

Here's the new exhaust, ready for our final welds and then installation. It has the same overall dimensions as the old piece, a straight pipe in the center, and should flow better than the old unit. We spent $50 on the pre-made parts and this took us about 2 hours—a significant savings over a muffler shop!

6 We decided to keep the Y-pipe from the front of the old exhaust system and the muffler and tips from the rear. So we cut them off the old pipe when we had the basic parts measured and we cleaned up the mating surfaces to weld them to our new material.

7 Finally, assemble your new pipe and match it up against the original. Just tack-weld everything together at first. Your part needs to match critical dimensions, and it's easy to get the length right, but lose accuracy on rotational orientation as you weld. When you've got everything close, go ahead and test-fit it to your car. You may need to adjust things a little bit to avoid rattles and knocks. That's another reason to build your pipe in sections: you can make adjustments without removing (or rebuilding) the whole assembly. Then when it's all just right, go ahead and weld it all into place.

As an extension of this exercise, you can spend some time grinding your welds smooth to give your new exhaust pipe a seamless, one-piece look. Even though most cars are never inspected that closely underneath, you'll know it's there.

The new aluminized steel of the resonator welds up nicely to the stainless of the Y-pipe. Most different steels will weld together quite well if you use the process approved for the more exotic alloy.

Building Headers With a Template

When you've gotten good at exhaust pipes, you can try your hand at exhaust headers. Working in tight engine bays and with up to 8 exhaust ports on a side, making exhaust headers can be a job for experts. One shortcut to making great headers is to make a mock-up kit. You can make these out of laundry vent pipe, PVC, or anything else that will slip-fit together. Get a good variety of 30-, 45-, and 90-degree angles and different lengths of short straight pipe. Then you can test-fit a design in the actual engine bay to see how it will work and how it will interact with the other pipes.

One other benefit is that header builders generally try to keep the pipes to each exhaust port the same length, and using a mock-up kit allows you to measure each pipe even when you're creating a complex header. Once you've got your design, you can build up your headers using the same techniques employed on the exhaust pipe project.

WORKING WITH CAST IRON AND OTHER MATERIALS

Cast metals are different from other metals in a few key ways. First, the alloys used for cast parts are different from those used to make forged or machined parts. Cast iron or cast steel, for example, has a much higher component of carbon than rolled steel. This presents specific challenges when you need to weld or adapt cast parts. For example, you cannot readily heat and bend cast iron—it just cracks and falls apart. But you can weld cast parts with the proper equipment and techniques.

Because they tend to be more brittle, cast parts have a tendency to crack and break. Therefore, most of this chapter is dedicated to fixing broken cast parts. At the end of the chapter, there is a short section on working with other metals, such as copper, lead, bronze, tin, and other alloys. While these metals cannot generally be welded, they are commonly used in brazing, soldering, bodywork, trim, and other automotive applications.

Cast metals can be welded effectively, but you need a slightly different set of skills and some special supplies to weld cast iron.

Fixing Broken Cast Parts

When cast parts break, they tend to break cleanly. That is, like a broken ceramic mug, you can fit the pieces back together and come up with a shape that's very close to what you started with. This is good news for repair work, because you don't have to deal with a bunch of bent parts. However, you may be dealing with cracks you can't see, so when you think you're done, have your cast parts checked for cracks at a good machine shop before you use them.

Exhaust Manifolds

Exhaust manifolds are among the most common cracked or broken cast parts. These parts are subject to regular heat cycles and vibration in normal service. Some manifolds are made of very thin cast iron, and what iron is there can get worn even thinner over time. Additionally, there are flanges where the manifold bolts to the engine, and these are especially subject to breaks. Most exhaust manifolds are made from basic cast iron, and are comparatively easy to weld.

Engine Blocks

Engine blocks have an advantage over exhaust manifolds because they're generally made from thicker castings and better materials are used. However, the application is correspondingly more critical, with precise machine tolerances required through most areas. Welding up engine block cracks caused by freezing water is within the capabilities of most amateurs, but always have your engine block checked for cracks by a professional before you use it. You may have fixed the obvious crack in the outer jacket, but if you missed a flaw in the crankshaft support area or a cylinder wall, you could waste a lot of money when that engine fails.

Suspension Components

Many suspension components such as spindles, brake flanges, and steering knuckles are also made from cast iron or steel. In general, vintage cars are more likely to use cast parts. If your project involves boosting the performance of a vintage car, have a good look at all your steering and suspension parts. They were designed for less engine power and much-less-capable tires, and the extra stresses added by hot rodding can spell disaster. The good news is that these parts can be reinforced and in critical cases, replacements are available that have been machined from modern high-strength materials. As always, if you want to use old parts, have them professionally crack-checked before it counts.

Fixing a Broken Cast-Iron Part

In this project, we'll weld up a crack in a 50-year-old cast-iron exhaust manifold from a British sports car. The manifold is made from good quality thick material, so it's a good candidate for repair.

For cast iron, there are two main types of stick welding rod—55 percent and 99 percent nickel. The 99 percent rod leaves a softer material in the weld and is suitable for machining if you need a flat surface when you're done. The 55 percent rod is a harder alloy and a little easier to weld with.

We chose 99 percent nickel stick welding rod for this repair, and used that rod with the stick welding attachment to a TIG welder. We set the TIG for DC operation and negative polarity, and used 75 amps of power.

Most cast-iron parts benefit from preheating before being welded. Heat the entire part uniformly to minimize the heat shear differential when you weld. You can preheat the part with an oxy-acetylene torch and a rosebud tip. Simply play the flame over the part until it's all hot. Be sure you do not heat any part of the piece to more than a dull red glow when viewed in a dark room.

If you're rejoining two parts that have broken apart, position them back in their original orientation. You can grind some bevels into them if they're thick and penetration is going to be a problem. But especially for auto parts, you want to preserve the key dimensions.

1 When you weld up a cracked part, you put a great deal of heat into the part. You want to be sure you don't cause the crack to propagate further as you fix it! So begin your repair by drilling two small holes at the ends of the crack. This helps relieve the internal stresses that caused the crack, and allows you to get the repair done without causing further damage. Also, sand or grind the surface "skin" away from the weld area. This skin tends to absorb impurities in the casting process, and can be hard to weld.

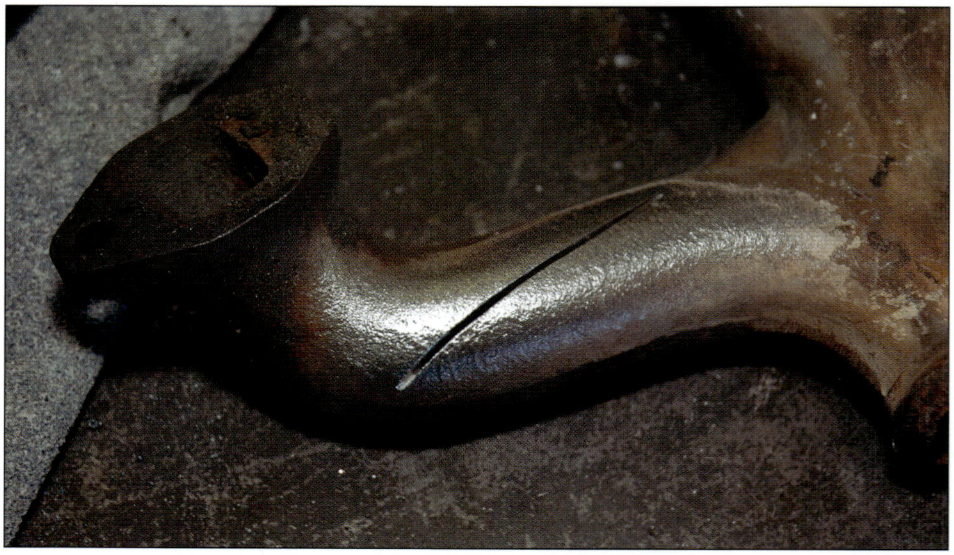

We made a cut in this old manifold from a British sports car. The metal is good and thick, so it will weld up very nicely.

2 Check the packaging and documentation delivered with your welding rods and start with the lowest power rating suitable for the thickness of the weld. Start at one end and slowly work your way along the crack. If you have not preheated your piece, you should weld no more than 1/2 inch at a time, and then stop to let the temperature differentials in the piece normalize. Also, stop every inch or so and clean the slag and crust from your weld before continuing. This also gives you a chance to check that the crack is not widening or propagating.

Remember that you need to chip away the crust on all stick welds. A good wire brushing never hurts.

You can use your TIG welder as a stick welder, which is nice because you then have your choice of AC or DC operation and you can choose the polarity of your weld according to the materials you're using.

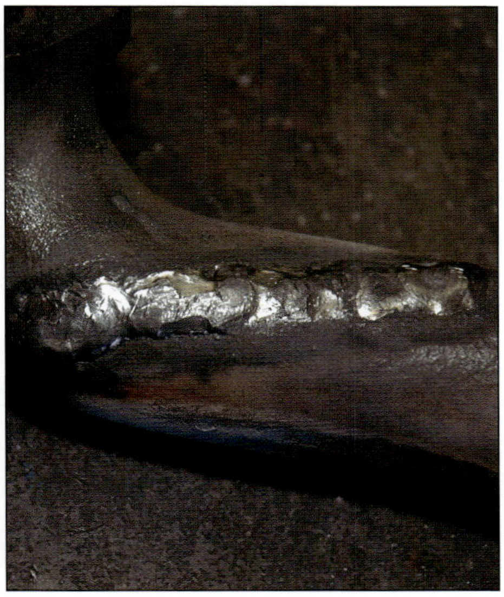

The finished weld can be ground down or just left raised for that much more support to the piece.

3 Finally, weld up the hole at the far end of the crack and then grind or machine down the weld, if necessary. If you're welding a part that must hold fluids or gases, plug one end and check for leaks. Small flaws in your weld can create holes in the material and cause leaks when the part is placed under pressure.

TECH TIP

JB Weld

If welding up a crack or a hole in an old part just isn't practical, I've had good results using JB Weld. This two-part epoxy has metal powder in it and it sets up just like a weld bead. Just apply it like body filler and smooth it over. You can even weld over it!

Welding Aluminum

Aluminum is the most common non-ferrous metal found in automobiles. Engine blocks, cylinder heads, oil pans, bearing carriers, suspension and steering parts, body panels, and structural beams and other components may be made from cast or rolled aluminum.

Welding aluminum is challenging even for experienced welders. The most common method used to weld aluminum is a TIG, but you can also use a spool gun and Argon gas attached to your MIG welder. If you have an oxy-acetylene torch, you can also weld aluminum with that tool.

Working with a MIG welder equipped with Argon and a spool gun makes fast work of aluminum projects. You must use aluminum wire in the gun—check with your welding supply shop for the correct material.

If you choose a TIG welder for aluminum, the machine must be set for AC operation. Direct current TIG welding on aluminum leads to splatter problems. You also need aluminum TIG welding rods.

Cleanliness is even more important than usual when working aluminum, as the smallest bit of grease, dust, or flecks of ferrous metal causes pitting and slag in the weld. All aluminum parts to be welded should be carefully cleaned to eliminate any oil or grease, and then handled carefully thereafter.

If possible, use dedicated aluminum saw blades and files. This helps keep small flecks of iron or steel from becoming lodged in your aluminum. Even tiny particles of ferrous metals in your weld will contaminate your bead, causing pitting and a porous weld.

Welding an Aluminum Oil Pan

Note that in this case, the depth of the two pieces is not the same. We need to fill those gaps with weld.

For this project we are adapting a BMW 2.5-liter oil pan for use in a 1.8-liter engine by removing about half an inch out of the middle of the pan. In addition to the cast aluminum upper pan, the stamped steel sump pan also needs modification. And when it's all done, the two pans have to line up on their bolt holes, and the mating surfaces must be smooth enough to seal. This is a delicate job.

1 Carefully clean all parts in a washer, then bake the aluminum upper pan in an industrial oven to remove oil and grease. When they're clean, mark the spot to make cuts.

2 Cut the aluminum upper pan with a dedicated aluminum saw blade, and the stamped steel pan with a metal-cutting bandsaw. Then use a dedicated aluminum file to smooth and cut the edges of the aluminum where you're going to weld. Also, wipe down the edges again to keep things as clean as possible.

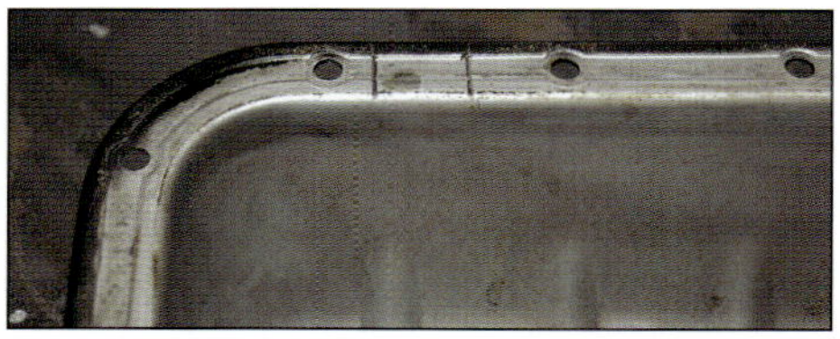

We marked the place on both the aluminum upper pan and the stamped steel sump pan where we're going to remove material.

The two parts of the upper oil pan are cleaned, filed, and ready to weld.

3 Clamp the aluminum parts to the steel table. This is important for two reasons. One is that you want the parts to stay perfectly aligned while you tack them together. The second reason is that aluminum has a tendency to warp under welding, and you want to make sure that the mating surface stays as flat as possible.

4 With the welder set at medium-high power, tack the two halves into place at several locations along the mating surface. Then fill in the entire length of the piece with weld, bit by bit. It's important to let each segment cool before continuing to the next step to help prevent warping.

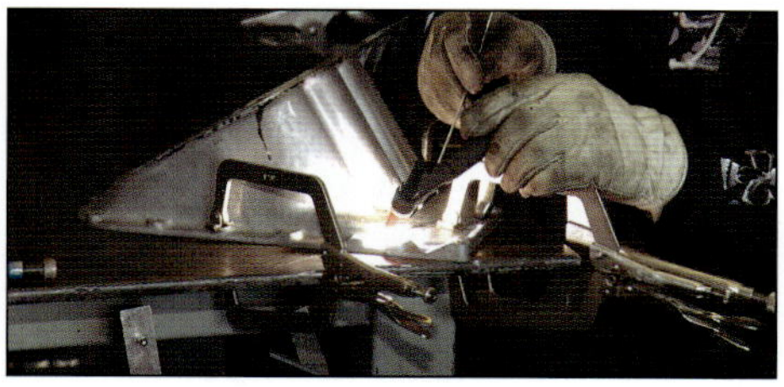

Tacking the piece into place at several points along the weld line helps avoid warping the part. If you weld solidly from one side to the other, the part will warp.

5 The aluminum welding technique is to move the arc and create a hot spot with molten aluminum, then push a bit of welding rod in to fill the gap, then move a couple of millimeters and repeat.

See how the heat, push, and move technique yields a nice, even result. Note the slight galling and impurities at the right hand side—we could have been cleaner!

6 With the outside welded, file off any drips that have formed on the inside. Then repeat the welding bead along the inside—this part has to hold oil without leaking. Note the V-shaped notch filed at each end on the gasket mating surface. Build that up with welding rod, then file it flat and smooth.

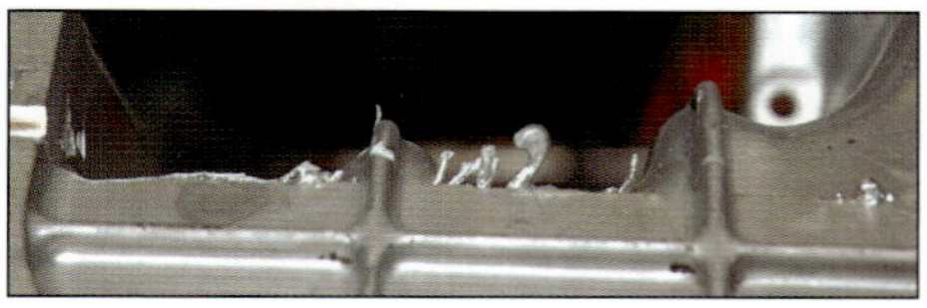

Molten aluminum dripped in and must be removed before the inside welding bead can be laid down. Note the V-shaped grooves at the sides.

When the bead is complete and built up at the gasket mating surfaces, use a dedicated file to flatten and smooth the surface.

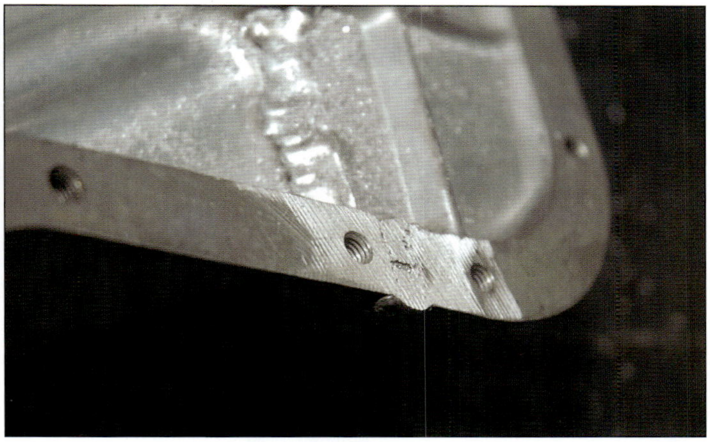

The finished mating surface. We'll want to use some gasket sealer on this, but it will work well.

7 When you're done, take a straightedge and hold it up against the part. Despite our best efforts, we still got some warpage as the aluminum cooled. There are a couple ways to fix this. If there was enough material, we could take the part to a machine shop and have it machined flat, but since the sump pan only attaches one way and the upper pan is only slightly warped, we'll just make sure the two halves fit each other.

A straightedge shows that there's a little warping from our work. We'll make the other pan the same way for a good fit.

8 Using a small sander/grinder, wire brush, and files, prepare the edges of the stamped steel sump pan for welding. You could do this part with a MIG welder, but we decided keep on with the TIG. Of course, you must switch to steel welding rod and use a lower level of DC power this time, because this part of the job is working with steel. To get a good fit, bolt the two pieces of the pan securely into their places. The important thing is that the bolt holes line up and the gasket mating surfaces are the same to seal in the oil.

Bolt both sides of the steel sump pan into place, then weld so you know your bolt holes and mating surface contours will match up.

9 As before, tack the two pieces together in several locations to fix the pieces in place without introducing warping. Stamped sheet steel may be very thin, so reduce the welding power. These tack welds also help make sure of good penetration without risk of burning up the thin steel of the pan.

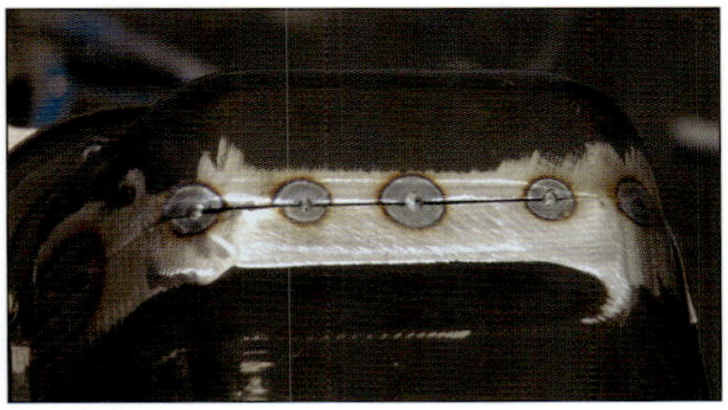

Tack the two halves of the pan together in a few places before you run a bead. This helps avoid warping.

10 Use the same heat-push-move technique to lay a bead along a sheet steel weld. Go over the pan from the outside, with it bolted firmly into place. Then take the pan off and repeat the bead on the inside to fill in any possible leaks.

11 Finally, file the mating surface of the steel sump pan smooth and make sure that everything bolts up cleanly to the aluminum upper pan. There's a bit of flex in the stamped sheetmetal of the sump, so this should hold oil nicely, and the bolts all line up, too. It's a job well done!

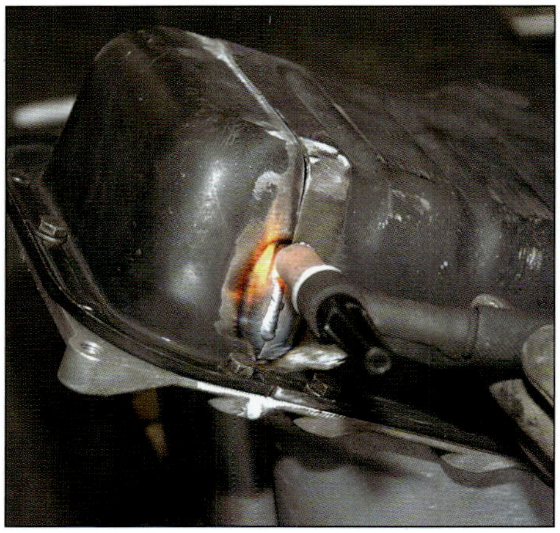

Heat-push-move to lay a bead on the stamped steel. Be careful of your welding heat—you don't want to burn your part, or blow a hole through it.

When you've welded the outside, go over it again from the inside to plug any holes that might leak.

The finished product. This took about two hours to complete and used just a couple sticks of aluminum and a couple sticks of steel welding rod.

Working with Copper, Lead, Tin, Bronze and Other Alloys

Unless you're working with a car from the first few years of the automotive era, there's not a lot of call for bronze, copper, and other soft metals. But these materials do merit some mention and can be useful to the modern metalworker.

Copper sheet is useful for cutting custom gaskets and making certain decorative pieces. Pure copper is quite soft and forgiving, so you can form it cold without too much trouble. You can also use thicker copper and brass sheets to make engine dress-up items such as brackets to hold your ignition coil, TDC pointers for your crankshaft, and other non-stressed items.

Lead has a long history in automotive work—it was used as the basic body filler before the invention of plastic based body fillers. Because lead melts at a little over 600 degrees F, you can melt it with a propane torch and let it fill a dent or gap, then easily file or sand it smooth. It's very cool and old school to do body-work with lead, but obviously take all due precautions as lead is poisonous to your brain and will accumulate in your body over time.

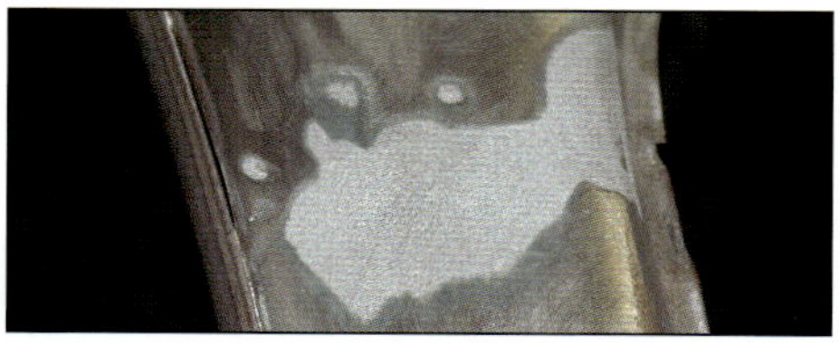

You can see lead in a car when the paint comes off. The lead has a silvery look to it and shows more effect from media blasting.

With older cars—European cars especially—you are likely to find some bushings and other components made of bronze. Bronze is an alloy of copper and tin and while it's harder than copper, most of the time the bronze pieces you find will be hopelessly worn out. Replace them with new bushings made of nylon, Delrin, or aluminum. The original automaker used bronze because it was inexpensive and we have better materials now.

Brazing and Soldering

Occasionally you need to join unlike metals together. Usually this involves fasteners—you bolt the aluminum part to the steel part, or rivet the aluminum sheetmetal to the steel bodywork. But sometimes the interaction requires a watertight seal or just a connection that is more solid.

Most people have used a soldering iron on electrical components. The theory is simple—you melt a soft metal filler material (usually an alloy of lead, tin, and other metals) and use it to glue a wire to a fixed point. The molten soldering metal flows and sticks to both parts and when it freezes, it has enough grip to hold the piece in place as long as no one pulls too hard on it.

A piece of copper sheet like this can easily be cut into a custom gasket for antique applications.

Brazing and soldering are similar processes in that they create an attachment without melting either of the two (or more) parts that are being held in place by the braze. Brazing rods are typically made of bronze, brass, or other soft metal alloys.

If you look at metal under a microscope, it's not as smooth as it appears to the naked eye. It has a rough surface with space between metal crystals and fibers. Molten brazing metals will flow and soak into those spaces and when the brazing material freezes, it holds to the surrounding metal.

You can take advantage of that property and use brazing to join aluminum to steel, for example, with a weld-like joint. The joint can be as strong as a weld, but make sure that the braze is cleaned, assembled, and performed well to get that strength.

This radiator tank is made of copper, with the seams brazed shut and AN fittings brazed onto the tank as well. It's lasted at least 20 years this way with no leaks.

Race car builders sometimes braze suspension parts onto a race car so that in the event of an accident, the braze is the part that breaks. If the suspension tears away in a crash without damaging the frame, it's easy to repair! This requires a detailed knowledge of the stresses on the parts in normal operation and a high degree of confidence in the quality of the braze.

On many older cars, you can also see evidence that brazing has been used to fix cracks in sheetmetal and to fill small holes. This was popular among amateurs for many years because brazing was easier and less expensive than a welding fix.

More often, brazing has been used to assemble radiators, oil coolers, and other tanks that require a fluid-tight seal. But the process has lost some favor with the advent of widespread and affordable TIG welding for aluminum.

To braze a joint, both parts must be absolutely clean. Wire brushing the parts at the mating surfaces helps, too. The two parts must be mated as closely as possible. Brazing is not as good for filling gaps as welding, because the strength of the braze depends on getting as much grip into the surrounding metal as possible.

A corollary of getting the grip in the parts to be brazed is that you need to have an ample mating surface. If you try to braze a butt joint between two thin pieces of metal, you won't get a strong joint because there's very little metal to take the braze—just a square millimeter or two. So, always plan to overlap your parts when brazing. The braze soaks into the joint between the two parts and that's what makes it strong. You can also braze fittings (such as aluminum and plumbing fittings) onto brass or aluminum tanks. The mating surface isn't large, but then again, it's an unstressed joint.

1 Get two pieces of aluminum and clean them thoroughly. Give them a little wire brush treatment to rough up their surfaces. Make sure that they fit well together—two pieces of flat 1/8-inch plate work well for brazing.

2 Set the pieces of aluminum up on your welding table and put some aluminum brazing flux powder on them. Overlap them by at least an inch. Make sure they're closely mated with no gaps!

3 Start a braze by heating the surrounding metal up to the melting point of the brazing rod, but not any higher! You'll know it's right when the flux melts and starts to flow. The aluminum itself is far from melting at this point.

4 Dip your aluminum brazing rod in a jar of flux and feed a little into the hot area. It should melt and create a puddle. Let the puddle flow into the joint and fill the area. Then move on as if you were gas-welding the joint. The molten rod will actually be sucked into the braze joint.

5 Turn your project over and braze the lap joint on the other side in the same way. Then let the parts cool normally and test your braze.

TECH TIP

Fumes

Be careful around brazing fumes. When you heat up the fluxes and materials used for brazing, you're releasing some poisonous fumes. Avoid breathing these fumes and always work in a well-ventilated area.

Source Guide

www.allshops.org
This is the online home of the Metalshapers Association, with many resources, tips and tricks, and input from some of the top metalworking professionals in the business.

www.bbssystem.com
Also known as www.metalillness.com, this forum covers all manner of metalworking and welding topics.

www.fabricators.com
Tremendously helpful site with a forum, reviews, and a few sample DIY projects useful to fabricators.

www.honda-tech.com
The welding/fabrication section of this forum is useful for general automotive metalworking information.

www.jalopyjournal.com
Fantastic resource for the home-building hot rodder. As they say about themselves, "The Jalopy Journal was formed to spread the gospel of traditional Hot Rods and Kustoms to hoodlums worldwide."

www.knucklebusterinc.com
Dedicated to custom motorcycle fabrication. If you want to race it or chop it, here's your online home.

www.lincolnelectric.com
The official site of Lincoln welders has a library of articles and resources for welders.

www.metalmeet.com
Billed as the largest online community of metalworking professionals and enthusiasts in the world, this site and its forums are great for getting your questions answered and learning techniques.

www.metalprojects.no-ip.com
This site offers a range of project plans for the metalworker. Just a few are directly automotive-related, but many are fun and useful exercises. Most plans cost between $5 and $20 to download.

www.metalwebnews.com/mf.html
A wide range of free project plans and other links and resources for the metal fabricator.

www.millerwelds.com
The official Miller Welding site offers a deep list of resources, including articles, tables, forums, videos, and prepared projects for welders.

www.offroadfabnet.com
This is a forum site with an emphasis on off-road fabrication, but the content is good for all automotive purposes.

www.stanford.edu/group/prl/documents/html/TIGweld.htm
This page offers some good information on TIG welding.

www.streetchopperweb.com
This is another site devoted to motorcycle fabrication, with a special focus on choppers.

www.thefabricator.com
Great site full of resources, articles, videos, and news for metal fabricators.